THE FOUR SUNS

By the same author

Mexique, terre indienne, 1935
La familie Otomi-pame ou Mexique central, 1937
La culture materielle des Lacandons, 1937
La pensée cosmologique des anciens Mexicains, 1940
Daily Life Among the Aztecs, 1955 (U.S.A., 1962)
Arts of Ancient Mexico, 1966 (U.S.A., 1967)
Mexico, 1967 (U.S.A., 1967)

with Ignacio Bernal
Mexico, pre-Hispanic paintings (1958)

Jacques Soustelle

*Recollections and
reflections of
an ethnologist
in Mexico*

TRANSLATED BY E. ROSS

THE FOUR SUNS

AN ORION PRESS BOOK

GROSSMAN PUBLISHERS, NEW YORK, 1971

All rights reserved
© *Librairie Plon* 1967
Translation © 1970 *by Grossman Publishers*
Published in the United States by Grossman Publishers
44 West 56th Street, New York, N.Y., 10019
Published simultaneously in Canada by
Fitzhenry and Whiteside Ltd.
Library of Congress Catalogue Card Number: 70-114945
Printed in Great Britain

Contents

Foreword

IN THE CENTER OF THE ENORMOUS STONE DISK called the Aztec calendar, a symbol shaped like a St. Andrew's cross frames the grimacing face of the Sun. Four smaller disks accompany it. The whole design reads *naui-ollin*, "Four Movement." This is the name of our world, "ours, the one in which we live and which was also that of Our Lord of Tula, the Plumed Serpent."[1]

The word "*ollin*" means both "movement" and "earthquake," and it is the name of one of the twenty days of the Mexican divinatory calendar. Our universe was born on the day of "Four Movement," when the Sun began to move in the heavens, and it will collapse amidst earthquakes and cataclysms. Then the monsters of the dusk, the skeletal-masked *Tzitzimimé* that lurk in the shadows of the west, awaiting their hour, will surge out of the darkness to exterminate mankind.

Our universe, according to the ancient Mexicans, is the fifth in a series. Four Suns have preceded it. On the Aztec calendar, their hieroglyphs are engraved within the four branches of the sign *ollin*. They are called:

Naui-Ocelotl, "Four-Jaguar." Tradition has it that men were devoured by jaguars. But for the most ancient peoples of Mexico, that feline was the symbol of the dark forces of the earth, symbol of all the mystery which prowls "in the heart of the mountains." For the more recent Mexicans of the Tolteco-Aztec period, the feline represented Tezcatlipoca, god of the night sky, strewn with stars as the robe of the jaguar is sprinkled with spots.

Naui-Eecatl, "Four-Wind." This time, it was the tempest that put an

1. *Codex Chimalpopoca, Leyenda de los Soles*, III, 10, Mexico City, 1945.

1*

end to the Sun; a magical storm since, under its influence, men were turned into monkeys. The emblem of this world is the mask of the god of wind, who, in turn, is but one of the forms of Quetzalcoatl, the Plumed Serpent and eternal rival of Tezcatlipoca.

Naui-Quiauítl, "Four-Rain." A rain of fire (*tlequiauítl*) came pelting down in this universe and annihilated it. This cosmic period is symbolized by Tlaloc, god of the beneficial rain but also of the thunder and lightning, the mountains and the volcanoes.

Naui-Atl, "Four-Water." The deluge lasted fifty-two years. A single couple survived, having taken shelter in the trunk of a huge cypress tree. But since they disobeyed the orders of Tezcatlipoca, this man and this woman who had escaped from the fourth universe were turned into dogs. The Plumed Serpent was obliged to descend into the subterranean world, steal the bones of the dead ancients from the darkness, and pour its own blood over them so that the present race of men could come to life.

The Indian mind, as we can see, was far from imagining a sure and stable world, far from believing that it had always existed or had been created once and for all until at last the time should come for it to end. Instead, the Indian looked on man as placed, "descended" (the Aztec verb "*temo*" means both "to be born" and "to descend"), in a fragile universe subject to a cyclical state of flux, and on each cycle as crashing to an end in a dramatic upheaval.

The Mayan priest-astronomers were the philosophical elite of American antiquity. Through their calculations, bearing upon millions of years, they succeeded in imagining the prodigious immensity of time past and time to come not as a linear duration but as an infinite series of periods comparable to the cogwheels of a clock.

The Aztec tradition was less sophisticated and more popular. It did not so much contemplate a superhuman order as recollect cosmic cataclysms and wait in anguish for more to come. Hence the feeling of insecurity in which all of recent Mexican civilization is wrapped, for never, at any time, does anyone forget that the fifth universe is destined to disappear like the first four Suns—and that the end may come tomorrow.

This vision, of a world forever pushed and pulled by alternating phases of creation and destruction, is related to the way in which the greatest thinkers of our own antiquity (particularly the Stoic philosophers) conceived the cosmos and to some of the concepts of our modern physics. Moreover, if we transpose that vision from the future of the world to the future of man, it corresponds closely to what our own science, still in its infancy, allows us to glimpse with respect to the birth and death of civilizations.

Civilizations are the infinitely precious and infinitely precarious creations of our species, so many monuments which tireless man has erected and which, until now, a pitiless law has always demolished. Each civilization appears to us as a separate cycle, each marked by the features peculiar to it, each coming into existence at a specific point in time, running its course and doomed to reach its inevitable end.

Today our civilization is bent on being triumphant but, faced with the perils born of its mastery over nature, and powerless at the same time to master itself, has it not fallen prey to the same profound anxiety that haunted the soul of ancient Mexico behind its façade of luxury and might?

Intuitively, daringly, the Indian probed reality to a depth of which we too are becoming aware, as the boastful confidence we enjoyed less than a century ago gradually fades away.

Now we know that every sun is doomed to extinction. A civilization may succumb to assault by barbarians—the jaguars of the first universe; it may founder in impotence and futility—men are turned into monkeys; it may collapse under the blows dealt by natural forces—the deluge and the earthquake; or, finally, it may explode in an ultimate conflagration— that hail of fire which, in our day, has become more than a mere legendary image. The Mexican myth, expressing an ancient wisdom, fits in with modern anxiety.

What is the attitude of the ethnologist, the researcher, who participates whether he wants to or not in the historical phase in which he lives and who may realize more keenly than anyone else how precarious and relative it is? In the Legend of the Suns, he finds the symbol of that human adventure, so often interrupted and begun again, to which he is committed even while he strives to contemplate and comprehend it.

J.S.

May, 1967

THE FOUR SUNS

Chapter One

Prelude to Research

WHEN IT COMES TO DETERMINING THE DIRECTION a life will take, how can we measure the parts played by innate taste, by training, and by chance? In my own case, as far back as I can trace my memories, I always had a passionate desire to learn about distant countries and, especially, distant peoples. This curiosity has never left me. I maintain that there is no richer or more moving sight for any of us than the spectacle offered by our own species. Often this spectacle inspires horror, more often still compassion, sometimes pride in being a man; but always it stirs that deep desire to understand others which allows each of us to escape from the small corner in space and in time where fate has enclosed us.

Curiosity, the proverb says, kills the cat, but there is no doubt that it makes the ethnographer live. It has to be very compelling indeed to make the researcher overcome the thousand minor, irritating obstacles that he finds along his path: exhausting pack rides, backbreaking marches, food shortages, foul water, insect bites, provisions that rot, the bearer or the mule driver who does not appear at the appointed place and time, the rain that comes too soon, the trail that is lost. . . . These are unimportant tribulations, trivial in themselves even if they harass you in the heart of Africa, but certain explorers make them the substance of their accounts, to the delight of the public which heeds them. Of course there is an appealing element of sport and adventure in the ethnographer's quest: I myself have appreciated, and still appreciate, that side of our work. But there must be no mistake. When we set out on the trail, we are not out to set records. In fact, honesty compels me to admit that the "picturesque" element of research, if properly or passably conducted, frequently boils down to tedious efforts and a quartermaster's job. And it may happen—it has happened to me, at any rate—that you expend all that effort and organize such an arduous trip for nothing at all. But what saves you is curiosity, and it is the object of your curiosity that counts. The object is that man or that people you tried to reach at the cost of a thousand difficulties, in the hope—possibly a vain one—that from him or through him you would learn something about yourself.

When I was a child, I spent the whole of every day when there was no school endlessly reading the books which a friendly neighbor allowed me to take from his library. I have always liked to leaf through books, open and close them, take them up again, consult a particular page, compare it with another, stop reading something so as to pick up where I left off a little while later. A real treasure had been opened to me— adventure stories and travel stories, books about discoveries, descriptions of exotic *moeurs* and customs. The tribes of central Australia wandering in the reddish deserts around Alice Springs, the Pueblo Indians with their *kivas* and their many-storied houses, Malayan navigators under the triangular sail of their *prahus*, Indians thronging the muddy banks of the Ganges and the dusky temples of Kali, the huts in the vast forest of Guiana, bearers advancing slowly through the tall grasses on the trails of equatorial Africa—all of these images and many more like them, imprinted on my mind as I read and reread and read again insatiably, must have marked me indelibly from the very earliest years of my conscious life.

As I write these lines, I can still smell the beehive odor of the freshly waxed floor in the library where I went to delve into all this wealth. I was accompanied by a Siamese cat. Outside the window, our gray street in Villeurbanne near Lyons, which was brightened in summer by the blossoms of the acacias shading a game of *boules*, became a sea of mud in wintertime. The Percherons that tried to haul heavy wagons sank into the mud and their drivers swore vehemently in the rain as they whipped the poor beasts. Meanwhile I pored over the engravings in books with red and gold bindings. I sailed down the Amazon on a *jangada*, fought my way through the jungle of the Orinoco, went along on a *koroboree* in

Australia, squatted by the fire next to Indians who were draped in blankets and who held high their heads crowned with eagle feathers.

Later on, when I was able to decipher a little Latin and Greek, I was engulfed in the universe of the past, as heady a change as any created by distance. A marvelous encounter with the civilizations of our Mediterranean Sea! I discovered the dimension of time and, although I did not clearly understand why as yet, I felt that one could seek out other men just as well by moving upstream on the river of time as by exploring distant lands. Soon I put the classics of the great ages aside and yielded to an instinctive preference for the periods of transition and mutation. Through the philosophy of Plotinus and Porphyry, the life of Apollonius of Tyana, the biographies of *The Augustan History*, and Ammianus Marcellinus, I dimly grasped how this ancient world and its sun-drenched beauty had slid, at first little by little, then collapsed into the misty chasm of the Middle Ages. This was a spectacle as majestic and terrible as an avalanche high in the mountains. So, I thought, there was a civilization which had been capable of producing such near-divine beings as Plato or Marcus Aurelius, or a genius like Caesar, had built the Parthenon and the Pantheon, reached the summits of art and intellect, lasted a millennium and a half—only to collapse, weakened from within as much as by the attacking Huns and Germanic tribes. If this had been the fate of Athens and Rome, shouldn't we deduce that a similar tragedy was written into the fate of every civilization?

In my student days, first in Lyons, then at the Ecole Normale Supérieure in Paris, the university teaching of philosophy was dominated by post-Kantian idealism. This was an intellectual game, and it could be brilliant when played by minds that had sufficient subtlety and practice. The history of ideas supplied the material and, especially, the pretext for those dissertations in which, by contrasting and resolving the theories of Plato, Aristotle, Hegel, and Kant, the views of Descartes, Berkeley, Locke, Malebranche, or Maine de Biran, by juggling with the conclusions of science and common sense (which was invariably ridiculed and reduced to silence), we managed to demonstrate that the human mind had never ceased to advance, on an upward path, from the groves of Academe to the main lecture hall of the Sorbonne.

Of course not everything about this eclecticism was worthless; at least it gave us a strong background and allowed me to go thoroughly into the Greeks, approach the Germans and discover Nietzsche. But it is easy to see how it could lead to verbal juggling. These metaphysical constructs were no more closely related to the concrete reality of human thought than the outline of the continents is to those early maps where you can barely recognize the shape of Italy or France, while Africa and northern Europe are lost in a sort of dim haze. It was very flattering to ourselves to overlook, arbitrarily, whatever did not belong to our world—and China was only one example; and even within that world, we deigned to consider only a certain category of safely identified authors.

This was idealistic scholasticism; it has been transmuted since, among some students, into Marxist scholasticism, and among others into existentialist scholasticism. In either case, it is characterized by the same disdain for the human fact in its diverse reality, and of course it neither could nor would take any account of what were called "the primitives." Durkheim and his school of sociological thought had gained a small place in the sun, but they were still held in only slight esteem by the philosophers. The day I was awarded my *agrégation* in philosophy, the inspector general of higher education, who was chairman of the jury, received me with an "Ah, so you're the sociologist," which expressed equal amounts of astonishment and regret. As a matter of fact, I had been the only one of all my fellow students (who were mad about mathematical-metaphysical speculation and were disciples of Léon Brunschvicg) to desert the summits of epistemology and the rarefied neo-Kantian stratosphere and prefer Indian linguistics as taught by Jules Bloch, and Chinese thought as Marcel Granet so magnificently explored it. I even took a course on mental pathology at the Sainte-Anne asylum. Most important of all, as soon as I arrived in Paris, the head of the Ecole Normale Supérieure, Bouglé, had introduced me to Marcel Mauss, who was teaching at the Institute of Ethnology founded just a year or two earlier.

No one who had the privilege of knowing Marcel Mauss will hesitate to agree that he was one of the greatest minds of our times. Our times, which place so much emphasis on the sciences, pay little attention to the scientists themselves. In terms of both fame and reward, they come far behind the most commonplace mountebank. At best, it is when they die that the newspapers notice that they had existed and give them an obituary. Physicists and biologists do receive some consideration in their lifetime because their work is expected to produce practical results. But in France, since virtually no one, and least of all in official circles, gives any thought to the social sciences or has any notion of how they can be applied, anyone who devotes himself to them is generally overlooked.

This is what happened to Mauss. Yet, as he was a prodigiously learned man and a thinker of genius, he profoundly influenced an entire generation of researchers. By a curious paradox, it was this man who never did field work (he was the last and the greatest of the armchair anthropologists) who inspired us to go out and follow trails in every corner of the world and who armed us with rules and advice which were more precious than any mere provisions: "Where? Who? When? How? What? With what? For whom? Why?" All his former students still remember that litany; his instructions for making ethnographic surveys always began with it. The nephew of Emile Durkheim and one of the leaders of the sociological school, he had freed himself of all dogmatism, like Franz Boas in America, whom he greatly admired. Mauss's memory was an unfailing storehouse of his exhaustive reading. For every aspect of human activity, dwellings, clothing, sacrifices, family institutions, law, magic, or trade, it supplied him with a whole gamut of facts with which he illustrated his teaching, so that at every instant we realized the stunning wealth and diversity of the cultures we would be studying.

He felt, and rightly, that it was still too early for ambitious sweeping syntheses. In a short essay on "culture areas," he incisively criticized the theories of the Vienna school, the *Kulturkreise* of Father Schmidt, not on the basis of some preconceived ideology but by demonstrating that reality was too varied and too complex to be squeezed into a rigid doctrinal framework. He had the keenest intuition of those actions and reactions that link social phenomena to form a number of wholes, each with multiple facets. Writing about the "realm of contracts and economic 'prestations' " toward the beginning of his essay on *The Gift*, he said: "On this subject there is a great mass of complex data . . . each phenomenon contains all the threads of which the social fabric is composed. In these *total* social phenomena . . . all kinds of institutions find simultaneous expression: religious, legal, moral and economic. In addition, the phenomena have their aesthetic aspect and they reveal morphological types . . . this necessary form of exchange . . . is nothing less than the division of labor itself."[1] Phrases such as "very complex patterns" or "multiplicity of changing social facts" are frequent in his writing. He drew away, and drew us away as well, from the temptation to schematize which is built into the science of man.

Lord knows Marcel Mauss was not an easy professor to have! His beginning students were thunderstruck when they heard that cavernous voice, emerging from an unseen mouth inside an abundant beard, run down a list of unknown authors and their unknown works, utter such aphorisms as "The most important thing to study in a society is its rubbish piles," and give them a kindly warning that unless they knew the tongues of classical antiquity plus Sanskrit, Hebrew, and Chinese, not to mention German, English, and Dutch, there was no point in their trying to tackle ethnology. The peoples and cultures that cropped up in his demonstrations ranged from ancient China and the India of the Vedas, Greece and Rome, the Celts and the Germanic tribes, to Polynesia, the Eskimos, the Kwakiutl in Canada, the Papuans in New Guinea, the Arunta in Australia, and a hundred others. He quoted in perhaps twenty different languages and made bibliographical references that were as obscure as they were varied. Some of his students were discouraged and lost their footing. But for the others, once they recovered from their initial panic, the seeming chaos took on meaning, and dazzling flashes of unsuspected links and piercing intuition illuminated the marshaled hosts of facts.

Marcel Mauss was never more himself than during his seminars at the Ecole des Hautes Etudes, in one of those dusty, old-fashioned rooms at the Sorbonne where I myself, many years later, was to guide my own

1. London, Cohen and West, 1954, p. 1.

students. There were rarely more than half a dozen of us at a time grouped around him, as he sat and commented on the book he had placed before him on the awkward table. In the crossfire of questions and answers, he drew, excitedly and profusely, from that boundless store of facts and examples he carried inside his head, and it was exalting to witness the birth, as it were, of his thought, vigorous and superbly free, agile and mighty. Sometimes it was like a turbulent stream, leaping from boulder to boulder, and sometimes like a broad and peaceful river.

To complete our initiation into the human sciences, there were courses and field work in prehistory, paleontology, and linguistics. For the study of physical anthropology we went to the laboratory of the Muséum National de l'Histoire Naturelle in the rue Buffon while, for ethnology, we visited the Muséum d'Ethnographie du Trocadéro. In this way I came to know Dr. Paul Rivet, who reigned over both places at once. The lab in the rue Buffon was pleasing, with its workrooms and their outdated furnishings, the prodigious library, the collections of skulls labeled "Serb, Orthodox, aged 28," for instance, or "Young Turkish girl." The ethnographical museum (known since 1937 as the Musée de l'Homme), where Paul Rivet had just taken charge, was an aggressively ugly building at that time, a cross between a Moorish bazaar and a Byzantine cathedral, which housed a gigantic jungle of dusty, half-open display cases and crippled boxes. Inside them, mingled with pottery fragments and pieces of moth-eaten cloth, were collections of the utmost scientific value and marvelous pre-Columbian, Oceanian, or African art objects. Enlightened amateurs regularly made raids upon the museum, which was supposed to get along with almost no staff at all and on funds that were barely adequate to buy labels. Rivet's first act was to close the museum altogether before beginning to reorganize it with the help of Georges-Henri Rivière. Volunteers were recruited, for lack of any better solution, and I was among them. My first experience in practical ethnography came when I plunged into the labyrinth of dark halls and storerooms and managed—how, I don't know even today—to find those Tiahuanaco copper hooks which Rivet wanted to submit to his friend, Erland Nordenskjöld, the Swedish scientist.

Paul Rivet had the gift of making any question he touched on crystal clear. Mauss's manner of thinking was like live coals: tall flames could shoot out of them, but so could clouds of smoke. Rivet's mind, by comparison, was more like a lamp giving bright and steady light. As a young army doctor at the beginning of the century, he went on the French scientific mission that was to measure an arc of the meridian in the Andes. From the five years he spent there emerged his first book, *Ethnographie Ancienne de l'Equateur*. It was the contact with living Indians and vestiges of the past which had shown him his vocation. The training he had received was more naturalistic than philosophic, and he did not have to make any effort to free himself from dogmatism, which would have been as incompatible with that training as with his own character. He was to realize very quickly, and with remarkable penetration, how complex human facts are, to what extent physical, cultural, religious, and linguistic data are intermingled, so that ethnography was at the crossroads of various disciplines, all converging toward an identical object: man. His method was to approach a problem from every possible angle—direct observation, reading, excavations —and, without any preconceived notion, to compare techniques, costumes, or vocabularies, to rely on prehistory, the chemistry of metals, or comparative pathology. In short, he would use anything he came upon that could help him grasp the segment of humanity he was studying. He began by applying that method to his research into the origins of the American Indians[2] and extended it to that obscure and tantalizing question, the relationship between the American continent and the world of the Pacific, Southeast Asia, and Oceania.

With the boundless energy and activity he brought to his roles as organizer and instigator, he was in a position to sway an entire sector of French science, through his museum, the Musée de l'Homme, the Institut d'Ethnographie, the Société des Américanistes, and the Centre National de la Recherche Scientifique. He was a great stirrer of minds. His own mind was constantly alive with projects, and he managed to extract from the clutches of government officials and the pockets of private patrons the funds needed to send young researchers, fresh out of

2. Paul Rivet, *Les origines de l'homme américain*, Paris, Gallimard, 1957.

the Sorbonne, to their first assignment in the field. Whereas in France he became known to some extent only when he launched into the political skirmish with an ardor that brought him many a disappointment, in Latin America his name was haloed with prestige, which often reflected onto the novice ethnographers he sent off to Mexico, Brazil, or Peru, and whom he spurred on until they had published their first books or articles and defended their doctoral theses.

It was a great stroke of luck for myself and a few others to be able to draw on those two sources at once, the encyclopedic knowledge of Mauss and the methodical, pragmatic, orderly science of Rivet. Undeniably, neither man was easy to get on with. Mauss often took refuge behind a thicket of vagueness, although he could also be disarmingly good-natured; and as for Rivet, his vast and lucid intellect was set off by an uneven and temperamental nature. But what good fortune it was to have met them both! As the years went by, I became attached to Rivet by an affection that lasted, untarnished, until his death.

And that, I might say in conclusion, is how the dreams of a child immersed in picture books come to melt into the mixture of adventure and routine, observation and reflection, which forms the ethnographer's life, and how a man becomes devoted to the science of man which (in France, at least) is still like a Cinderella whom no good fairy has yet equipped with a carriage.

At the rate things are going, we will soon know more about the Selenites or the Martians, if there are any, than about the inhabitants of our own planet—our own brothers. Our civilization is not very concerned about the motto of Greek civilization: Know thyself. What a stunning contrast between, on the one hand, the energy we expend and the huge sums we spend in our determination to explore nature, penetrate the secrets of the atom, and probe the endless reaches of space and, on the other hand, our negligence, our stinginess, our lack of organization when it comes to knowing ourselves! Apart from medicine and some aspects of psychology, economic and demographic surveys, the study of man and human cultures is vegetating or is simply written off as a branch of metaphysics or an amusement for talkative travelers. In France particularly, a young researcher must feel the impetus of a very compelling vocation indeed before he launches into a career from which he can expect to derive strong intellectual satisfaction, certainly, but little respect and even less money. The funds spent in France on ethnology and the related disciplines, such as prehistory or comparative mythology, are infinitesimal; there is no doubt that the social sciences remain the most underprivileged of all the departments of the Centre National de la Recherche Scientifique.[3] It was pitiful to see such scholars as Abbé Breuil, Leroi-Gourhan, or Lévi-Strauss struggle to wrest a mere thousand francs from close-fisted officialdom to prevent a researcher who was doing indispensable work from starving to death. In the thirties, Paul Rivet did manage to arouse some interest in our branch of science, but since then it has waned to such an extent that a single atomic mushroom bursting into the stratosphere costs more than all the social sciences put together.

But just think about the enormous problems latent in the future of the human species! Think of the sometimes crushing errors which the Western nations could have avoided, either in colonizing or in de-colonizing, if their conduct had been guided by some accurate notion of ethnic realities. Think of the helpless dead end of relations between "developed" and "underdeveloped" countries. Think of the damaging intensity that racial antagonisms are taking on throughout the world. Think of these and a hundred other questions of like importance, and it becomes clear that, even from a pragmatic standpoint, ethnology deserves as much attention and as much support as the physical and biological sciences receive. Governments leave no stone unturned when it comes to discovering mineral or petroleum resources, but what on earth makes them overlook man himself, the raw material of any policy? This is a difficult oversight to explain, except as a survival of the prejudice which combined the study of man together with a certain branch of literature; it is one of the ruts in which governments and elected bodies get stuck. They have not yet caught on to the idea that human technicians can be as vital to the public welfare as agronomists or prospectors and speleologists.

3. I had the honor of belonging to that department for over ten years; in 1960 I was ousted for my political nonconformity, not for reasons of scientific capacity.

Besides, even if ethnology did not have immediate practical applications, why should it be brushed aside? It is a method for understanding men, in the same way as mathematics constitutes a method for understanding things. Sometimes certain mathematical calculations or speculations are arrived at before there is any practical use for them, but later they prove indispensable.

In the meantime, every day that goes by means another language lost, more techniques and customs that disappear, more ethnic groups that are broken up, and all the while our civilization, whose very existence is the cause of this destruction of a thousand different cultures the world over, does nothing to salvage even the wreckage of all those sinking ships.

In order to understand the present in which he lives and try to peer through the veils surrounding his future, man must reconstitute his past as fully as possible. Vestiges of that past are rotting underground everywhere in the world, and every year only a minute fraction of them can be brought to the surface because the means at hand are so slight.

By virtue of a great collective effort, renewed from one generation to the next since the Renaissance, it has been possible to take inventory of the living world, to list, describe, and classify the genera and species even of extinct insects and vertebrates. But no such effort has yet been applied to man himself, to past and present ethnic groups and cultural bodies, to a point that would make it possible to arrive at a generally acknowledged descriptive nomenclature. Of all living beings, man is the one least known to man.

Why don't we in France follow the example of our English-speaking colleagues and simply call this science of man "anthropology"? In France, that term was applied to the study of man considered as a branch of natural history, and the museum laboratory was the laboratory of anthropology. Rivet himself, Broca, Quatrefages, and Deniker were illustrious exponents of that discipline, which was based on the measurements of living beings and skeletons and extended to human fossils. It goes without saying that the physical traits of the various human groups are of great importance, and all of us, in one way or another, have done that sort of research. But anthropology conceived along those lines and taken in the strictest sense of the term could never define more than a fraction of the science of man—that is, ultimately, the science that studies societies and cultures. Accordingly, the word "ethnology"—equivalent to the German "*Völkerkunde*"—came into common use to designate the science whose object is "peoples," or human groups, while "ethnography" is the more specific term for the descriptive study of those groups. As a result, I am an ethnographer when I observe and describe a society and an ethnologist when, going beyond description, I try to penetrate further into an understanding of the structures of that society, or when I compare that society to others, or when I try to retrace the influences, borrowings, diffusions, and evolutionary phenomena which affect one or more societies. It is a pity, perhaps, that in French there is no counterpart for the German term "*Kulturmorphologie*." But, in the last analysis, any nomenclature is largely arbitrary and convention-ridden and I, for my part, shall take this one as it is commonly in use.

As I have just said, ethnology *lato sensu* applies to man living in society and to all cultures. Clearly then, there is no space limit or time limit on its subject. There is no reason why ethnology should specialize in the so-called "primitive" peoples, whether living or recent, and rule out any study of more developed civilizations, past and present. A Parisian or a New Yorker is just as legitimate game to the ethnologist as an Arunta or a Papuan—begging their pardon. Yet why is it that the ethnographer almost always goes looking for his field of observation in distant places, among aborigines who, rightly or wrongly (mostly wrongly), are looked on as the survivors and witnesses of an extremely ancient form of society? There are several reasons. First of all, there is the illusion of "primitiveness," which I will be coming back to; then, the fact that when a population is small and a society is not very extensive, it is easier to grasp them than it is to grasp a more massive civilization. And, also, the fact that a change of surroundings, as total and as abrupt as possible, and the heterogeneous picture formed by certain structures and customs compared with our own do a great deal to make up that sense of relativity without which the research scientist would remain bound by the prejudices of his own civilization and unable to understand any other. Just remember what a healthy effect the first Indians from Brazil had on the inquiring mind of Montaigne!

Then, too, there is a matter of urgency to be considered; one of the most pressing jobs is to note down certain phenomena before it is too late, for they are disappearing faster and faster. At Pastora, for instance, in San Luis Potosí, there were four or five very old men who, between them, and with great effort, could barely manage to recall four dozen words of their ancient language. In Michoacán I arrived too late to record the last vestiges of the Pirinda tongue, for the old woman who still spoke it had just died. Time is running out for the research scientist, who must work faster than the erosion that is wearing away facts which may be crucial to the knowledge of a given culture.

Even so, and at all costs, we must get the idea out of our minds that an observation is more valuable and interesting because it was sought out in some wild and remote spot, twenty days away by boat or on foot from the last village, where the inhabitants have coppery skin and wear feathers in their noses. Just as much—perhaps more—can be gleaned from a study of a village in Auvergne or of a district of Paris or from archaeological research done in Mesopotamia, Rome, or Chichén Itzá.

Inevitably, each of us comes to have his "favorite" series of cultures or "his" continent or region. The great weakness of world-wide syntheses is that their authors have worked them out on the basis of their thorough knowledge of one civilization, or perhaps two or three, and have had to be content with more superficial reading to gain knowledge of the others. For instance, when I see what Toynbee has written on the Mexican civilizations which I believe I can say I know quite well, I realize how imprudent I would be if I were to start lecturing on China. Spengler has no peer when he is dealing with the "Arabian" Orient or with Gothic Europe, is erudite but full of prejudices concerning Greek and Roman antiquity, and sounds vague and arbitrary on the rest of the world. I prefer the modesty of Alfred Kroeber: his posthumous *A Roster of Civilizations and Culture* (Chicago, 1962) shows that at the end of a life of research and study centered chiefly on the American natives, he made an effort, and rightly so, to break out of that field of specialization and take a look at civilizations as a whole, but he was very careful not to contrive one of those artificial constructions which are as vain as they are brilliant, and whose time has surely not come yet.

The fortunate feature of Americanist ethnology—to which Paul Rivet introduced me and where he guided my first steps—is that the specialist is very naturally and constantly led to link the past and the present. As soon as you set about studying the Aztecs or the Maya of today, how can you help but look at those of yesterday? The transition from ethnography to archaeology is both imperceptible and indispensable. It has become commonplace to photograph a Chiapas Indian in front of a stela over a thousand years old, to show that the profile of stone and the face of flesh and blood are like two coins made with the same die. This is an everyday experience in Mexico. There, duration is always present and palpable; there, time is felt as a dimension.

Ideally, the perfect ethnology should make a synthesis of all human activities, all cultures, all periods, and all countries. Just as Laplace dreamed of an intelligence which would embrace the movements of the largest bodies in the universe and those of the lightest atom in a single set of terms, and just as the natural sciences aim to penetrate into the remotest nook of the entire physical world, so we can imagine a science which would bring the whole world of man before our gaze. Then it would really deserve to recover the title of anthropology. But there is no need to say how far we are from that ideal. Our science, more than any other, is subject to the interference of philosophical, theological, or even political dogma, and still has to work hard to defend its autonomy and gain recognition for its existence. Take a thinker such as Teilhard de Chardin, for instance, who was also an outstanding paleontologist. It is remarkable that in his work he left aside all the concrete evolution of man over several hundred millennia past and thought it possible to jump, without transition, from the remotest origins to the present time, which, in his view, is already turned toward a future colored by the most glowing tones of his own poetical metaphysics.

Of course it is tempting to replace the study of various cultures as they really are and really were, with their reciprocal influences, their births and rebirths and their declines, by the convenient outline of a single and continuous evolution toward a culminating point, or toward the Messianic ideal of the classless society, or toward the ever more elevated degrees of infinite progress. If that is their outlook, the Catholic thinker and the Marxist theoretician go along with the "average" Westerner, who is convinced that the whole human adventure amounts to an ascending development from the savage to the pre-eminently civilized man—who is none other than himself. Whereas ethnology, even though it is still in its infancy, does at least dispel these illusions. It shows us mankind grouped in societies of varying sizes and structures, groping for the way and managing not more than one in a thousand times to build up a civilization which will decline anyway, after a few hundred or a few thousand years, from full flower to decay and death. The ethnologist accepts this reality for what it is. His task is to describe, know, and understand it as best he can, and not to hide it under a heap of tempting or consoling postulates. The ethnologist studies history but does not glorify it. He does not fondly imagine that he has found the key to all these various phenomena, assuming that such a key could even exist, which he doubts. He knows that it was chance which caused him to be born into a certain society at a certain time, and that they constitute only one phase of one culture among others. In many cases, because he is aware that our knowledge has its limits, he prefers not to pass judgment at all.

If, as Voltaire said, "the occupation of a prophet is exceedingly irksome and dangerous,"[4] then in some respects, and for the same reasons, the business of being an ethnologist is no easier. Like the prophet, he inevitably runs up against preconceived notions. Simply because he is so aware that cultures and their arts, morals, and cosmologies are all relative, he cannot help annoying the dogmatists. But, still, what an absorbing business it is for anyone driven by that unremitting curiosity I mentioned earlier to explore bookshelves and museums, the crumbling ruins of cities, and the trails that wind through forests and mountains!

---

4. *Philosophical Dictionary*, Vol. IX, article on "Prophets", London, E. R. DuMont, p. 26.

Chapter Two

The Men of the Forest

It WAS OVER THIRTY YEARS AGO THAT I MET SOME Lacandon Indians for the very first time.

We were on the swampy shore of a lake, in the shadow of one of the densest forests in the world. My companion was Adolf von Schmeling, an experienced brush explorer, Pomeranian by birth but Chiapanec by adoption. Together we fired into the air to inform the "Caribes," as they are called locally, that we were there. Like the pillars of a cathedral nave, trees rose all around us to the lofty, leafy vault that hid the sky, and the shores of the lagoon, though it was very close by, were hidden by the trunks of the trees. After the sharp bark of our guns, the silence had returned, heavier than before. We waited in the stifling hothouse heat.

Then suddenly they were there, four furtive little silhouettes in off-white robes, long hair loose on their shoulders, noiseless bare feet. Minutes later we were out in the open air and gliding in their dugout canoe over the still gray water. Far away, the lake broadened out at the foot of high chalky cliffs where vines hung down in tangled skeins. Soon the scorched-leaf roofs of a *caribal*, a Lacandon village, came into sight on a promontory that had been cleared of brush. Columns of smoke climbed from the hearths up to a cloudy sky.

Although this was the so-called "dry" season, it rained every day in this Lacandon country, and the same was true when I went back there the following year. At the limit of Mexico and Guatemala, between Palenque and the Lacantún River, between the Usumacinta and the Jatate, live perhaps two hundred Indians, in small groups scattered over an area of nearly 39,000 square miles, in the folds and crannies of

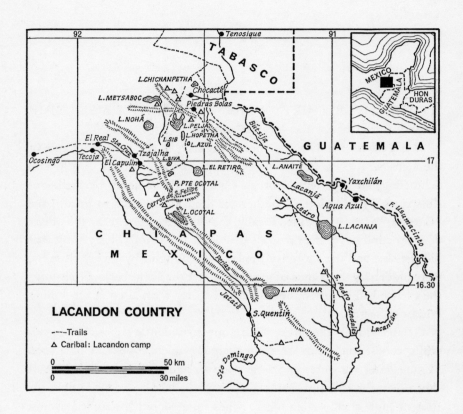

LACANDON COUNTRY

----Trails
△ Caribal: Lacandon camp

0   50 km
0   30 miles

a vast mountain chain grown over with jungle, pocked with lakes, crisscrossed by countless rivers, streams, and creeks. Relentlessly, the wind that blows off the Gulf of Mexico pushes toward this forest the clouds and mist that hang in the tops of the trees, lazily wind down the slopes, and break up at any minute into showers of rain over this ocean of vegetation choked with water.

What a relief it is, what a feeling of comfort you have when you reach the huts of a *caribal* and at last you are out of the wet! Huge logs, laid starwise, glow day and night; the Indians always sleep with one eye open, and more than a dozen times in the night they will get up to keep the fire going. Often a small fire is lighted under the hammocks as well to keep mosquitoes away and ward off the damp. The palm leaves of the roof have been lacquered black by the smoke.

Even today, if I go by one of those autumn fires at home where we burn dead leaves, the harsh smell of smoke suddenly carries me a dizzying way, through space and through time, and I am back under those blackened roofs near the Caribes with whom I lived and shared meals of cassava roots roasted in the ashes. I still see the little cabins in the midst of the jungle, the crops planted in tiny plots between the felled trunks of trees, the green wall of the forest, the lake growing dim in the hazy distance. Once again I am sitting in a hammock while the everlasting smoke stings my eyes and throat and Tchank'in ("little sun") is at work delicately sharpening flint arrowheads.

If I am not mistaken, I saw six Lacandon hamlets or villages, accounting for nearly half the total population. Some were cleaner and neater than others, with bigger and better-built houses. The wealthier ones were brightened by large light-green tobacco leaves and the darker clusters of banana leaves, while others were overrun by the thorny, sterile brush. One feature common to them all is that the artificial clearing where the cabins are built is carefully hidden. Each *caribal* is several days' march away from any of the others and access to it is protected: either you can reach the *caribal* only by water, or else the paths leading to the hamlet fade out and disappear as they come near it. You can be scarcely twenty yards away and pass by a group of huts without seeing them.

The Lacandones form a very distinct society. If you compare them with the neighboring natives of Chiapas, their originality becomes very obvious. For instance, with minor local variants, they speak the "classic" Maya of Yucatán, not the Tzeltal dialect. Not one element of their clothing is European style, and they have no hats; the men wear a tunic and the women a blouse and skirt, except in the southern zone, where the women wear tunics similar to the men's.

Since they have never been evangelized, their religion is the old polytheistic one. Far from grouping together to form villages under the authority of "*principales*," like the *katinabs* of the Chiapas tribes, they scatter in an infinity of small autonomous groups which sometimes burst and subdivide into still smaller ones. While there are men among them who might be considered leaders, or chiefs, the type and extent of their authority varies from one *caribal* to another. The chief may be the oldest father in the group, or the eldest brother, or the man who is said to know more about the gods and rites than the others do. Sometimes it is the man who, by his violent or even tyrannical nature, has come to dominate the others. However that may be, whenever a Lacandon can no longer bear to live with the other members of the group for some reason or other, he takes his wife or wives and his children and he leaves. Somewhere in the brush he clears a small area and there he settles, far from any contact or constraint.

What may surprise us most about their existence is that the Lacandones manage to live day after day and year after year without a single element brought in from outside. For food, they grow maize, cassava, sweet potatoes, pimento, beans, *chayotes*, tomatoes. They hunt the birds of the forest as well as monkeys, tapirs, and wild pigs. They fish in the lagoons and rivers. They make their bows and arrows of guaiacum wood, reeds, flint, and the parrot feathers they have obtained themselves. Their houses and temples are built of branches and leaves. They grow cotton, which the women spin and weave into cloth for their clothing. The big cigars they smoke are made by rolling together the barely dry leaves of the tobacco they grow. They fell mahogany trees and hollow out the trunks to make their canoes. Not to mention the *baltché* bark they ferment with maize to produce the ceremonial beverage, or another bark which they pound and use for clothing, or the red urucu and other vegetable dyes the women use to decorate their skirts, or the multicolored feathers they put in their hair, or the clay which is shaped into sacred incense burners, or the fibers which are twisted to make string, nets, and hammocks, or the calabashes and gourds used as recipients, or the reeds that are made into mournful flutes. And there is still more.

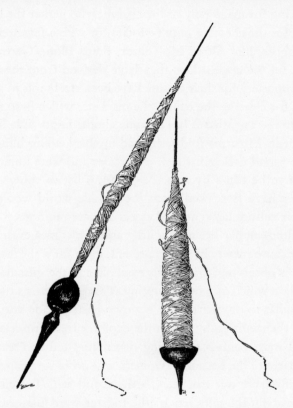

Fig. 1. *At right:* Wooden spindle with cotton thread; tortoiseshell balance made by the husband of the woman who spins. As she spins, she holds the lower end of the spindle in half a calabash shell. The left hand holds the fibres and the right hand makes the spindle turn. Lacandon Indians. Lake Peljá. State of Chiapas.

At left: A wooden spindle with a *corrozo* fruit for a balance. Used in the same way as the spindle on the right. Lacandon Indians. Jetjá River. State of Chiapas.

Every single part of their life—from food to leisure occupation, from weapon to toy, from shelter to ritual—has been wrested from the ground or the forest or pulled from the water, built, fashioned or woven by their own hands.

At one time or another, of course, since the beginning of this century, the Lacandones have come into contact with the *monteros* who come looking for mahogany or the *chicleros* who gather the latex of the *chicozapote* for the chewing gum factories, or with a few archaeologists or ethnologists, like Alfred M. Tozzer, Frans Blom, Gertrude Duby, or myself. Of the acquisitions they have derived from these contacts, the most important for their culture have been steel tools in general and especially, for clearing the brush, the machete, which is so superior to their old stones axes that it has become almost impossible for them to do without it. Firearms (old-fashioned mouth-loading blunderbusses) were soon found useless for lack of powder and were hung up on the cabin roof to be eaten by rust. All in all, a list of things which the Lacandones have borrowed from the outside world would be negligible. Their culture has remained essentially autonomous.

The ethnographer hesitates a little and sometimes even feels some remorse because merely by being present, even for a short time, in the society he is observing, and by his example and the gifts he brings, he carries a germ which may be corrupting. This problem is a transposition of one familiar to physicists. For my own part, I made very little concession to the tradition by which the explorer totes trinkets with him, although I must confess to having distributed red scarves and glass-bead necklaces to the Lacandon women, who were very eager for them, but I readily gave out machetes, knives, and salt. To tell the truth, those were about the only articles the Indians were interested in. They would also have liked some dogs, since they believed that the mere presence of dogs would guarantee them a successful hunt. Dozens of times a day I heard *ts'aten pek'* ("give me a dog"). But they were never willing to taste our food and, in particular, could not overcome their disgust at our frying fat. When we traveled together, they made a point of preparing their own meals separately and found our dish of beans cooked with lard no less repugnant than we found their little monkeys, roasted whole with their skin and their hair, like horrible charred babies on a cannibal hearth.

The Caribes are the only non-Westernized descendants of the ancient Maya—or rather the only non-Orientalized ones since, for the Indians, Europeans are people from the east. Like their ancestors, they are farmers, and especially growers of maize. The staff of life for them, and the tree of life for the seventh-century priests and sculptors of Palenque, is maize. Certainly, they do hunt, fish, and pick fruit, and these additional food resources are often more varied and more nourishing than the monotonous diet of *tortillas* and black beans that the Indians of central Mexico are reduced to. Nonetheless, the basis of all Caribe food is maize. It is made into the big *"wa,"* a kind of *tortilla*, which the women prepare on large banana leaves, where they often mix a reddish cassava paste with the precious and all too rare maize. Maize is also blended with fresh water to make the strengthening beverage called *k'ayem* (*"pozol"*), ambrosia itself, since it is pre-eminently the food of the gods, especially the Sun.

From the earliest times, the Maya of the arid Yucatán peninsula, where the scanty brush is burned by the heat of the sun, have worshipped Chac, the rain god. His nose, shaped like an elephant's trunk, and his mask with the long sharp teeth are depicted obsessively on the façades at Uxmal, Labná, and Kabah. Even today, the Yucatec peasants who have been converted to Christianity direct their prayers and their invocations to Chac. The Lacandones, on the other hand, far from needing to beg the rain to fall, dread the torrential downpours that make gullies in the ground and drown the seeds. Metsaboc, their rain god, is more formidable than benevolent.

My wife and I were the first—and I believe we were the only—non-Indians to go on a pilgrimage to Metsaboc. He is supposed to live in the cliffs rising above a large lake, which we named after him, at the northern tip of the Lacandon territory. This region is dominated by Indians belonging to the *K'ek'en* (*"wild pig"*) clan. They are considered slier, less hospitable, and more warlike than the others, and although we had no complaint to make of the way they treated us, it is a fact that we felt less at home among them than among the Indians of the

2*

Maash ("monkey") clan. Their *caribal* was messy and dirty, littered
with half-burned tree trunks, their faces expressionless, their silence a
little disturbing. To persuade them to lead us to the lake of the rain
god, we had to negotiate at length. Tchank'in Maash, the Indian sage of
La Arena who gave us a very warm and friendly welcome, intervened
on our behalf, bringing the weight of his recognized authority in
sacred matters to bear. His brother K'ayum had been delegated to go
and bring back the chief of the "wild pig" group, a sly figure with the
pointed little beard of a prophet. After two exhausting days' march,
we saw the wall of foliage open ahead of us and the great bluish sheet
of Lake Metsaboc spread before our eyes.

That day, exceptionally, the weather was very fine. The mountains
that line the lake were reflected with perfect accuracy in the utterly still
waters. After the stifling half-darkness of the forest, this vast and sunlit
landscape, with not a single bird or cayman to disturb its silence and
charm, was radiant with an unhuman and unreal beauty. Our companions were more silent than ever. It was easy to feel that a divine and
invisible presence was hovering over these deserted waters.

The sanctuary of Metsaboc is nothing other than a shallow cave,
just above water level, in the cliffs covered with petroglyphs—mysterious drawings reminiscent of those made some seven or eight thousand
years ago on the walls of the ravines in the Tassili-n-Ajjer, in the heart
of the Sahara. The Lacandones attribute these drawings to the gods
themselves. In the grotto are countless incense burners, masses of copal
gum burned as incense, and human skulls—doubtless those of Caribes
for whom their relatives chose this last resting place. Once again, on
the day we visited this sanctuary, Metsaboc had summoned the mist and
rain to hang above his lake.

In order to reach an old abandoned *caribal*, our canoes followed a
narrow, twisting channel through the flooded forest, its dead trees lifting their gnarled branches like arms to the sky. Never have I felt so
clearly as I did then that I was really at the end of the world.

Although Metsaboc is feared as a god, it is from *k'ak*, fire, and *k'in*,
the sun, that the Lacandon—a peasant, after all—expects his survival to
come. In order to plant maize, he must take a great deal of trouble to

clear away the brush and undergrowth, then wait until the heat of the sun has dried it enough for him to burn it. This is done in the spring, when there is a lull in the rains before the long humid season begins. At the foot of the trees that have been left standing, the Lacandones pile up enough dead branches to set fire to the trunks themselves. Then they await a favorable day. The fire is lighted by means of a very simple device. A piece of soft wood, with a hole hollowed out of it, is placed on the ground. A piece of harder wood is placed upright in the hole and the Indian turns it back and forth between his palms, producing a sort of incandescent wood powder which ignites some cotton fluff. The Lacandon then invokes the fire god before taking the blackened cotton, blowing on it softly, and placing a few very dry twigs on the cotton. Soon flames are rising into the air, and the firebrands will be used to set the whole field burning.

All of this physical-ritual technique dates back to the earliest antiquity, about 3000 B.C., when farming first began in Mexico. It was with exactly the same fire stick, the *tlequiauitl*, that the Aztecs lighted the New Fire every fifty-two years at the top of Uixachtecatl Mountain. The Lacandones never allow the fire for their daily use to go out; when on an expedition, they use a flint which they strike with an old piece of iron above a cotton wick, kept dry in a snail shell. But the sacred flame that must burn the forest so that men may sow and live can leap only from the fire stick that has been a tradition for thousands of years.

Obviously, a premature rainy season or a series of unseasonable storms and downpours would be a genuine catastrophe. The survival of an entire group of human beings hangs on a precarious equilibrium between the forces of water and the forces of fire (and of the sun). So Metsaboc must be appeased, and K'ak and K'in must be propitiated.

From what little we know of the ancient religion of the Maya in the classic period, between the fourth and ninth centuries, we are inclined to think that it was strongly dualistic. Not only were there benevolent gods and fierce gods, but some of them could be either favorable or harmful, depending on the case. In the main, the Lacandones of today hold the same beliefs. Whereas the Sun is the good god at his best—

Fig. 2. Fire sticks used to burn off the forest before sowing time. The stick with the two round holes is held down on the ground with the foot. The other stick is placed vertically with its point in one of the round holes and is turned between the palms of the hands, which move rapidly up and down the stick, over and over again. Some cotton fluff is placed near the hole. Rubbing produces and ignites wood powder from the horizontal stick; the powder sets fire to the cotton, which is gently blown on before being touched to the dry grasses or wood. Lacandon Indians. San Quentin camp. State of Chiapas.

especially among the southern Caribes, who worship him almost exclusively—it is Kisin, his counterpart, god of the world underground, who causes earthquakes and sickness. After the Sun has gone to bed in the west, he must travel under the earth during the night; and to combat fatigue, he has to drink many a calabash of *k'ayem*. This obliges him to cross the dark realm of Kisin, but, fortunately, the Sun is protected by Usukunkyum, "his venerable elder brother," a benevolent though chthonian deity who carries the Sun on his shoulders to the eastern exit from the nether world.

Fig. 3. Lacandon kitchen-hut.

Near the southernmost *caribal*, I explored a series of caves where the Lacandones ventured only in fear. These caves were once inhabited, or at least used, by a native population who existed even before the Lacandones and which they know nothing about. At any rate, so it would seem from the remains found there: pottery objects much better finished than those our Indians make and very well aligned little stone walls built at the entrance to certain hypogea. The strong sulphur waters of a spring close by have dug a labyrinth out of the hill, but we had neither the time nor the equipment to explore it. The air there was heavy, almost impossible to breathe. Our Indian companions were sure we had inveigled them into the realm of Kisin. One of the Indians, Bor, was an excitable and unstable young man. He reproached me violently, assuring me loudly that we were all going to die. But as time passed and the god did not wreak any vengeance on us and we did not succumb to any supernatural disaster, our prestige was at its peak, and Bor did not hesitate to let a little of it reflect onto him.

The long-forgotten sacred book (*Popol Vuh*) of the Quiché, who are Maya Indians in Guatemala, was brought to light by the tireless research of Abbé Brasseur de Bourbourg. It shows that this subterranean world that the natives called Zibalba has always had a powerful grip on their imaginations. The wise man I mentioned earlier, Tchank'in Maash, had countless stories to tell about that shadowy realm where rivers of ice and rivers of fire flow side by side, and where K'in, the Sun, transformed into a hero of mythical-historical dimensions, foils the malevolent designs of Kisin. Similarly, in Quiché antiquity, bold explorers of the infernal regions overcame the magic obstacles which the rulers of the dusk placed in their way.

It was at the San Quentin *caribal* that I had a dramatic revelation of what the myth of the bad god signifies for an Indian. The chief of this group was a placid, sturdy old man with knobby limbs. He owned the largest cabin in the village and gravely presided over ceremonies in the well-built temple. He had two wives. The older of the two—and this was a very important privilege—"knew" how to prepare the *k'ayem* for the gods. In other words, when making the maize beverage, she knew what gestures and ritual phrases to incorporate into it. If these were missing, the supernatural beings would not accept the offering with pleasure. When a rattlesnake bit the chief in the foot, I performed a rudimentary operation on him, using a razor blade and alcohol. He bore this without a murmur, though his jaws were clenched and his eyes filled with tears. He began to talk about what he remembered. His life had been a continual flight from illness, flooding rivers, and the arrows of other, hostile Lacandones: one long struggle against hunger and the elements. Suddenly he was describing an epidemic that had struck the group he belonged to—just at the time, I estimated, when "Spanish flu" was rampant in the world following the First World War. Panting as he uttered the hard and emphatic Maya syllables, he made a whistling noise to reproduce the deadly flight of the arrows released by illness, the invisible archer, and imitated the convulsions and death rattles of their victims. "Kisin! Kisin!" Immediately, I was reminded of the *Iliad*, when the arrows of Apollo rain death upon the camp of the Greeks.

The idea that an archer-deity hurls his arrows at the victims of certain illnesses is common to more than one culture. For the Aztecs, it was the god of the morning star, "Lord of the House of Dawn," who performed that sinister task at certain dates in the divinatory calendar.

According to their aged chief, the inhabitants of this southern *caribal* came from the Guatemalan jungles. Their entire religion is dominated by the cult of the Sun and the cult of the Forest. Among the other Lacandones, a throng of divinities occupies the three superimposed heavens, the incense burners that represent them in the temples, and certain specific places. Kanank'ash, for instance, the "Protector of the Forest," dwells in a cliff (of which I had a fleeting glimpse) in the heart of the jungle separating the Chocoljá River from the La Arena River. The forest all around this cliff belongs to him, and my Lacandon guide forbade me to cut or break even the smallest branch. Another cliff-dweller—this time in the cliff overlooking Lake Peljá—is Itsanohk'u, "the great god Itsana"; I believe we can recognize in him the Itzamna of the classical Maya. The Indians who live on the shores of that lagoon call it "the lake of Itsanohk'u." The high limestone wall is marked with petroglyphs like those of Lake Metsaboc, as well as the imprints of open hands, and a drawing of a plumed serpent in a style unlike that of the petroglyphs and akin to ancient Maya art. Still other gods haunt the ruins of Yaxchilán, the great Maya city on the left bank of the Usumacinta. It was at its zenith in the seventh century.

There is no doubt that Yaxchilán was a religious metropolis of utmost importance. Palenque impresses us as the city of refinement and grace; Piedras Negras seems to have been the city where powerful lords and priests wanted the evidence of their grandeur to be preserved in carven stone; Tikal stands out from all the cities for its pyramids, sheer and lofty as skyscrapers. But it is at Yaxchilán that bas-reliefs and statues achieve an extraordinary feat: they make us share a little of the sacred feeling which a religion that disappeared over a thousand years ago and that we know nothing about aroused in its believers. Despite the gulf of centuries and the gulf of mentality between our civilization and that one, we are touched and moved by the serpent-gods, the jaguar-priests, the officiating priests brandishing feathered banners, and the faithful in their embroidered mantles heavy with jewels and plumes. We can still see them carved on the stone lintels just as those skillful sculptors caught them, in their hieratic poses.

Even today, for a handful of Indians scattered throughout the forests, Yaxchilán remains a holy site and a place of pilgrimage. Every year the Lacandones trek to it, bringing their incense burners and their copal resin, which they call *pom*. They place their crude ritual pottery in front of the carved lintels, at the feet of the statues, on the steps of the crumbling palaces and temples, and they burn their incense and chant their prayers. They do not seem to make any distinction between the natural caves where certain gods, like Metsaboc, "live," and the ancient buildings of Yaxchilán. For them, both are "houses of stone," as compared with their own branch-and-leaf huts.

In 1897, Teobert Maler, a German who explored these solitary regions on behalf of the Peabody Museum, noticed that one of the statues at Yaxchilán had been decapitated, probably by some logger looking for mahogany. Now, the Lacandones in the northwest are convinced that the beheaded statue shows the god Atch-Bilam, and that on the day when his head is put back on his shoulders, the end of the world will come. Then the jaguars will appear and devour mankind, just as, in the Aztec cosmology, the *Tzitzimimé* monsters will surge up on that last day, when a final earthquake will make our universe collapse. The Lacandones are frequently concerned with the end of the world, and in this they resemble the other Mexican Indians, including those who built up the most brilliant civilizations. Since antiquity, the idea has been found everywhere—even among the Indians now living in the southwestern United States—that several other worlds (the Four Suns) preceded our own, that each of those cosmic eras finished in cataclysms, and that our world will know a no less tragic end. This notion of a sort of pulsation of the universe, a cyclical flux interrupted and resumed by the alternation of the creative and destructive phases, is curiously reminiscent of Stoic doctrine and, at the same time, of certain theories of modern cosmology. We begin to suspect that when the human mind, whether that of a poor forest-dwelling Indian or of a refined and subtle Greek, is faced with the mystery of things, it has only a limited number of hypotheses from which to choose. After all, in all the million years that a creature has existed that we may call man, and in the five or six thousand years since he began to build civilizations, none of us—not even we Western peoples so proud of our science—has done more than skim the surface of the great mass of the unknown. Why should we laugh when we see how a handful of Lacandones, huddled in their forests, try to answer the silent questions put by nature as it surrounds and often crushes them? Instead, we should recognize in them, weak and unequipped as they are, what makes the dignity of all men.

No Indian ever made me so clearly aware of that dignity as the "sage" I have mentioned twice. Like many Caribes, he was called Tchank'in, and he belonged to the "monkey" clan, Maash. With his brother K'ayum, he lived near the small and limpid La Arena River in a man-made clearing with two huts and two temples. We lived with him, his wife, and his young son Nushi, a graceful little boy who wore a robe of beaten bark. Tchank'in, whom some logger had nicknamed "Anacleto," wore a long and spotlessly white tunic. He was fairly tall, light-complexioned and fine-featured, with slightly wavy jet-black hair that fell to his shoulders. Generally he stood very straight, with a mixture of gravity and benevolence. He often chewed a huge cigar, and had some fine tobacco plants growing all around his cabin. A tireless worker and skillful hunter (peccary skulls whitened where they hung on the roof of his hut), he performed to perfection all of a Lacandon's tasks and his duties toward his family, and visibly held sway over his brother. As a result, that *caribal* was the most orderly, the cleanest, and most healthful that I ever saw. He gave up part of his house to us. A bark partition separated it from the rest, and, in the night, Nushi would slip in noiseless as a shadow to tend our hearth.

My most lasting memory of our stay in that clearing is one of still-hazy dawn, the gray-lighted hour when humidity fell from the leaves and rose from the ground, and the howling monkeys greeted the sun with their long metallic-sounding cries from the tops of the trees that towered over us.

But above all, Tchank'in was the wise man, he who knew the myths, the cosmogonies, and the rituals better than anyone else in the Lacandon country. We knew of his reputation long before we met him, for his fame extended from Lake Peljá to Lake Metsaboc not only among the members of the "monkey" clan but also among the people of the "wild pig" clan. Several days before reaching his camp, I was given some idea of his moral ascendancy: the chief of the small group living along the Chocoljá River had begged me not to tell "Anacleto" anything about the violent quarrels that had shaken his family (out of jealousy, his youngest wife had drowned one of the sons of the first wife), because he feared the disapproval of the wise man of La Arena.

Morning after peaceful morning we spent with him, painstakingly filling our notebooks. We conversed in an odd and often comical mixture of Maya and Spanish—if Spanish is really the term that suits the obscenity-ridden jargon of which Tchank'in had picked up a few scraps in the course of his brief contacts with the mahogany prospectors. He talked about the gods, listing their names and their dwelling places in the heavens and on earth, describing their clans and their marriages, evoking the disturbing subterranean world and the charmed reaches of that heaven where, after death, the Lacandones find splendid forests free of brush and jaguars, plentiful game, and abundant maize. He showed us the incense burners he kept in his temple. Those of the gods had vertical stripes, while those of the goddesses had a checkered design in red and black. He explained how *baltché* was prepared in a tree trunk hollowed out like a canoe; this fermented beverage is named after the sacred bark which no woman can touch without dying. He prepared the red *k'oshop* ("urucu") dye made from crushed berries. Tunics are bespattered with it when rituals are celebrated, and in the same way are dyed the strips of beaten bark that are placed around the incense burners when copal is burned in them and when crumbs of food and tobacco are placed on the lips of the little figures that decorate them.

Fig. 4. Terra-cotta incense burner which may represent the god Itsanohk'u. During ceremonies, incense or copal is burned in the bowl and crumbs of food are placed on the lower lip of the sculpted head. The native who is officiating wears a bark band around his head and places another around the incense burner. Lacandon Indians. Lake Peljá. State of Chiapas.

As a profoundly religious man, Tchank'in did more than merely explain his conception of things or the ritual observances on which the favor of the gods and the lives of human beings depend. His attitude and everything he said reflected a certain ethic. Above all, he abhorred violence and felt the deepest repugnance for the often deadly rivalries, with their whirring arrows and bloodied machetes, that split the Lacandones when the men of one group tried to kidnap the women of another. The world this man had lived in from birth was a hard one, where everyone had to wrest his own survival from nature and defend himself more than once against his fellow men. But from his sober gestures, his quiet voice, his whole being radiated a serenity and goodness that were expressed day after day in a hundred touching little ways: he presented us with an incense burner, or went to pick a bunch of bananas for us, and when at last we had to leave, he offered us a net full of *chayóte* fruit to roast over our campfire.

Often, in an ethnography book, you cannot see the forest for the trees. By this I mean that the book talks so much about the society that it forgets the individuals, as if "primitive men," who are assumed to be more subject than "civilized men" are to a crushing conformity with regard to religion and magic, were all cast in the same mold. We are told what "the Arunta tribe" of central Australia do or think, and not what a particular Arunta does or thinks. It is true that any society, by the mere fact of its existence, places its stamp on the conscious and subconscious life of its members, and even on what would seem to be their most elementary reactions and attitudes, such as the way of walking or sitting, or expressing joy or sorrow. But judging by the Lacandones, the range of individual variations is as broad in a society like theirs as it is in our own. I would even go so far as to say that we, who are so inclined to consider ourselves "independent-minded," are more conformist than they are. Among the Caribes, in any case, even though there are so few of them, and to take only one example, that of religion, I knew a genuine theologian and moralist like Tchank'in Maash, unsubtle believers like the Lake Peljá Indians, and, near the Jetjá River, a bad-tempered, evil, alcoholic old chief whose concern with metaphysics was reduced to a minimum, if not totally lacking. And I remember that although the chief of the Chocoljá group, who was first cousin to Tchank'in the sage, had a temple and incense burners, he openly admitted that he was ignorant of the rites that went with them.

In fact, it is worth considering to what extent a certain amount of initiative and individual innovation comes into play within the limits of the collective tradition. Of course, every *caribal* and every head of a family honors essentially the same gods, harbors the same general conception of the universe, believes in the same myths. But that observation is more or less valid. A closer analysis[1] brings out the changing, unstable side of the myths and the rites, whose texture becomes poorer or richer depending on what the individual Indian—member of a very scattered society that has no specialized clergy, no books, and no writing, for that matter—forgets, leaves out, or adds, and so alters what he has learned from the generation before him. Among the San Quentin Lacandones, the pantheon is reduced to the Sun and the Forest, and *baltché* is almost unknown. But the sage of La Arena, in addition to being an expert on the preparation of *baltché*, can list dozens and dozens of gods, with their genealogies and the myths in which they appear. I even suspect that he personally made up certain myths, especially one that focused on Metsaboc and told how he married the daughter of a *santo* (Christian) among the Ocosingo mestizos!

All in all, religion weighs heavily on the daily life of a Lacandon. Already we are staggered when we try to measure the time, the energy, the ingenuity, and the physical strength that each of these Indians has to devote simply to the job of overcoming the hostility of nature in order to survive in surroundings that have nothing at all in common with the paradise of the happy savage, as the centuries of enlightenment were pleased to imagine it. Every new day means that the same ceaseless labor and exhausting effort must begin all over again: to cut down enormous trees; repel the perpetual assault by the brush; burn the jungle; build and clean the cabin; grow maize, cassava, cotton, tobacco; look for, find, and pick more than a dozen other plants; manage to shoot arrows through birds, monkeys, peccary, and fish! And yet the Indian will go to the trouble of building a temple as well, often making it bigger and arranging it better than his own hut, with an altar table or shelves. With care he makes incense burners, shapes figurines that represent the gods, uses urucu, sootblack, and chalk to decorate them. He goes into the forest to search for the aromatic copal gum and berries from which to make dyes. He beats the bark for the ritual strips, hollows

1. See, among others, the study by Georgette Soustelle, "Observations sur la religion des Lacandons du Mexique méridional," *Journal de la Société des Américanistes*, Vol. XLVIII, Paris, 1959.

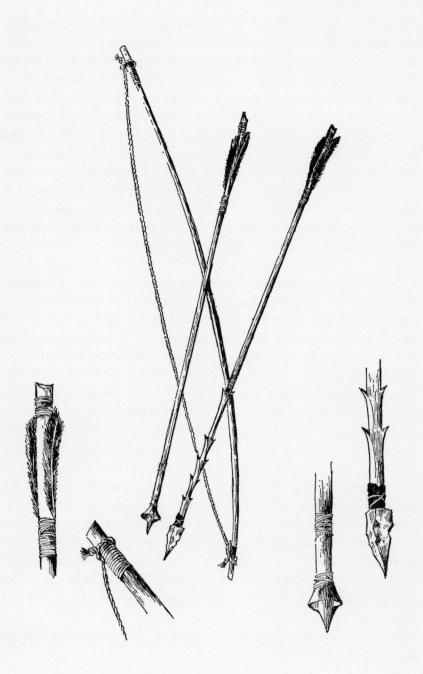

out a tree trunk in which to make *baltché*, puts up a shelter under which to prepare *k'ayem*, makes long and wearying pilgrimages to Yaxchilán. In short, the Indian, who already has so much difficulty in obtaining and producing what is strictly necessary for himself and his family, forces himself to work almost as hard again in order to serve his gods.

Gordon Childe noted[2] with some asperity that the Sumerians "wasted in futile rites" most of the surplus which their society produced. The Lacandones, whose society has no surplus at all or only an infinitesimal one, are an even more striking case. But of course *Homo sapiens* is not always and everywhere *Homo oeconomicus*. It is our own mercantile and utilitarian civilization which has invented the latter type of human being and is astonished at not finding it at other points in space and time. We are the exception, not the rule, and there is nothing to prove that the exception is admirable. We place work and money on a very high pedestal, but in Genesis work is looked upon as a curse, and the Bible warns us that it is more difficult for a rich man to enter the kingdom of heaven than it is for a camel to pass through the eye of a needle.

Social and family structures among the Lacandones, by contrast with the importance of religious ideas and practices, may be compared to one of those Maya monuments which have been eaten away by the jungle; whole sides have collapsed so that all that is left is a fragment of wall here and there between two gaping holes, or a lintel suspended

---

2. *The Prehistory of European Society*, London, Penguin Books.

Fig. 5. Hardwood bow; the bindings are cotton dipped in black wax, and the rope is made of *henequén* (*Agave rigida var. Sisalana*). This small bow is used along with the toy arrows at right as a plaything for boys. Lacandon Indians. Chocacté and Lake Metsaboc camps. State of Chiapas.

At right: Arrow with reed shaft and lentoid wooden point; used to kill birds without spoiling their plumage. Small, used as a toy. Lacandon Indians. Chocacté and Lake Metsaboc camps. State of Chiapas.

At far right: Arrow with reed shaft, barbed wooden shank, stone point; used to kill monkeys (because it is barbed, the arrow remains in the wound). Small, used as a toy. Lacandon Indians. Chocacté and Lake Metsaboc camps. State of Chiapas.

above a void. At the beginning of this century, Alfred M. Tozzer, an American ethnographer, found that among the Lacandones there was a system of exogamous clans with animal names, which in turn were grouped into two "phratries" or "moieties." But even at that time the system had become very lax, and I myself was able to find only remnants of it, chiefly among the Lacandones of the northwest. The clans are named for ten different animals, including the monkey, the peccary or wild pig, the jaguar, the forest pheasant, the coati, and the white-headed monkey. Each of these animals is called the "relative" ("*wonen*") of the clan members, but the taboo on eating it has disappeared, supposing that it ever existed. Indians of the Maash clan blithely eat their monkey "relative" and the K'ek'en do not deprive themselves of wild pig. The clan name is transmitted by the father to his children and, in principle, a man will marry only women belonging to some other clan than his own. In the area stretching from Lake Peljá to Lake Metsaboc, men of the "monkey" clan do in fact look for women of the "wild pig" clan, and vice versa. Each of these two clans belongs to a distinct "moiety."

In the south, the system has fallen into such disuse that only infinitesimal traces can be found. One of the women bore the name of *Tchanuk*, which, in the northwest, is given to the women of one of the two phratries. From this it may be inferred that the structure which can still be observed in the north must have existed in the south as well, just as it is inferred, from the tooth of a mammoth found in an excavation, that that pachyderm used to live there.

What is more important is that, if I am to believe my wise man of La Arena, the stars and the gods are considered to belong to one or the other of the two exogamous "moieties." But the sun and the moon, who belong to the same "moiety," are husband and wife, and therefore incestuous. The incest of the Sun and the Moon is found in a goodly number of American mythologies, beginning with that of the Eskimos.

The inclusion of gods and heavenly bodies, even if only to a very slight degree, in purely social systems shows that like many other peoples (especially Indians such as the Pueblo in New Mexico), the Lacandones have tried to bring some order into their world by casting the net of human categories over it. This is a special instance of those "primitive categories" which Durkheim and Mauss studied. Just how far should we go in assuming that this system of social structuration and classification of natural and supernatural beings used to be more complete and flourishing than it is today? The ethnographers of my generation, like Claude Lévi-Strauss,[3] have abandoned to some extent the notion of "totemism" at which the specialists had arrived by taking phenomena observed in perhaps twenty different societies and kneading them into one conceptual model. But nothing proves that the same term can cover facts which are Australian or North American, Arunta or Ojibwa, and we have still less right to tack on to that theoretical concept what may be observed among the Lacandones. What is clear is that the structures of the Lacandon society have atrophied and so, as a corollary, has the system of categories which stemmed from those structures; for that vision of the world reflected human society, and not the world itself. No structure can persist when the society itself falls below a certain density. The demographic collapse of the Lacandon ethnic group, the indefinite scattering of minute groups throughout the vast expanse of forest, and then the fact that those very groups are torn apart again and again by rivalry because women are scarce while the chiefs continue to be polygamous—these are factors which, in the long run, make it impossible for matrimonial rules to be strictly observed or complementary clans and "moieties" to maintain a peaceful and reciprocal basis of exchange. The young men go out on kidnapping expeditions without being very concerned about what clan the women they take belong to. The result is fights, reprisals, and rancor that further divide a society already becoming more and more thinned out in the vastness of its natural surroundings.

Judging from my conversations with Lacandon men, their ideal is polygamy. A man who has several wives has prestige and authority. Certain women, because they know the ritual that accompanies the preparation of *k'ayem* for the gods, enable their husbands to have an enviable rank in the ceremonials. Of course, the man who has several wives has to feed them by bringing back to the hut enough maize,

3. *Totemism*, Boston, Beacon Press, 1964.

game, and fish for all of them. On the other hand, he will always have a better supply of clothing which they have woven and, on his return to the clearing, will always find wild plants, roots, and fresh-water shellfish that one or the other of his female companions will have gathered during the day.

As I have already said, among the Lacandones of the northwest, the rule of matrimonial exchanges between clans works just about in the normal way. I say "just about" because I knew of at least one attempt at kidnapping, near Lake Metsaboc; it ended in the kidnapper's death by arrows. Among the Lacandones of the south, a man cannot find a wife except within his own group. If there is no woman available of roughly his age, he will marry either a very elderly widow or else a very young girl, generally one of his paternal uncle's daughters. Whereupon he goes to live in the hut of his uncle–father-in-law, works and hunts with him and for him, and places the maize he gathers and the game he takes in the common family fund. For several years, until he can set up house in his own cabin, he has no land or hearth of his own, although a separate fire is kept burning in the family house for his cousin and himself. Little girls of four and five can be seen trotting through the *caribal* alongside their "husbands" or sitting near the fire being taught the techniques of Lacandon cooking. I even saw a two-year-old, who from time to time still sucked her mother's breast, and was already "married." Under these conditions, it is not at all surprising that two young men from San Quentin undertook to raid the *caribal* of the Jetjá River, a week's journey away by foot and by canoe, in the hope of finding or kidnapping women. They did not succeed.

So we see that one portion of these Indians lives in a system of exogamous clans and another in a system of endogamy—which means, without putting it into technical jargon, that some of them look for wives outside their own group and the others marry within their group or even within their own family. The first structure corresponds, I imagine, to what the Lacandon society was when it was larger and organized into two "moieties" and at least ten clans; at that time it assured its own cohesion through matrimonial rules which bound the different social segments to one another. Far more important in such an organization than the taboo on certain marriages is the obligation to contract certain others. Like an optical illusion—where the variations of attention and the movements of our own eyes alternately make certain elements of the drawing stand out or recede—any matrimonial rule can be "read" two ways, negatively or positively. The prohibition that prevents a man of the "monkey" clan from marrying a woman of the same clan (thus, in particular, from marrying his female cousins on his father's side) is only one side of the coin. The other is that he is obliged to go and look for a wife elsewhere and especially by marrying a "wild pig" girl who, for that matter, may be his cousin, daughter of his maternal uncle. Each time that such a union takes place, an additional bond is created between the "monkey" clan and the "wild pig" clan, despite the traditional distrust and antipathy that separate them.

Clearly, the endogamy practiced by the Lacandones of the south is only a second-best solution; a man marries into his own group and within his own family only because he cannot manage any other way. The proof is that if he could kidnap women from somewhere else, even if that meant using violence, he would willingly forgo his female cousins.

Both endogamy and kidnapping are expedients which extreme isolation and decline of numbers have made necessary. Like the most beautiful girl in the world, a society cannot give any more than it has.

At various times and in different areas of the world, exogamous matrimonial systems have contributed mightily to the solidity of human societies by weaving a stubborn network of reciprocity among groups, which have been either indifferent or hostile but at any rate distinct. Like a rushing stream tamed by a hydroelectric dam, the sexual instinct, asocial if ever an instinct was, has been directed and channeled for the sake of social cohesion. Obviously, any exogamous pattern functions within a broader endogamous pattern. A man does not marry within his clan but must marry within his tribe; a Lacandon will not marry a Tzeltal woman (although I knew of a Lacandon woman who married a mestizo from Tenosique, the legendary "Pancho Caribe") any more than a Christian man will marry one of his close relatives or a Moslem woman. Most often, then, there are two limits—internal and external—on the possible types of marriage. The causes of endogamy among the Lacandones of the south are collapse of social structures and demographic impoverishment. The endogamy of the Incas and the Pharaohs, which went so far as to become incest, stemmed from the dynastic pride which would not allow kings of divine essence to mingle their blood with the blood of inferior beings. The endogamy which persists in the area around the Mediterranean and especially in Moslem countries[4] is based on an exalted and exclusive notion of the purity of one's descendants and a determination to keep one's property in the family at all costs. So it is that in the reality of human history identical or analogous phenomena can be the results of totally different causes. This means that a social fact must not be abstracted from the over-all context in which it is placed. The facts that an ethnologist studies differ from those with which a mineralogist or a botanist is concerned in that they have a meaning. Light is shed on each of them by the entirety of the culture to which it belongs. The vanity of those comparative constructions (such as Morgan, in the nineteenth century, and later Engels liked to produce) becomes obvious. They were a handy sort of inlay of fragments drawn from the grab bag of literature on the subject. For instance, by taking the family institutions of two or three Australian tribes, of some Polynesians, of certain North American Indians, and of classical antiquity, and by stringing them together like beads, you acquire the illusion of having reconstituted the development of the family throughout several millennia and over several continents. Actually, you haven't reconstituted anything at all, except a chain of concepts. But I will have more to say later about the hundreds of ambushes that await the ethnologist when he shifts from observation to reflection.

Observation itself, for that matter, is deceiving. What we call "a fact" is a hybrid, fruit of the person who is looking and of what he is looking at. Ethnology is the only science which considers man as man and not, as biology does, as a living being among others. The observer belongs to the same species as the observed and would not in fact

4. Germaine Tillion, *Le Harem et les cousins*, Paris, Editions Stock, 1966.

understand anything about what he is studying if he were not able to feel and experience within himself the mental processes and behavior of the strangers who are also his fellow creatures. You cannot remain indifferent and detached before the aborigine you are questioning and whose attitudes and words you are noting down. He may repel you at times, but most often you will feel sympathy for him and his people, and that is the indispensable vehicle of your investigation. But because of that sympathy, your science will be imbued with subjectivity just at the very instant when you are getting at its object; will that distort your perception? It is hard not to become attached to a people when you have lived among them, shared their cabins and their maize, learned their language, known what their work and their worries and their fears are. One of my masters was the pastor Maurice Leenhardt, once a missionary in New Caledonia; later on, as minister of the French over-seas territories, I could see for myself in what veneration the Kanaka still held his name. From listening to him, it quickly became clear that the thinking of the aborigines had had at least as much influence on his own thinking as his had had on theirs. Sahagún, the famed Catholic missionary, is another example. We are indebted to him for that extra-ordinary opus on pre-Columbian Mexico, *Historia General de las Cosas de Nueva España*. It shows to just what an extent a sixteenth-century Spaniard, a priest and a profoundly devout man, had come to identify himself with the Aztecs. He even called them his sons, at the same time as he considered their beliefs and their rites abominable and demoniacal.

There is no such thing as observation in the raw state. The ethno-grapher uses cameras and recording machines; he is not in himself a camera or a tape. Any observation includes a dose of judgment, and no judgment can be totally objective. The researcher has to force himself to find an imperfect and unstable equilibrium between cool detachment which, if carried to an extreme, would even cancel any possibility of research, and a sympathy (or an antipathy) which would completely corrupt his judgment. The ethnographer's field work, even if he makes use of all the modern techniques, is actually an art which is "all in the doing." Like a medical diagnosis, and to a degree that varies with the individual, it involves a certain flair, and an ability to take things in at a glance.

While the ethnographer and the aborigine have their human condition in common, the ethnographer is set apart from the aborigine by the fact that he belongs to a different culture. No matter what effort he makes to free himself from it—and he would not be an ethnographer if he had not made such an effort or even if he had not wished to make it—nothing can alter this reality: he is a twentieth-century Westerner who was born and has grown up in a cultural environment which is localized in time and space, structured in a certain manner, and marked by a religious, legal, and aesthetic tradition that has become as instinctive for each of us as our mother tongue. His birth has placed him on the surface of that planet which is his culture, and from there he observes another planet which is the aborigine culture. The astronomer sees the heavenly bodies from the angle imposed by the situation of the earth in the universe and by the configuration and speed of its movements, and from those heavenly bodies he receives light which, before reaching his eye, has already traveled for thousands or billions of years. In the same way, *mutatis mutandis*, the ethnographer cannot escape the culture of his origins. One of his tasks, and not the easiest one, is to become sufficiently aware of that fact to adjust his observations and his judgments accordingly. He must also keep in mind that any culture, at the particular time when he is studying it, is only the present aspect of an historical reality or duration of which it transmits the message, just as the glow our eyes see today is the luster of stars dead before our world was born.

In the case of the Lacandones, for instance, the European who comes in contact with them will have trouble avoiding a double mistake. Immediately, these creatures scattered throughout the forest and carrying Stone-Age weapons will be "primitives" to him. Although they are survivors of a distant past and are lost in the present, it will also seem to him that they have never had any history, as if the life of this people for thousands of years had been only a biological duration. The illusion of the "primitive" does not yield easily. It is doubtless one of those prejudices which our culture injects into our thinking while we pay no attention. Classical ethnology in France or Germany or England was based on the exegesis of the beliefs, structures, and ritual of peoples like the natives of Australia, who were looked upon as "primitives" and were assumed to give us some idea of what all human societies must have been like in their elementary stages. By labeling them *Naturvölker*, the German scientists even expelled those men from culture itself, and in so doing reverted to the man-in-a-state-of-nature myth which was so important to eighteenth-century French philosophy. One of the fundamental features of Spengler's theory is the notion that only civilizations have a history, whereas the "primitives" before them and the "fellahs" after them merely live a certain continuity, in the way that animal societies do. Even Kroeber, in talking about the native cultures in North America which he knew so well, went so far as to state that in the beginning they seem "almost a still pool, a historyless, unstructured ethnographic reservoir."[5]

But do primitives exist? Nothing is more doubtful. When Arnold Toynbee maintains[6] that every society has had a history, and yet at the same time he calls certain societies "primitive," it seems to me that this is a complete contradiction in terms, for whoever says history says change, evolution, mutation, and whatever has changed cannot thereafter be "primitive." If some Neanderthal men had survived until our own day in the caves of a mountain range cut off from the rest of the world, and even if the making of stone tools still characterized their way of life, nonetheless we can safely assume that their customs, beliefs, and family structures would inevitably have evolved over the past 150,000 years and so could not be termed "primitive."

The Australian Negroes, who fit the description of typical "primitives" which has been inculcated into generations of students, have few or no dwelling places, wear no clothing, and do not raise crops or animals. But the amazing complexity and sophisticated subtlety of their clan and family structures are evidence of a refinement which has been focused on something other than technology and of a development which presupposes an extensive history. As much time has passed since

5. A. L. Kroeber, *A Roster of Civilizations and Culture*, Chicago, 1962, p. 58.
6. Toynbee, *A Study of History*, Abridgment of Vols. I–VI, pp. 48–49.

the beginnings of these so-called primitives as since our own beginnings, but they have put it to a different use. We would be deluding
ourselves if we thought that they had remained static for tens of
thousands of years and as a result were a living demonstration of what
the origins of all cultures must have been like.

The culture of the Lacandones is not "primitive" to any degree.
Unlike certain Indians of tropical America, such as the Nambikwara
whom Claude Lévi-Strauss has studied, they are not reduced to grub-
bing a few seeds, roots, and insects here and there in order to survive.
They belong to that part of the population of the Americas which
accomplished its agrarian revolution about 3000 years B.C., just as our
ancestors in the Old World had done some three thousand years earlier.
It is true that the Mexican Indians do not have cows, pigs, sheep, or
goats. Accordingly, their agricultural economy has not been able to
include animal breeding, and they grow maize without benefit of
plows. Nonetheless, and no matter how strange it may seem at first to
apply the word to these men of the forest, the Lacandones are peasants.
Although a large part of their food resources comes from hunting and
fishing, and although they use sharpened stone arrowheads as the prehistoric Europeans did, they are distinct from the nomadic hunters and
collectors whom the Aztecs called "Chichimecs." Along with all the
other Mexican and Central American tribes, both the famous and the
less famous, the Lacandones must be included among the farming
peoples; that is, among the peoples it would be arbitrary to call
"primitive." Isn't the discovery of agriculture the most significant stage
in the forward movement of mankind, the stage that marked the most
decisive break with the past?

Should the Lacandones be called "primitive" because of their way of
thinking, where religious and mythical concern forms such a large part?
The French school of sociology, which was derived from Auguste
Comte and is responsible for the rebirth of the social sciences in France,
has set positivism, or the supreme phase of human evolution, apart
from the theological and metaphysical forms which are said to have
gone before. Starting from that premise, we would assume, as Lévy-
Bruhl did, that the "primitive" is characterized by "prelogical thought,"

a mentality which is radically unassimilable to our own, lost in a mystical haze, and innocent of the principles of identity and contradiction. It is true that in his last books, Lévy-Bruhl himself, who combined great subtlety with inexhaustible learning, softened the rigor of his theory, acknowledging that a certain degree of "*prélogisme*" remained among us "civilized" men and adding, "Even I don't mind a good fairy tale from time to time. . . ." But like a badly exorcised phantom, the notion of a difference of nature, an unbridgeable gap between prelogical thought and positive thought, continues to haunt the sociology that is taught in the universities.

It takes no more than a week of living with the Lacandones to realize that in their daily existence they behave with an acute sense of the reality about them. They are not daydreamers on the verge of succumbing to illusion. They have to cope with very hard natural surroundings and must survive in a pitiless world. Every day they apply a whole series of very skillful, very specific, and very complex techniques (for instance, just try to work the pre-Columbian loom used by the Caribe women) which indicate a very positive outlook. Without it, there would not be any Lacandones.

And that is not all. They do not just automatically repeat the gestures needed to grow maize, to hunt, and to fish. Their actions are based on knowledge. Time and time again I marveled to see how unhesitatingly they knew how to find what they were looking for in the midst of the jungle, at so many days' march in a certain direction: a clump of trees whose bark can be beaten, a colony of parrots, a lone plant with edible fruit, a deposit of clay or flint; how knowledgeably they could distinguish the different varieties of berries, vines, animals, or stones; how signs that were invisible to us guided them in the great shadowy forest. In this world of theirs, they were the experts and I the novice; it opened before their eyes like a book and they read it with ease. For me it remained a closed book. Undeniably, that book is the only one they know, and only by memory and experience is their knowledge passed on from one generation to another. That does not detract in any way from the fact that the Indians have taken inventory of the natural setting in which their lives are lived and that they keep it

3

constantly up-to-date. This is a genuinely intellectual process, and I do not find any intrinsic difference to set it apart from the most rational of our mental processes. In the mind of every adult Lacandon, there is a body of geographical, botanical, zoological, and mineralogical knowledge, all unwritten but very well adapted to its objects.

We belong to a civilization which has carried its technology very far, so far in fact that we have become accustomed to obtaining what is essential for our survival in exchange for money, and to pressing a button or lifting a lever in order to have light and heat and to move from one place to another. Where the Indians survive, we would certainly die of hunger and privation. We ought to stop and think just how unlikely each discovery or invention made by "savages" in the past really was. How much fumbling, how many mistakes and failures did it take, over a period of centuries, before they learned, for instance, to tell the edible from the inedible plants and found out just how each one of them should be treated? Just think of the way in which the Indians of the Amazon region and the Guianas turn cassava, which contains a violent poison, into food safe for human beings by grating it and pressing it in a woven cylindrical basket. The principles of practical chemistry were discovered over the hearths, the clay cooking pots, and the calabashes, under the shelters of the tropical peoples, and were probably, to a large extent, the work of the women, while among the men, who were more mobile, knowledge extended to the vaster areas they ranged over in search of game.

On top of the foundations formed by techniques and knowledge, the mythical and religious symbols are placed. The Aristotelian pattern: first physics, then metaphysics. The Indians do not consider that there is any gap between the two. It is we who make the distinction; it does not exist outside of our own minds. But for a Lacandon who sets about burning the brush and sowing maize, it is just as necessary to invoke the god of fire as it is to light the fire itself. For successful hunting, he obviously needs a bow that has been carefully made and arrows that have been well-balanced, but if, in addition, that bow and those arrows have not been kept free of any contact with the women, they will have lost all their effectiveness. As a puny mortal, the Lacandon tries to inject his will, his prayer, and his hopes into the workings of the world. A rite that is performed meticulously and at the right time neutralizes the threat of jaguars, appeases the storm god, and assures the Sun of nourishment when he reappears each morning after his perilous voyage through the subterranean darkness.

This is one aspect of the Lacandon's religious beliefs. It is closely bound up with his positive outlook and realistic actions, both of which condition his survival as a human being. It also assuages the anxiety he feels, as a creature besieged by the universe. But it has another aspect, as an attempt to introduce some order into the immense and threatening variety of things. The Indian does not confine his efforts to finding and using resources, nor even to performing rites to influence the interplay of cosmic forces. He tries to understand the world and to represent it to himself in a coherent way. His cosmological myths, his beliefs about the structure of the universe, the superimposed heavens and the hells, about life in the afterworld and about the end of this world are far more than a merely utilitarian undertaking. The names given to cliffs, lakes, rivers, and the ruins of cities are determined by a sacred geography, just as the animal species, the gods, and the stars appear to be bound by categories which have been transposed from social reality to the natural and supernatural creatures. The purpose of this effort to know and to organize is to fit reality inside a framework of order molded by thought.

Of course it is legitimate to say that there are two poles to that thought: the sacred and the positive. But how much subtlety and shading go into the transition from one to the other! All meditation is utilitarian to some degree, and every practical activity has a sacred background. Whereas from a formal standpoint these two aspects of thought and action are antithetical, in fact they are complementary. Man as he really is and lives constantly achieves a synthesis of them. The "primitive" is not "prelogical" any more than the "civilized man" is "positive." Both of them, each within his own culture and his own era, perform on two keyboards at once.

The only way to make the conventional contrast between the

modern Westerner and the "primitive" is to amputate reality in two
ways: overlook all the Westerner's metaphysics, whether implicit or
overt, and strip the "primitive" of all the knowledge about his surroundings that he has acquired and adapted to practical ends. If we do
this, then we will undoubtedly come up with a rationalist and a mystic,
each in the pure state. But clearly they would be abstractions, largely
born of that naïve feeling of superiority which any culture or society
instinctively harbors with respect to the others. We like to think we
differ more widely from the Indians than we actually do.

Within any given civilization, the proportion accounted for by each
type of thought varies with the period. In Mediterranean antiquity, the
terminal phase of the Roman Republic and the beginnings of the
Empire probably mark the lowest ebb of mysticism and the highest tide
of positivism. The scientism of the times is voiced in Lucretius' great
materialistic poem. Then came the engulfing wave of mysticism. From
it Christianity emerged victorious—after a long struggle with Mithra,
the Sun, and the syncretism of Julian—to conquer souls and the State.
I do not agree with Spengler and Toynbee that all civilizations necessarily go through the same cycles. Yet we cannot help but be struck by
the similarities between the present phase of our own Western civilization and the phase that the Mediterranean world went through some
two thousand years ago. Perhaps the next wave of religiousness is not
far off in our own future. But who is qualified to state the laws that
govern that wave? Has it any laws at all, for that matter?

In all events, no known culture, no matter how far back we look in
time or to what remote corner we search the continents, has ever been
purely positivistic or purely mystical. Whether Maya, Babylonian,
Aztec, or Egyptian, architects, mathematicians, and astronomers have
included a strong dose of myths, divination, and magic in their calculations and their science. When, as in our own case, scientific knowledge
becomes the property of laymen, the realm of the sacred merely shifts
but does not disappear. Even when this is carried to an extreme, in a
civilization reputed to be the most detached and liberated from any
metaphysical tradition, there still remains, as at the bottom of a
laboratory retort, an insoluble deposit of unproved and unprovable

axioms, principles and attitudes, cosmic and ethical concepts. The content of this irrational minimum varies from one culture to another and one age to another, but it is never altogether absent, and each culture secretes it as a flower gives off scent.

The Lacandones are an example of the fact that man must act in order to survive. In order to act, he tries to acquire knowledge. In order to organize his knowledge, he projects the mental structures pertaining to his own society upon the reality outside it. There is no reason why we should not believe that it has been this way ever since the first human—or even hominoid—being existed, since the adventure of our species began a thousand millennia ago. The act of choosing a certain stone to make a weapon or a tool from it, as the first hominoids of China and Indonesia did, implies foreknowledge as to what that weapon or tool will be, how it will be used, and what a future action will be. For tens or hundreds of thousands of years, this awareness projected beyond the present may have remained obscure, but it was already a way of looking at things and arranging them. From examples closer to home, starting with Neanderthal-type man at Monte Circeo, then the mural paintings of Lascaux or Altamira or the cliff sepultures of Grimaldi, it becomes clear that at the same time as they developed better tools and weapons, these elements of long ago mankind were constantly looking beyond the immediate requirement of utility for ways to make contact with the cosmic forces and the dead.

We do not know at just what point in human evolution language appeared. I personally find it difficult to call any creature not endowed with language a man. What is established is that any language expresses a system of categories, a classification of things, a structure which the mind of speaking man imposes on objects and beings. We may find that classification rational or irrational: the masculine and the feminine, the animate and the inanimate, the singular, the dual and the plural, or round objects and long objects, what is hard and what is fluid, what has to do with I-who-am-talking and what has to do with others, and so on and on. The fact remains that in all of us—white or Negro, Mexican Indians or Ionian Greeks, swarthy Egyptians or blond Vikings—the mind is not content to give back a passive reflection of the world and uses the symbolic system of language to organize the world so as to replace the enigmatic chaos all around us with an intelligible order.

There is no such thing as an elementary language. The least civilized of the American Indians I know have the most complex tongues. The Pame language is only one example. I found the last vestiges of it as it is still spoken by a few thousand Indians isolated in the rare fertile valleys of the Sierra Gorda Mountains, like oases scattered over this rock-and-cactus desert. Their language has been handed down, probably without any noteworthy changes, from nomadic hunting tribes who knew virtually nothing about agriculture and so represented the most rudimentary form of mankind indigenous to Mexico. It is a diabolically complicated and astonishingly refined language. Everything is ingeniously built on three numerical combinations (singular, dual, plural) and four possible relationships between the object being designated and the persons: "me" (I who am talking), "you" (to whom I am talking), "him," and "them" (or some unspecified person). These uncultivated and illiterate Indians constantly use a whole set of particles and internal inflections, subtle as a delicately mounted mechanism, which reflects a vision of the world characterized by a geometry, as it were, wherein men and things, the speaking subject and the objects, are always precisely situated with respect to one another.[7]

Similarly, every language contains an implicit philosophy and reflects a *Weltanschauung*.

When a Lacandon wants to say, "I am a Lacandon," he uses the Maya expression *"winken"*: literally, "man-I"; in other words, "I am man." To designate us, he will borrow the Spanish words *"la gente"* ("people"). This is certainly a case of ethnocentrism, which is frequent, as each people tends to identify itself pre-eminently with man as a whole. From another standpoint, however, the Lacandon is right: no matter how strange and different he may seem to us, he is first of all a man, one form of the phenomenon man. Whereas under the double

---

7. I discussed the language of the Pame Indians in *La famille Otomi-Pame du Mexique Central*, Paris, Institut d'Ethnologie, 1937, Chap. III, and in "Documents sur les langages pame et jonaz," *Journal de la Société des Américanistes*, Vol. XL, Paris, 1951.

pressure of history and natural surroundings, the use he makes of his faculties has been bent in another direction from our own, nothing in those faculties themselves is inherently unassimilable to ours. I, too, am the heir of a past and the world in which I live is also a jungle. I, like the Lacandon, can proclaim that I am man. He and I are made of the same clay, though we have been shaped differently. Or, to take another metaphor, the two of us are variations on the same theme; we are neither identical nor radically strangers to one another.

Earlier I compared the ethnologist to the astronomer. It is quite true that in relation to one another, the various cultures are situated like planets in space. The universe, as we know, does not revolve around our earth and is not arranged in terms of earth. In the same way, our civilization is only one specific case among others and is neither an ultimate stage, a vantage point, nor a frame of reference intrinsically preferable to others. But the fact remains that those planets are comparable. It is not impossible to know those farthest from us, since all are formed from the same substance. Yet once we have grasped the notion of the relativity of social phenomena and resisted the temptation to yield to an illusory ethnocentrism, we realize that a human condition common to even the most diverse cultures links them all and bridges the gaps between them.

Diderot was certainly mistaken when he had his Tahitians utter speeches which only a Parisian philosopher of the eighteenth century could have shaped. The "savage" is not the virtuous, reasoning man described in his *Supplément au Voyage de Bougainville*. But neither is he walled within an uncommunicable affectivity, a prisoner of dreams, a slave to a static society shut in upon itself. Isn't it we, instead, who are fooled by our own abstractions?

The very first lesson I learned from the coppery-skinned little men of the Chiapanec forest was that I must recognize what, in any human group, relates it to the others and at the same time what is peculiar to it.

APPENDIX TO CHAPTER 2

I had already finished this book when I received a letter from Chiapas, written by someone who knows the Lacandones well and loves them. The letter describes the plight of those Indians today. First of all, their forest is overrun by a horde of natives who come, in greater numbers every year, from the Ocosingo, Yajalón, and Bachajón regions in search of new and unworked land. The Indian newcomers are also Maya, but they speak other dialects and have been superficially converted to Christianity. Because erosion has made their own fields sterile, they prefer to clear the jungle. Furthermore, it appears that the hunt for mahogany is on again, after a lapse of over thirty years. A logging company is setting up its sawmills between the Usumacinta and the slopes of Monte Líbano. And, finally, in the Lacanhá region near Bonampak, where there is a small landing strip, a missionary is striving to convert the Lacandones.

Certain small groups have reacted to this multiple intrusion by falling back toward Lake Metsaboc. Others are holding out at Nahá, in the southwest. Still others have been completely scattered. In the Bonampak region, perhaps fifty Indians have abandoned their native religion and call themselves Protestants. They wear European-style clothing, cut their hair, use modern rifles, and no longer make bows and arrows except to sell them to the tourists who come to see the ruins. These Indians even have transistor radios.

So it seems that this culture, which had survived for over a thousand years following the fall of the ancient Maya civilization, is on the verge of total collapse. In a short time, the ethnic group which shored up that culture will have merged with the half-Indian, half-mestizo mass of eastern Chiapas. Or at least this is the picture I get from that letter. There remains only a very slim chance that some families will be able to find a refuge that is safe enough and remote enough, near Lake Metsaboc or possibly near the Lacantún, to preserve the essential elements of their cultural tradition.

3*

Chapter Three

The Depths of the Past

At THE NORTHERN LIMITS OF THE LACANDON country, where the forest-clad mountains taper off in foothills above the swampy plain, the gray and golden monuments of Palenque stand out from the dense greenness of the jungle.

Though only part of the city has been uncovered as yet, we know that it reached its height in the seventh century A.D. Then, toward the ninth century, the life that had filled it seeped out of Palenque, as it did out of the other Maya cities, and the city became overgrown with brush and trees whose roots gradually broke up its walls. Mute and solitary, Palenque persisted, while in Yucatán and in Mexico peoples and empires fought and built and disappeared each in turn; the Plumed Serpent triumphed at Chichén Itzá in about the year one thousand, the Toltecs fled their highland capital, the bloodthirsty sun worship of the Aztecs became law from one ocean to another, and the Christians of Spain came suddenly over the sea. Cortés must have passed close to Palenque without seeing it in the course of his extraordinary expedition toward Honduras. Neither wars nor revolutions troubled the slumber of Palenque. It took almost a thousand years before Palenque (we do not know how the city was named by those who built it), rediscovered at last, was stripped of its gangrenous green growth and revealed as the amazing spiritual and material masterpiece of a people lost in the night of time.

When I visited Palenque several years ago, under the friendly guidance of Alberto Ruz L'Huillier, the Mexican archaeologist, the single-minded efforts of the experts and their teams of helpers had brought to light what must have been the vital center of the flourishing city: the palace, the group of three temples (of the Sun, the Cross, and the Foliated Cross), the Temple of Inscriptions. Other ruins are visible in the part that has been unearthed, and still others are mounds that can barely be made out in the dusky forest, its great trees swarming with monkeys and parrots.

Judging not only from Palenque but also from Copán, Piedras Negras, Tikal, Uaxactún, and Yaxchilán, the ancient Maya cities were not laid out in a system of avenues and streets but instead were organized around artificial terraces, platforms or pyramids on which the public monuments were erected. The dwelling places, at least those of the common people, must have been scattered about man-made clearings near the fields of maize and probably resembled the leafy-branch-and-wood huts of the Lacandones today. Nothing remains of them now. Only the edifices of stone have withstood, to some extent, a thousand years or more of torrential rains, encroaching vines, and the pressure of gigantic tree trunks.

The spectacle offered by the remains of Palenque, in the midst of exuberant nature, is a subtle alloy of strength and grace. The three temples on their squat pyramids are grouped like pale ivory carvings in a green velvet case, and the openwork roof combs atop these small sanctuaries show a fine harmony of proportion. The Palace is vast and majestic; its halls and galleries give onto four cool and shadowy patios, its arcades are vaguely reminiscent of a mosque, its windows are curiously shaped like a letter "T," and its square tower is three stories high. The portico of the Temple of Inscriptions opens onto an expanse of hieroglyphic panels. Despite the gap of centuries, anyone who gazes on these monuments today feels the silent message of those who built them pounding within him. Immediately and without the slightest hesitation, he knows that he is in the presence of a style, fruit of a lofty civilization that had achieved perfect mastery of its expression. The inarticulate eras have no style, and still less style is produced by those phases that copy and borrow and juxtapose helter-skelter without creating anything. Here, simplicity of conception, the perfect relationship of the detail to the whole, the sureness of execution have left their mark everywhere, on pyramid and temple, sanctuary and palace, bas-relief and stucco, inscription and jade jewel, the carved lintel and the piece of shaped pottery. Not a single object in Palenque, from the stela to the statuette, is ugly or even ordinary. Everything has been stamped with the inimitable seal of style, beautiful in a way that is Maya first of all and then peculiar to this particular city.

A style is a difficult thing to define. Yet who would confuse a statue by Praxiteles with an angel on the cathedral of Chartres? In the same way, you instantly recognize a Tula bas-relief, an Aztec idol, or a Maya sculpture. Let us confine our comparisons to just two neighboring cities: we have no trouble telling the bas-reliefs of Yaxchilán, showing figures frozen in ritual attitudes expressing the presence of something sacred, from the lords and priests of Palenque. Refined and aristocratic on their carved panels, with elongated profiles and uncannily elegant gestures, they are framed by marvelous hieroglyphics combining the rigor of mathematical signs with the fantasy of an arabesque.

Few experiences can be as moving as a trip down into the crypt of the Temple of Inscriptions. In 1952, Alberto Ruz became the first living being to penetrate into the monumental tomb since it had been sealed, over thirteen centuries earlier. The stairway, so carefully hidden and filled up with stones that it took three years to excavate it, leads down from the platform summit of the pyramid to a vaulted crypt more than seventy feet below and supported by massive stone cross-struts. The crypt is almost entirely filled by an enormous sarcophagus, and the bas-reliefs on the slab that covers it are among the most perfect I have found in the Maya country. They symbolize death and the hope of resurrection by showing, with the immediacy of a snapshot, a delicately beautiful adolescent in the very act of drawing his last breath as he lies down upon the monster of the earth. Above him rises the abundant foliage of the tree of life and at the top is a quetzal bird with its precious plumage. The hieroglyphics of the planets form a border around the slab.

Under a transparent cloak of stalactites, nine gods in luxurious robes—the nine Lords of the Night, divinities of the dead—stand guard around the sarcophagus. A skeleton lies beneath the slab. It is that of a

high priest or priest-king, buried with his rings, a jade pectoral ornament, and a mask of jade over his face. Two stucco heads have been
laid beside the sarcophagus; they are young men's faces with refined
features, feather and flower headdresses, and faintly smiling lips. From
a date engraved on the slab, we know that this grandiose tomb was
sealed—for all time, it must have been thought—on what corresponds
to January 27, A.D. 633 of our calendar.

At that time, Teotihuacán dominated the high Mexican plateau
farther to the north and Monte Albán was flourishing in the warm
Oaxaca Valley. East of the Mediterranean, Byzantium had just brought
the Persian expansion to a final halt; but the prophet Mohammed died
eleven years after the Hegira, and the great wave of Arab conquests
was to break over the East. An impoverished and barbarized Europe
struggled feebly in the chaotic ruins of the defeated Roman order. In
the world as it was at that time, and as an omniscient intelligence floating above the continents might have contemplated it, the Maya country,
like a scarf stretching from ocean to ocean, from Yucatán to the
Pacific coast, dotted with white cities, bristling with pyramids, spreading its lush fields of maize over ample expanses of cleared land, would
have appeared as a patch of civilization and peace on the surface of the
planet.

Thirteen centuries later, on the same soil long since reconquered by
the tree and the vine, the serpent and the jaguar, a handful of Indians
barely survive, speak Maya and burn incense to the ancient gods. For
anyone who has known the Lacandones and admired the monuments of
Palenque, the poignant contrast between what is and what was raises
questions that probe the most profound human problems.

But, first of all, can we consider the Lacandones the direct descendants of the builders and sculptors of Palenque and Yaxchilán? What
happened on this land between the end of the ninth century (the last
known engraved date, found at Uaxactún, is 889—the time of the
Norman invasions in France) and the Spanish conquest? We do not
know. It seems that allogeneous peoples came from the coast and occupied Palenque. In the Palace they built a certain number of rooms in
which to live or worship, and they left one of those enigmatic stone

"yokes" that characterize the cultures of eastern Mexico. It is also very possible that even when the cities had ceased to build, to erect stelae and carve inscriptions, they did not die suddenly like a candle that is blown out but, rather, that they slowly dimmed like a lamp without oil, "not with a bang but a whimper." Part of the elite of priest-astronomers and architects, of governing classes and artists must have emigrated northward toward Yucatán, and the rest must have gone back to the fields and huts, melting away and disappearing over a period of several generations. The people of farmer-hunters, scattered throughout a jungle that grows more densely every year around the skeletons of dismantled cities, has preserved only the most rustic forms of the former life. The Lacandones descend from the "plebeians" of the ancient cities.

Although this historical sketch is probably accurate on the whole, it is oversimplified. Neither the shores of the Usumacinta, the Lacantún, and the Jataté, nor the mountains and the nearby lakes were ever sealed off and separated from the rest of the world. It is true that European influence in that area was negligible. In his *Historia de la Conquista de la provincia de el Itza*,[1] the eighteenth-century chronicler Villagutierre y Soto Mayor described the successive attempts launched from Guatemala or Chiapas to reach the Lacandones and evangelize them. None succeeded, not because the Indians put up very strong armed resistance but because the expeditions found nothing but a void. Yet there was a larger Lacandon population in those days than there is now, and an attempt was even made, again unsuccessfully, to regroup them into one large village named Dolores.

But although the massive incursions into the forest were as futile as bullets shot into a swamp, occasional contact did occur at peripheral points of the Lacandon country, and that explains why the Indians have imported the banana tree (which they call *patan*, from the Spanish *plátano*), and why some of them grow sugar cane or raise a few chickens. Nordenskjöld noticed, from studying the reports of explorers in the Amazon region, that the banana tree and domestic fowl traveled faster

1. Madrid, 1701. Reprinted in Guatemala, 1933.

than the Europeans who had brought them into that continent, and that they were very quickly passed on from one native tribe to another, before the pioneers themselves arrived. The same thing must have happened in Chiapas.

Similarly, certain features of the Lacandon culture can be explained only by borrowings from other native groups—their hammocks, for instance, which are very different from those in Yucatán but like those in the Antilles and South America. In spiritual matters too: the gods listed by Tchank'in Maash included one Nawat, whom the wise man of La Arena described as "very ugly." Nawat is not a Maya name but is reminiscent of the little Aztec god Nanauatzin, always shown as a repulsive being covered with sores.[2] According to Tchank'in, this god was worshipped only among the Lacandones of the *K'ambul*, or "wild pheasant," clan, along the Chancalá River. Since it was in Yucatán that the incursions and influences of central Mexico were strongest starting with the end of the tenth century, it is possible that a group of Indians from Yucatán imported this god from the high plateau regions and "Maya-ized" his name slightly.

J. Eric Thompson maintains[3] that the present-day Lacandones are all emigrants from the Yucatán Peninsula. There is no doubt that he is partly right, but only partly. When you see the Lacandones at close range and when you live among them, you cannot shake off the impression that, although they live in isolation, two or even three widely differing physical types are to be found among them. There is the "classical" Maya type, which seems to be a flesh-and-blood reproduction of the figures in the Yaxchilán bas-reliefs or the Bonampak frescoes, with their long convex noses and high cheekbones. Another type of which Tchank'in Maash was a rather good example, has a straight narrow nose and thin lips. A third type, with broad flat face and slightly flattened nose, I found at Lake Peljá and especially at San Quentin. This particular physiognomy bears a striking resemblance to that of the bound captives on Stela Number 40 at Piedras Negras (on the Guate-

2. Georgette Soustelle, *op. cit.*, pp. 150, 158.
3. "Sixteenth and Seventeenth Century Reports on the Chol Mayas," *American Anthropologist*, Vol. 40, No. 4, 1938.

malan shore of the Usumacinta). They are kneeling in fear before a magnificently garbed lord, a *halach uinic* ("veritable man"), who is probably about to decide their fate. The hieroglyphics engraved on their naked bodies must certainly have indicated where they came from. Once these strangers, who may have been non-Maya, were captured and reduced to slavery, perhaps they settled down in Lacandon country. Or perhaps the tribes they came from mingled with the Maya peasants much later, after the cities had declined, and adopted their language and their costumes.

The Lacandones do speak Maya as it is used in Yucatán, but there are very clear phonetic differences between the northern and southern parts of the territory. In the south, the liquid *l* which is so common in Maya has disappeared and given way to a resounding rolled *r*, recalling such other Maya dialects as Chorti or Quiché.

In the light of all this, I am inclined to believe that, contrary to what Thompson claims, the Lacandones descend essentially from the lower class of the civilized Maya society but that, over the centuries, other indigenous elements were added and mixed with the original nucleus. Where did they come from? Probably from Yucatán, and from Guatemala as well. As a result, the Lacandon ethnic group and its culture, simple though they seem, are actually quite complex.

There are even hints that still other ingredients went into the mixture. Among the present-day Lacandones, I found a stringed musical instrument,[4] like a zither on a plank, that they call *pash*—a Maya word which, in the classical tongue, meant drum. But the Lacandones have no drum, except for a pottery instrument reserved strictly for ritual use and which they call K'ayum ("god of song"). So it would seem that they have simply applied an old word to a new object. No native American culture, for that matter, has ever had a stringed instrument, aside from the musical bow. This type of zither is entirely African, and I have found numerous examples of it either in the black Africa collections of the Musée de l'Homme in Paris or at the Musée du

4. "Culture matérielle des Indiens Lacandons," *Journal de la Société des Américanistes*, New Series, Vol. XXIX, Paris, 1937.

Congo in Tervueren-Brussels. The only way it could have been introduced into the Lacandon culture was by African Negroes, doubtless
slaves who were fugitives from the plantations and took refuge in the
impenetrable forests. A detail, but it makes us realize what we might
otherwise overlook, namely, that however inhospitable this forested
area may be or seem, it has offered and continues to offer asylum;
groups or individuals, paying the price of freedom, have availed themselves of this inviolable "sanctuary".

That has sometimes been too high a price to pay, as the story of
Pancho Caribe shows. I have mentioned him already. He was a mestizo
from Tenosique, a large market town in Tabasco State, on the Usumacinta. In about 1900 (everyone in Chiapas knew the story of Pancho
Caribe but no one could give an exact date for it) or, at any rate,
under the dictatorship of Porfirio Díaz, Pancho Caribe fled Tenosique,
either because he was in trouble with the law, or had debts, or was
afraid of some revenge. He went into the jungle, cleared a small plot of
land and built himself a hut, where he lived like the Lacandones.
Eventually, he married a woman of the Maash clan, Tchank'in's sister.
But things went sour between him and the Lacandones, who thought
he was a witch and could cast spells. Perhaps he succumbed to nostalgia.
At any rate, twenty years after fleeing from his native town, he went
back to it, and no one recognized him. With his Indian wife, he
languished there some time until he died. Immediately, his widow left
Tenosique, went back up the Usumacinta, and resumed her place
among her people. She married a man from the "wild pig" clan. When
I knew her, near Lake Metsaboc, she was still using a few words of
Spanish.

So, that attempt at assimilation had come to nothing; but very
possibly other grafts of one stock upon another were successful.
Villagutierre mentions an Indian whom one of the Spanish expeditions
encountered in the woods and who spoke some incomprehensible
language. This indicates that he did not belong to any of the known
Maya fractions of Mexico and Guatemala.

It takes from two to three months for a sturdy man who knows the
area and is traveling on foot to cross the thick jungle that covers the

Lacandon country and Petén until he reaches the Gulf of Honduras. But small groups of Indians who live off the country, staying in one place for two or three years to sow their maize and moving on once the soil has been exhausted, can wander slowly in the interior of the country, meet up with one another at times and possibly mix. This is probably how the Lacandon ethnic group we find today came into being.

If we take the Lacandones to be Maya, for the most part, distant great-nephews of the people whose brains and hands have left us incomparable marvels as evidence of their time, then we are led to an inescapable conclusion: *they are not primitives but rather decadents*, vestiges of a segment of mankind which, for seven centuries, was able to rise very high above itself before falling very low. The history of the Lacandones is a striking example of the processes of regression that our minds tend to overlook because we are obsessed by the myth of uniform, continuous progress. And I am inclined to think that many so-called "primitives," far from representing the hesitant beginnings of our own species and having been frozen in a timeless, changeless past (but, by what miracle would that have happened?) are really products of a history that has pulled them down a long, declining curve, marooned survivors of some long-ago shipwreck.

Take a Lacandon and show him the complex glyphs that his ancestors carved into the stone of temples and palaces. Even though he speaks the language, or a variant of the language which those signs expressed over a thousand years ago, not only is he incapable of reading a single sign (whereas we can decipher part of them), but he does not even grasp the fact that those figures are symbols conveying ideas, figures, or words. The notion of writing remains foreign to him. This gives us some idea of the degradation wrought upon what had been the most brilliant civilization on this continent. But did the shepherds of medieval Rome, who let their herds graze among the ruins of the Forum, know how to read the Latin inscriptions?

The most striking feature of the ancient Maya civilization is an extraordinary intellectual development in the fields of mathematics, the observation of heavenly bodies, and the reckoning of time. This was a people without industry or machines and even without metal of any kind; their techniques never went beyond the level of Old World Neolithic, and in fact they did not have either animals or vehicles. Yet they produced an elite, doubtless a sacerdotal one, of astronomers and arithmeticians. For the basis of their numbering system, the priest-scientists used the twenty digits of the hands and feet, and even today the word *uinic* ("man") is used with the meaning of "twenty" to form numerical nouns. The twenty-day "month" was called *uinal*. But the Maya's special genius was revealed in the double discovery they made no later than the third century A.D. and probably long before: the notation of numbers by the position values of the figures, and the zero. None of the civilizations of Mesopotamia or Asia Minor or the Greeks or the Romans had found those two reckoning tools that make it possible to designate any number simply and clearly. Europe owes those two discoveries to the Arabs, who in turn had imported them from India.

Equipped with these intellectual tools, the Maya succeeded in calculating the length of the year more accurately than our own Gregorian calendar does and in drawing up correct tables of the phases and eclipses of the moon and of solar eclipses. In calculating the movements of the planet Venus, they made an error of scarcely two hours over a period of five centuries. Without any danger of ambiguity, they could determine any date—for instance, the year in which a monument was inaugurated—in relation to an initial date corresponding to our year 3113 B.C., which, at the same time, was the terminal date of an earlier period of over five thousand years. Nor were they content to plunge as far back into the past as the ninth millennium B.C.; the inscriptions on certain stelae refer to millions of years.

Very early on, it seems, this Maya elite had arrived at a notion of duration which had two aspects. On the one hand, there was infinite time, stretching uninterruptedly into the past and the future. On the other, there was the arrangement of periods and cycles—the day, the twenty-day month, thirteen figures and twenty names of days combining to make twenty "thirteen-day series" and a divinatory cycle of

260 days; the 360-day *tun*, which, when five "hollow" days were added to it, was equivalent to the solar year *haab*; the *katun* of 7,200 days; the *baktun* of 144,000 days; and the longer periods, each of them always equal to the preceding period multiplied by twenty. The Maya are perhaps the only people in the world to have worshipped time. In every one of their cities they erected dated stelae at the end of each *katun*, or about every twenty years, and sometimes every ten or every five years. At Quiriguá, there are columnar stelae, quadrangular in cross section, some of them over thirty feet high, and carved with lace-work intricacy; they were put up every five years, although at certain periods, between 780 and 795, they were replaced by admirable mono-liths covered with bas-reliefs. The most famous one is known as "the Tortoise." Each date was accompanied by corrections as to calendar and astronomy, with a wealth of mathematical and chronological detail that staggers the mind.

How profoundly our industrial civilization deludes itself in classify-ing civilizations according to a technological criterion: the age of chipped stone, the age of polished stone, the bronze age, the iron age, the machine era, the age of electricity, the atomic age. This vision of things give us the flattering impression that we have reached an apex. The Maya of the classical era never had any metal. Their tools were made of hewn or polished stone. Does this mean that they should be classified with the cave men of the Dordogne in France or with the Swiss lake dwellers? Should we say that the Celts of La Tène represent a superior degree of civilization than that of Palenque because they had iron weapons?

Clearly that would be absurd. The case of the Maya—which is an extreme one, because their technological level was very rudimentary, while their intellectual level was prodigiously refined—obliges us to dissociate two notions which we Westerners are all too prone to con-found: technological progress and cultural development. Yet we should have been warned by the distant past of our own world. The Greek barbarians who dealt a fatal blow to the brilliant civilization of Crete in about 1450 B.C. had iron and knew how to use it, which may partly account for their victory, just as the Spaniards' steel swords and breast-plates explained the triumph of Cortés over the Aztecs three thousand years later. The development of a given technique, particularly if it is put to military uses, among others, has nothing to do with the value of a civilization taken as a whole. A technique is no more than a servant. For eight centuries Byzantium was kept safe from the Moslem fleets by its "Greek fire," but in 1453 Constantinople was crushed by the Turkish artillery.

The Maya seem to have been notoriously weak where the military arts were concerned. Their weaponry included nothing more than lances and spears, large and cumbersome shields, and helmets that were more decorative than useful. Warlike scenes do not occur very frequently in the classical art of Chiapas and Petén; virtually the only examples are the famous battle painted on the walls of Bonampak and the stela of the captives, already mentioned, at Piedras Negras. Apparently, the other Mexican civilizations of the same period were no more bellicose and may have been even less so. I can think of only one picture of an armed man at Teotihuacán, and, even then, his spears seem to be more ceremonial than anything else, since the point of each one has been replaced by a ball. A vase from Teotihuacán, now at the Musée de l'Homme in Paris, shows a hunter with a blowpipe, which propelled round pellets of terra cotta. It could scarcely have been used to hunt anything bigger than birds, although the *Popul Vuh* describes it as the instrument by which the earthly heroes of Maya antiquity triumphed over the subterranean demons of Xibalba. The art at Monte Albán, in Oaxaca, is purely religious, with nothing warlike about it. Thus, throughout the entire first millennium A.D., these grandiose civilizations of the high plateau, the temperate valleys, and the torrid forest remained peaceful for the most part. Undoubtedly, the Maya city-states, analogous to those of ancient Greece in this respect, must have come into conflict with one another from time to time, in battles like that shown in the frescoes of Bonampak; but there is all the difference in the world between this sort of fleeting and limited conflict and the systematic militarism that caused so much blood to flow in the

Mexico of the second millennium. Toward the year 1000, the Maya, who still used weapons of the classical era, found themselves face to face with the fanatic and methodical Tolteco-Itzá fighters, who had shields that could be wielded with relative ease and long-distance spear throwers. Inevitably, the Maya lost. Then the bow and arrow, which nomadic peoples had brought in from the northern steppes, began to appear everywhere from central Mexico to Yucatán. Whereas military technique had remained in the embryonic stage for a thousand years, during the second phase of the native civilizations it was perfected considerably. During the same phase, gold, silver, copper, and bronze metallurgy, imported from South America, spread to the Mixtecs and the Yopi-Tlappanecs of Oaxáca and Guerrero, to the Tarascans of Michoacán, to the Aztecs, and throughout all the empire that Mexico City (Tenochtitlán) brought under its control. Without going as far as Toynbee, who calls the recent civilizations of Yucatán and central Mexico "second rate," we certainly must admit that they did not show any degree of superiority over the Maya civilizations of Palenque, Yaxchilán, Tikal, or Copán.

But what is a civilization? This question seems all the more pertinent to us today since our own civilization, while displaying potent vitality in certain technical areas, is showing clear signs of exhaustion in others. Like an anxious sailor scanning the sky for signs of storm, we pore over the past and the present not so much for the sake of pure and disinterested knowledge as in an attempt to discover, if possible, some omen which will shed light on our future. I will be coming back to this topic, but, before I go any further, I feel I ought to define some of the terms the ethnologist is obliged to use and which are not always as accurate as one could wish. There is no generally accepted definition in this field and often the meaning of the terms that are used varies from one author to another. So, for the sake of greater clarity, I would like to state what these key words mean to me.

I call "culture" the whole sum of types of behavior, techniques, beliefs, rites, and institutions which characterize man and human societies—in contrast with animals and animal societies—and which

are, therefore, the opposite of "nature." There is no such thing as man
without culture, man in the natural state, the *Naturvölker*. However far
back we look into the past, as soon as we find a creature whose bony
remains are analogous to ours (despite the striking differences found in
Sinanthropus or Neanderthal man), and who knew how to make tools
and fire and lived in groups, whether large or small, we call him man,
which implies the existence of a culture. Bees, ants, and termites offer
examples of societies without a culture, for culture has to be learned,
then passed on by tradition, education, or imitation. It evolves and
changes, borrows and innovates, whereas the structures and behavior
patterns of insect societies are perpetuated unchangingly throughout
millions of years by the immutable application of instinctive mechan-
isms. Thus, any culture presupposes a society, but a society does not
necessarily presuppose a culture. Since the only thing that prehistorical
and archaeological studies have to work on is the material remains
preserved in the earth, such as stones and pottery, we are inevitably led
to think in terms of technological criteria, like the way tools are shaped,
stone is worked, and flint, bone, and clay are used. But although that is
necessary and implicit in the very object of those sciences, we must be
careful not to overestimate the *homo faber* aspects of our species, as we
are too prone to do. The existence of language cannot be demonstrated
until we come to the more recent ages; yet how can we imagine a
human culture without language?

Where should we draw the dividing line between "nature" and
"culture"?

My feeling is that we often draw it inaccurately; either we leave too
much scope to nature or we grant too much to culture. Types of
behavior which we believe are the signs of culture are actually to be
found among animals. Most vertebrates, for instance, have the territorial instinct; that is, they defend a certain territory in one way or
another. Monkeys living in permanent troops, such as baboons, have a
hierarchy, and they move about their circuit in a specific pattern.[5]

5. S. A. Washburn, and Irven Devore, "Social Behavior of Baboons and Early Man,"
Social Life of Early Man, Chicago, 1961.

Conversely, types of behavior that we consider instinctive largely reflect the traditional habits of a given society. I mean the social or cultural facts, such as what Marcel Mauss called the "bodily techniques"[6]—positions of the body, way of walking, running, sitting, climbing trees, swimming, and so forth. A study like the one Bronislaw Malinowski conducted on "the sexual life of savages" shows that even in this area where one would think that instinct was dominant, suggestion, convention, in short, cultural pressure on individuals, play an important part. Some specialists even maintain that young apes, once they have attained sexual maturity, need to imitate the example set by their elders. Hediger writes, "Sexual behavior is not inborn among the hominids but has to be learned."[7]

I call "civilization" the state that has been reached by certain cultures in the course of human history. Whereas a great many cultures have existed and do exist today, we know of only a very limited number of civilizations in the past and in our own day. As far as we know (but archaeological research almost everywhere in the world is still somewhat incomplete), the most ancient civilization must have been that of the Sumerians, in southern Mesopotamia, about 3,500 years B.C. I believe the oldest civilization in Central America was that of the Olmecs, on the coast of the Gulf of Mexico, which must have begun about 200 or 300 B.C. and flourished about three centuries later.

Counting, classifying, and characterizing civilizations is such an appealing job, affording so many opportunities to extrapolate and compare, that philosophers and historians and scholars are always eager to tackle it. The mind derives a singular pleasure from moving through the labyrinth of history and occasionally, as from a mountain lookout, coming upon a majestic panorama. Although there is a bewildering variety of cultures, civilizations are easier to grasp, and we are even able to trace some of them—such as the Egyptian or the Greco-Roman—in detail from their birth up to their death.

6. "Les Techniques du Corps," *Journal de Psychologie*, Vol. XXXII, Nos. 3–4, Paris, 1936.
7. Heini P. Hediger, "The Evolution of Territorial Behavior," *Social Life of Early Man*, Chicago, 1961.

Such words as "birth" or "death" or "flourishing" naturally spring to mind; hence the idea that civilizations can be compared to living organisms or even, as Oswald Spengler maintains, that they really are organisms. But a metaphor is not a proof. No matter how brilliant it is, the Spenglerian theory—a genuine poem studded with attractive insights and penetrating visions—is not convincing. According to Spengler, the "soul" which awakens in the springtime of each *Kultur* instills all its innate richness into art, politics, and science, then contracts and hardens in what Spengler terms "civilization," the phase of decline and ultimately of death. But this "soul" does not constitute an explanatory principle any more than the alleged *virtus dormitiva* explained the action of opium. Furthermore, when we try to apply this outline to civilizations other than those of the Old World, we soon find that the facts will not fit the theory, unless they are forced and mutilated.

Although Toynbee's masterly work is less metaphysical in its principle, it suffers from comparable defects. It is one thing to state that down to our day there has been only a limited number of civilizations; but it is quite another to sit down and list them. When the British historian lists twenty-one civilizations, he is being arbitrary. For instance, why distinguish between a Minoan civilization and a Hellenic civilization, an Indian ("Indic") civilization and a "Hindu" civilization, and then wrap up in a single "Andean" civilization all of that diversity of historical developments which took place in Peru and Bolivia starting at least with the beginning of the Christian era and down to the sixteenth century? Why distinguish only three civilizations in Mexico— the Mayan, the Yucatec, and the Mexican?

There is still less justification for labeling a drawer "arrested civilizations" and tossing into it, pell-mell, the Polynesians, the Eskimos, the nomads of the Old World, the Osmanlis, and the Spartans. The first three of those groups are clearly cultures and not civilizations. The Osmanli Turks—former nomads who fought until they became the ruling caste of an empire, heir to Byzantium—shaped one fraction of the Islamic civilization. And as for Sparta, it was only one special case within the Hellenic civilization as a whole.

Like Kroeber,[8] I believe that we are not yet ready to discover and set down general laws which could be applied to all civilizations. Nothing proves that such laws even exist, or that each civilization must necessarily go through the same phases of an always homologous cycle. Of course we can say that various civilizations have tended to do certain things. For instance, a civilization which has lasted a certain number of centuries and extended to various countries and ethnic groups tends to become concentrated in a single state, which Toynbee calls the "universal state" of that civilization. This was true of ancient China and the Mediterranean areas. But there has never been a universal state of the Islamic civilization. The Aztec Empire in Mexico might have succeeded in extending its hegemony to all of the civilized peoples in the center and the south, but the fact is that it never did succeed in so doing, and I cannot accept Toynbee's statement that it was an "alien substitute," the Spanish viceroyalty of New Spain, which provided the Mexican world, so to speak, with its "universal state."

Generally speaking, accidents and chance happenings play too great a part in history to let human phenomena lend themselves to general explanations, and it is an interpretive error to try to pattern the study of civilizations along the lines of the physical and natural sciences. When Toynbee speculates on what might have happened in Europe if Abd-al-Rahman had defeated Charles Martel at Poitiers in 732,[9] or when Spengler regrets that it was Augustus, and not Marc Antony and Cleopatra, who won the battle of Actium,[10] they are implicitly paying tribute to the element of chance which their theories attempt to eliminate.

Every civilization is born of a culture, or of several related cultures, or of another civilization. In Egypt, Syria, and Mesopotamia, the first civilizations emerged from such Neolithic agricultural cultures as those of Jericho, El Fayum, Catal Hüyük, and Hassuna, which had developed between the seventh and fourth millennia B.C. In Mexico, the peasant village phase lasted approximately two thousand years before the Olmec

8. *A Roster of Civilizations and Culture*, p. 16.
9. Toynbee, *A Study of History*, II, p. 427.
10. Spengler, II, p. 191.

civilization appeared. In both the New World and the Old, the transition from culture to civilization was marked by a new phenomenon: the city. The city was the focal point of ceremonies and ritual, the seat of government, the trading center, and also the crucible of ideas. It swallowed up the villages and drew its strength from the rural world and, in so doing, both upset and regulated the existence of that world.

Although we can observe the shift from village to city via the urban revolution, we cannot discover the causes. Why did Teotihuacán spring up, massive and imposing, from the midst of the villages in central Mexico, whereas the villages of Nayarit continued for many centuries to live in the traditional way, prosperous enough but essentially peasant? Consider the Pueblo Indians of New Mexico and Arizona, with their beautifully organized towns, intense social and religious life, and very elaborate symbolism. Although they would seem to have been preparing to cross the border between culture and civilization, they never actually did it. Or take the Olmec civilization, the first native civilization as far as we know. Why did it develop in an unhealthy, swampy coastal zone, half drowned and covered with dense vegetation? Why did the Olmecs insist on carving huge monoliths that they had to carry for more than sixty miles?

We assume that the Olmecs went through a "formative" period of some two or three centuries before they perfected their art and symbolism, their delicately chiseled carvings, and a system of hieroglyphic writing and chronology which prefigured that of the Maya. But a difficulty is not any easier to solve for having been spread over a period of two or three hundred years. Moreover, the conveniently abstract use we make of language is likely to delude us into thinking that we are describing a phenomenon, whereas all we are actually doing is putting a name on it. We say that a civilization emerges or is born at a particular point and a particular time; but we must not forget that in the last analysis we are talking about men who, at a certain moment, must have invented new ways of life, deciding, for instance, to build monuments, carve stone, or organize a social or political hierarchy. Why did they do so? How? Of course we may suppose that most cultures (but clearly not all of them) tend to grow and to turn into civilizations. But just as countless trees in a forest vainly try to reach the sun and die before coming to maturity, so history is made of far more failures than successes. Civilizations stand out only here and there in the vastness of time and space and, like giant trees, tower over the countless cultures that vegetate or prove abortive. But again the question arises: Why did the Olmec tree and the Maya tree grow, and not the others? I have no satisfactory explanation to offer.

Of the three regions which were and still are peopled by Maya-speaking Indians, the one that appears best suited to human endeavors is the zone of mountains and high plateaus in Guatemala, for its climate is tempered by the altitude, while the lay of the land, broad and open, makes communication easy. It is a land of perpetual spring, and nature seems to have prepared it so that men could work and build there. Despite these advantages, the zone remained only marginal throughout the stupendous burgeoning of the classical era, and the only art in which its inhabitants excelled was pottery-making, judging from the exquisite painted pieces found at Nebaj and Chama. Meantime, architecture, sculpture, frescoes, hieroglyphic writing and astronomical calculation were wrought to their highest pitch in the stifling tropical forest of Petén and along the torrid, brush-covered chalky plateau of the Yucatán Peninsula.

The oldest chronological inscription discovered in the Maya country was found at Tikal. It corresponds to our year 292 A.D. Here again, if we allow for a "formative" period two or three centuries long, it seems reasonable to suppose that the nascent Maya civilization—contemporary with Olmec civilization at its height—borrowed such essential features from the mysterious people of La Venta as the chronological system itself, and the monolithic altars and stelae. Unless —and this seems more likely—the Olmecs and the proto-Maya, who were neighbors in this forested world of the tropics, both belonged to a single, common mother-civilization.

However that may be, the fact remains that these two civilizations emerged from the great humid forest and that they were developed not with the help of natural surroundings but despite those surroundings.

To use a Toynbeean expression, they met nature's challenge. What we do not know is the reason why the Indians along the Gulf Coast and in the inland forests were able to meet this challenge victoriously while other Indians, living in analogous circumstances, were not. In any case, it was an astonishing feat for a society with very simple and inefficient techniques to have tackled the most hostile environment and a destructive climate, and to have won.

Once launched, the native civilizations, born of one another and reacting upon one another, can be grouped rather easily in two cycles. The cycle of the classical era (first millennium A.D.) included the theocratic, peaceful civilizations of Teotihuacán, the coast (El Tajín), Oaxaca, and the Maya country. Beginning with the second millennium came a cycle of bellicose civilizations which left their mark on the Yucatán Peninsula and on the later Maya, as well as on Mixtec Oaxaca and the Nahuatl center. The Toltec civilization (ninth to twelfth century) was transitional. It began as a classical renaissance dedicated to the peaceful Plumed Serpent, Quetzalcoatl, inventor of the arts, of writing, and of the calendar, and enemy of human sacrifices. But in the end, and under the impetus of the barbaric and warring peoples who came from the northern steppes, it was dedicated to the bloodthirsty gods, astral divinities like Tezcatlipoca, god of Ursa Major, of the night sky, and of war. According to the mythico-historical Toltec tradition, still vivid in Mexico at the time of the Spanish invasion, the symbolic struggle between Tezcatlipoca and Quetzalcoatl had occurred at the end of the tenth century. The Plumed Serpent was defeated by the ruses of his rival and fled eastward, abandoning Mexico to the new gods and their macabre rites. And from Tula to Chichén Itzá, from Mexico City to Mayapán, sculptors began to depict warriors with their weapons, eagles, and jaguars devouring the hearts of sacrificed victims, and skulls piled up on the skull racks of the temples. Carvings also decorated the *quauhxicalli* used to catch the victims' blood, and bas-reliefs showed the sun god exacting his bloody tribute.

We can imagine the Mexican civilizations as a diptych, with Tula as the hinge between the two halves. The direction forced upon the later cycle by the immigrants from the north, with their star worship

Palenque. Stucco head found in the crypt of the Temple of the Inscriptions. Classic Maya civilization. (*Soustelle Archives*)

Palenque. Palace, patio between Buildings A, B, and C. Detail from the bas-relief of the slaves. Classic Maya civilization. (*Henri Lehmann*)

Where no other source is given, all photographs on these pages are by J. Soustelle

Woman from Lake Peljá, State of Chiapas. Lacandon Indians (*Gertrude Duby*)

Lacandon Indians. San Quentin *caribal*, State of Chiapas

Lacandon Indian camp: a few huts in a clearing still littered with tree trunks. This is called a *caribal*. State of Chiapas

Interior of a house in Chocacté, at night, State of Chiapas. Lacandon Indians

The author with a Lacandon Indian

A Lacandon Indian from Chocacté, State of Chiapas, with his wife

Lacandon Indians from La Arena, State of Chiapas

Lacandon Indians from the northwestern region, State of Chiapas

The men of the San Quentin *caribal*, State of Chiapas, In this camp the men have pierced noses and on certain occasions they wear feathers there. Lacandon Indians

Woman making maize *tortillas*. Lacandon Indians. Chocacté camp, State of Chiapas

Tchank'in, Lacandon Indian from Lake Peljá, State of Chiapas

Kitchen-shelter where the women make *pozol*, for offerings. Lacandon Indians from San Quentin, State of Chiapas

Otomi woman weaving. Santa Ana Hueytlálpam, State of Hidalgo

Otomi woman weaving. Santa Ana Hueytlálpam, State of Hidalgo

Otomi women and children.
Santa Ana Hueytlálpam, State
of Hidalgo

Otomi woman preparing a loom.
Santa Ana Hueytlálpam, State of
Hidalgo

Feast day in Atlacomulco, State of Mexico. Otomi and Mazahua Indians

Otomi Indians dressed for dancing. San Pedro, State of Hidalgo

Otomi Indians on their way to the pilgrimage of Atlacomulco, State of Mexico

Little girl from Santa Ana Hueytlálpam, State of Hidalgo. Otomi Indians

linked to a belief in cosmic war, militarism, and the expansion of states, reflected a vision of things which was profoundly foreign to the Maya. As a result, it is not surprising that after the short-lived renaissance of Chichén Itzá between A.D. 1000 and 1200 the recent cities of Yucatán, sucked into a whirlwind of armed battles in which the people of central Mexico played a vital role, withered away behind their fortified walls. At Mayapán, for instance, the architecture is merely a pitiful parody of the ancient monuments. Even the taste for good workmanship disappeared; masonry and colonnades were covered with thick layers of stucco in an attempt to hide their defects.

In the area where the Lacandones now live, the Maya civilization died out in the ninth century and, on the central plateau, the Teotihuacán civilization had already ended a little earlier. How can we account for this virtually simultaneous decline of the great classical civilizations? There is no basis either in archaeology or in tradition for suspecting that there was an intrusion of barbarians from outside. It would seem that these magnificent social edifices fell in upon themselves, succumbing to their own weight. Economic factors were probably influential. In the Maya country, especially, as the soil became exhausted and the undergrowth endlessly threatened to reclaim the areas of cleared land, the effort required of a people without animals or machines was so difficult and so protracted that in the end it was too much for human resistance. Yet I cannot believe that that is enough to explain such a surrender to nature on the part of men who, for as long as seven or eight centuries, had been able to overcome the obstacles of vegetation and climate and, moreover, who had rapidly erected a complex of works whose quantity and quality, volume and plastic perfection, over-all plan and details awe and amaze us. Furthermore, the agricultural problem was clearly not the same at Teotihuacán. On the high plateau, even a very severe and prolonged dry spell, like the one which caused famine in the middle of the fifteenth century, was not enough to leave the cities depopulated and abandoned. The people of Teotihuacán did not have to protect their fields from the assault of creeping undergrowth. They asked Tlaloc to send rain and, in addition, a network of small rivers watered their valleys. I am inclined to think

4

that in both cases civilization was destroyed by an internal revolution; it may have been a slow and gradual process. The small elite caste of priests, and the artists who worked for it, imposed the authority of the cities upon the villages only by the sacred weight of its prestige and not, or hardly at all, by force. Generation after generation of peasants had to give up a large portion of the fruit of their work to feed that elite, build monuments, provide the cotton, the plumes, and the semi-precious stones, all for the sake of fostering an esoteric body of knowledge which continued to be very remote from them and was expressed by hieroglyphics they did not read. Probably the Maya farmer, with the same practical spirit and resignation that he displays today, put up with that existence for a long time because in exchange the priestly aristocracy guaranteed him the protection of the gods of the rain, sun, and maize. But eventually the charm wore thin, perhaps because the mathematical and astronomic speculations of the clergy had become farther and farther removed from the daily cares of the rural masses. The social link weakened. Either the peasant turned in anger against his masters or, more probably, he simply eluded their grasp and returned to the little family plot of land, to his cabin and the gods of his tiny village, worshipping them in simple, unpretentious rites like those the Lacandones perform today. Possibly the "plebeians" scattered over the countryside in order to escape the demands of the city. The city was deprived of its labor force and its food supply; it became a brain without a body and died of starvation. The elite caste itself was dispersed, the avenues disappeared under the advancing brush, and the first sprouts of the future jungle appeared on the steps of the pyramids and the roofs of the palaces.

From this we may conclude that a civilization can perish in a variety of ways. The civilizations of Palenque and Teotihuacán were consumed by an evil inherent in their very structure; that of the Aztecs, on the contrary, was assassinated by the emissaries of another civilization, who had actually come from another world. Tula succumbed to terrible internecine struggles, whereas the Zapotecs of Monte Albán must have given way before the conquering thrust of the Mixtec mountain people who boldly settled down in their temples and even in their tombs.

But regardless of what causes the death of a given civilization, one thing is certain. In the five or six thousand years since civilizations have existed, every one of them so far, without exception, has perished. By what miracle should our own civilization escape that common fate?

When a civilization disappears, the ethnic groups which it had organized and borne along with it remain. They fall back from civilization to culture. In the course of time they may be used as the raw material of a new civilization, as in the case of the Gallo-Romans and the Germanic peoples after the western Roman Empire collapsed, the natives of Egypt and Syria after the Arab conquest, and the Indians of central Mexico after the Spanish Conquest. Or, if no other civilization comes to rule the area which they inhabit, such peoples can remain for centuries on the level of a culture. This is what happened to the Lacandones.

Human history, far from lending itself to a description as a continuous and ascending line, appears to the untrained eye as an ocean of chaos where waves rise and break and become troughs, endlessly. Progress at one point, regression at another, evolution and involution, expansion and decadence: everything, and the opposite of everything. Civilizations are the masterpieces of our species. Like distant fires scattered over the countryside, they light the vague and shadowy reaches where mankind struggles. And each in turn, these lights are dimmed and extinguished, either by exhaustion of their material or spiritual resources, or by the brutal thrust of a handful of ignorant barbarians, or by a battle to the death with another civilization. Cycles of civilizations are born from cultures. Some of them come to nothing, while others continue to rise, only to sink back. And so on, forever, to no apparent purpose.

In the second century A.D., the philosopher whom fate had placed at the summit of the ancient Mediterranean world gazed upon this spectacle and, finding it as grandiose and senseless as a storm-whipped sea, compared it to the comings and goings of ants, the frantic scurrying of panicking mice, or the jerking of puppets on strings.[11] But in the

11. Marcus Aurelius, *Meditations*.

notes which Marcus Aurelius jotted down "for himself" at the end of
a long day in Rome or on the banks of the Danube facing the Barbarians, he urged himself to look upon that nonsensical world with
"benevolence and humility." And indeed it is true that no man can
leave himself out of the picture when he contemplates his species. The
same mankind or, rather, branches of mankind that have stumbled,
forward or backward along hazardous paths, waded in torrents of blood,
tottered from folly to folly, devoted their energies century after century
to destroying and clawing at one another are also those that caused such
exquisite flowers of wisdom and beauty to blossom as those we asso-
ciate with the names of Buddha, Epictetus, or Jesus, with places like
Athens, Palenque, or Florence. Each of us, at the point of history
which we have reached and possibly before a new tidal wave carries us
off toward new horizons, can measure just what he owes to those
cultures and those civilizations blindly launched into orbits they were
unaware of. We are as indebted to the obscure efforts of the remote
generations which discovered wheat and maize, weaving and pottery,
as to the genius of the empire builders of China, Rome, and Tenochtitlán, and to the thinking of the philosophers and founders of religions.
Monuments, statues, bas-reliefs, frescoes and paintings, books and the
works of musicians—all of these are certainly perishable. By far the
greater part of them has already been destroyed, and all are doomed to
disappear just like men themselves. But meanwhile they form that
marvelous treasure which all this cruel and disorderly agitation has
placed at our feet, like the gold and gems which the ocean has brought
from a wrecked pirate ship and washed up on the shore. A fleeting and
precarious triumph, but the only victory which an ephemeral being can
achieve over the indifference of things and the enigma of fate.

Chapter Four

Cold Lands

IN THE WINTERTIME, ON THE MONOTONOUS PLATEAU that stretches north of Toluca to the mountains crowned by the dark and peaceful dome of the Cerro de Jocotitlán, the temperature falls to freezing every night. Every day, the sun gleams out of a dark blue, cloudless sky. Alternating frost and heat split the ground open, crevices meander over the sterile crust, and the wind stirs up whorls of whitish dust. At an altitude of nine thousand feet, the shade is icy cold, the air light and dry and so clear that the belfries of the mestizo villages—Ixtlahuaca, Jiquipilco, Atlacomulco—are distinct in the distance, while the small brown adobe (dried-brick) huts of the Indian hamlets are scattered over the slightly undulating steppe like so many affrighted sheep.

Not a single tree, not one blade of grass grows on this desolate plateau. The only plants that thrive are the sharp-pointed agave plants and the cochineal cacti, with their broad bristling joints.

In the last weeks of the dry season, in March and April, nature and men anxiously await the rain. After six months of drought, the plain has been burned by the cold, scorched by the sun, harried by the endless raking of the wind, traversed in every direction by lofty columns of dust. The plain seems as dead as a bleached skeleton. Day after day the Indians gaze toward the mountain peaks where the clouds of the wet season should gather, light at first, then blackish. Maize has been sown in the dry and pebbly fields. But now, will the rains come to bring those seeds to life under the ground?

This is what the Indians of antiquity begged for, in cruel and pathetic ceremonies. Although the Indians in the Valley of Mexico, the

Aztecs and their neighbors, lived on a more fertile plain, where the climate was less extreme, drought represented as great a threat to them. Their annals tell us that in certain years the rulers had to open the state granaries to the people in order to save them from famine. So there were invocations and sacrifices to Tlaloc, the powerful rain god, to the Tlaloque, the little gods of the mountain who echoed and served him, and to the bloodthirsty Xipe Totec. They begged him to "don his suit of gold" (the yellow-dyed skin of a sacrificed man) to make the rain come.

Finally, the clouds pile up on the mountaintops, lightning rips through their somber bulk, the thunder growls, and the first squalls or rain drum loudly on the hardened surface of the ground. Then the peasant can cry, just as his ancestors did, "The Plumed Serpent has defeated the Fire Serpent," for the green and silky undulating feathers of the marvelous quetzal which, two thousand years ago, became the attribute of the mythical and venerated serpent symbolized abundant vegetation, the leafy luxuriance of plants, in contrast to the ravenous serpent of the sun. Tlaloc was addressed in prayer as *naualpilli* ("magician-prince"), and there certainly seems to be good magic in the abrupt change brought about by the first rains. Pink and violet flowers suddenly appear where all had been arid such a short time before; the metallic leaves of the agave plants gleam as if they had just been waxed, and soon the first delicate sprouts of maize thrust toward the light between the humid lumps of earth. And so men know that with the help of the gods one more battle has been won, still another year of existence has been wrested from nothingness.

That is the rhythm of life on the high central plateau. Although each of its great valleys, separated from one another by wooded mountains, has its own particular altitude, hydrography, and climate, in all of them daily life and work are governed by the same alternation of dry winter and rainy summer. The gentle Valley of Mexico undeniably enjoys a privileged situation, and the peoples who have installed their villages and cities there have left the thankless lands of the Toluca Valley and Mezquital to other people. Yet even the rich milpas of Coyoacán and Texcoco, the fields of flowers at Xochimilco have been ruled by the law of Tlaloc down through the centuries.

Some fifteen or twenty thousand years ago, the mammoth and other large mammals, now extinct, grazed on the shores of the lagoons in the central valley and splashed about in the swamps; the climate was hotter and more humid than it is today, and men lived by hunting. Sharpened stone spear points have been found stuck in the bones of a mammoth at Tepexpan. The scant human population was probably wandering and scattered, like our Paleolithic ancestors, who could not have numbered more than a few thousand throughout all of what is now France. These nomadic hunters very likely lived the way all the peoples of Mexico and North America lived during that period, across the steppes and the prairies to the forests and even to the snowy Arctic reaches. Only shortly before—in about 25,000 B.C.—the icecap which had covered the whole northern portion of the continent down to Kansas had receded, thus offering the human beings who came from Asia a vast and empty world to discover and to people.

We can imagine what a revolution, what a total change the invention of agriculture introduced into this universe of small, scattered groups, widely separated from one another and drifting from one horizon to the next in pursuit of game. There is every indication that maize was first grown in the Hot Lands of the southern Gulf regions, by the ancestors of the Olmecs and the Maya, some five or six thousand years ago. In all events, the practice of growing maize spread surprisingly fast, first to Mexico, then to what is now the southern part of the United States from Arizona to Florida. Maize throve in the driest and most unpredictable climates and on the semi-arid plateaulands. The next step, when the golden grain was safely put away in wooden or earthern granaries, was the permanent village, rooted in the midst of the fields and organized for the purpose of cultivating and defending them. With the reassurance of a good harvest came the discovery of leisure and time for meditation, hitherto impossible for the hunter, who was compelled to go out every day in the exhausting search for food. Other discoveries included the security of the sedentary life, and the techniques of pottery-making and weaving; a social hierarchy, as we can see from the turbans, the jewels and the elaborate hair styles of the most ancient Mexican statuettes, found at Zacatenco;

4*

and fertility rites, which probably account for the broad-bellied, heavy-thighed female figurines reminiscent of certain prehistoric "Venuses" unearthed in the Old World.

The difference between the sedentary farmer and the nomadic hunter or breeder is the oldest division known to mankind, the one that separated Cain from Abel. The agricultural revolution, like any other revolution, was accepted by some people and rejected by others. In Mexico, virtually all of the Indians living north of a horizontal line extending from Tampico on the Gulf of Mexico to the Pacific and east of the Sierra Madre Occidental pursued their preagricultural way of life. These were the Indians the Aztecs called *Chichimeca* ("barbarians"). They wandered over the cactus-strewn steppes and the prairies, hunting, pulling up roots, picking the fruit of the *mizquitl* (a thorny type of mimosa), which they pounded and made into a sort of flour. Warlike tribes, using bows and arrows, they were monogamous and worshipped the sun and the stars. For centuries these Chichimecs were a permanent threat to the northern frontier of the civilized empires, invading them every time they showed signs of weakening, like the Germans and the Slavs at the confines of Rumania or the Mongols prowling at the limits of China. Most of the Chichimecs, once they had come within the area of influence of one of the various civilizations, quickly assimilated its forms and customs. But some of them never overcame their repugnance for the peasant life. In the fourteenth century, part of the Chichimec tribe which had settled in the Valley of Mexico simply refused to obey the king, Quinatzin, and take up farming. Refractory hunters, they preferred to emigrate toward the mountains and live there in their traditional way.

The hunting tribes resisted the Spanish Conquest inch by inch for two hundred years. The *indios de arco y flecha* became the nightmare of the viceroys and governors of New Spain, attacking and destroying newly founded villages, and ambushing mule trains. On the rare occasions when they did agree to group themselves into villages, they fled from them soon afterward. Only the joint efforts of Spaniards and Indians from the center—the Otomi from Jilotepec and the Nahua of Tlaxcala—finally got the better of the hunting tribes. Most of them were exterminated, and a few of them settled down to the sedentary life. One of the generals who led the struggle against the "barbarians" was Don Luis Andrade y Moctezuma, descendant of the Aztec emperor who died in 1520. Under the flag of Spain, he continued his ancestors' struggle against the nomads of the steppes.

Farther to the north, the legendary hard-riding "redskins" were the result of the encounter between Indians and Europeans, since it was the horse, imported from Europe, that enabled the Indian hunters to follow the herds of buffalo and, at the same time, to fight the new-comers. But it was the Sioux and the Cheyenne who disappeared after all, and the maize-growing Pueblo Indians who remained. Evidence from all over Indian America shows that under the impact of the meeting between European civilization and the natives, the peasant peoples were virtually the only ones to survive. In South America, too, only the maize- and potato-growing peoples of Peru and Bolivia have subsisted since the collapse of the Inca Empire, while the Guayaki and Nambik-wara have disappeared except for a scant handful or two who live by hunting, fishing, and picking fruit.

A goodly part of the world's history is composed of the struggle between nomadic and sedentary peoples. Again and again the hordes from the great steppes of central Asia, the Arabian desert, and the plains of northern Mexico made onslaughts on the civilized areas of China, Persia, Asia Minor, North Africa, and Mexico. Often, only destruction, ruin, and death came in the wake of these invasions, like the raids by Genghis Khan and Tamerlane, or the Hillali invasion of the Maghreb. In other cases, the nomads in turn have become sedentary people and picked up the pieces of crumbling civilizations or have been capable of creating new civilizations. This was true of the Turks in Anatolia, the Arabs in Syria, Iraq, and Spain, and the barbarians at Texcoco in northern Mexico. But once the nomad has gone over to the other side, once he has settled down close to his fields or in cities, he becomes the scornful foe of those who continue to dwell on the steppe and in the desert. Ibn Khaldun, for instance, harshly criticized the destruction wrought by Arabs in North Africa, and the rulers of the central Valley of Mexico put up fortresses facing the plains their own ancestors had swept down from two or three centuries before.

In the over-all Mexican picture, the Indians of the high plain stand out as pre-eminently sedentary peasants. This is true of the Otomi. I lived among them for a long time and studied their obscure language, from the plateau of Toluca to the plateau of Jilotepec, from the icy slopes of the volcano Malinche to the eastern rim of the Mesa, on the edge of the more temperate lands that go down to the Gulf. Their territory forms a sort of crescent north of Mexico City. About twenty years ago, the Otomi tongue was still spoken a few miles from the capital city, and I would not be surprised if the language was being used even today among the woodcutters and charcoal men who look down at night from their mountain hamlets to the countless winking lights of the modern city.

The Otomi call themselves *Nyan-Nyoû*. *Nyan* means "language" and "to speak." To be an Otomi means to speak the *nyoû*. From this we can see that the Indians' criterion for belonging or not belonging to their ethnic group is the criterion of language. I remember how the coppery face of an Indian I met on my way lit up with a smile of mingled astonishment and satisfaction when I asked him, "*Gui pandi nyan-nyoû?*" ("Do you speak Otomi?"), and he joyfully replied, "*Hein-hein*" ("Yes"). In certain regions, like that of Ixmiquilpan, the Otomi tongue is so predominant that even white Mexicans and mestizos have to use it, as the lingua franca. The guttural and nasal sounds can be heard as far away as in certain villages of Guanajuáto, founded by the Indians in the central part of the country at the time of Spanish rule. There are a great many local variants, as is only to be expected with a language which covers so vast a territory and is neither taught nor set down in writing, but the various dialects are quite close to one another.

There is no clearly discernible link between Otomi and the other important languages of Indian Mexico, such as Aztec or Maya, any more than there is between Turkish and Spanish. The Aztecs, who inclined to snobbery, applied condescending terms to any language that was not theirs. Anyone who did not speak Aztec "stammered" or "babbled like an infant." (Similarly, the Slavs call the Germans "mute.") Moreover, the Otomi were considered an unusually limited and stupid people. In Mexico City, when someone wanted to scold an awkward or foolish person, he cried, "*Uel totomitl* [You're a regular Otomi], *quatilacpol* [thick head]!" And the list of things with which popular tradition reproached the Otomi went on at length. They were greedy and improvident eaters; it was said that they ate up their maize while it was still green and then fell back on game and even, if nothing better was to be had, on such unclean animals as rats and lizards. They got drunk on fermented agave juice, which is called pulque today; the Aztecs called it *octli*, and in *nyan-nyoŭ* it is *sêy*. They were pretentious and had no taste, and their way of dressing was ridiculous. Their women, even the old ones, used make-up, dyed their teeth black, and stuck red feathers on their arms and legs.[1] Everything about the Otomi, including that erotic fervor so lavishly attributed to them, shocked the highly puritan Aztec society. It was acknowledged, however, that the Otomi women were good at weaving.

The truth, it seems to me, is that the Otomi, who had settled on the high plateau long before the Aztecs ever set foot there, never took the decisive step from culture to civilization, village to city. Only once, between the twelfth and the fourteenth centuries, did some of them found a small state—on the island of Xaltocán, in the middle of the northern branch of the central lagoon—but this was a belated attempt and had no sequel. Their villages continued to be dominated by cities created by other peoples. They probably provided the labor force for the architect-priests of Teotihuacán and later for those at Tula, and soldiers for the warring states around them. One of the warrior classes in Mexico City was even called Otomi; its members were not from that tribe, but their "uniform", and their weapons did come from the Otomi, just as we have hussars or spahis in our armies. It was Otomi soldiers, fighting for the Republic of Tlaxcala who put up strong resistance to Cortés and the conquistadores when they emerged onto

1. Sahagún, *Florentine Codex*, Book 10, University of Utah, reports what he was told by his informers, "upper class" Aztecs from Mexico City.

the central plateau with their backs to the coast. Later, after the battle of Otumba (Otompan, "Otomi country"), the exhausted and hungry Spanish received help and asylum among the simple Otomi villagers.

Ixtlilxochitl, descendant of the kings of Texcoco, tells how his ancestor, the famous philosopher-king Nezaualcoyotl, "Famished Wolf," was chased into the mountains by the ruffian soldiers of the tyrant Tezozomoc and saved by an Otomi chief.[2] When he saw that the assassins who were pursuing the young prince were drawing near, the chief ordered his men to form a circle and dance to the rhythm of a large drum. And inside the drum was the aristocratic Nezaualcoyotl, deafened undoubtedly but safe.

At a later period, when all the Otomi had been absorbed into the Aztec empire, those who lived in Jilotepec, on the northern outposts, traded with the "barbarians" to the north, bringing them salt and cloth in exchange for hides. When one of these traders, called Konni ("Thunder"), learned that the Spanish had arrived, he decided he would be safer living in no man's land and set up a village at the foot of the cliffs. The conquerors caught up with him, baptized and Hispanicized him, and made him the first governor of Querétaro. The chronicles[3] show him living the life of an important Castilian nobleman, presiding over a well-laid table and drinking—not *sêy* any longer, but Spanish wine.

The history of the Otomi has never been written by themselves because, in fact, they have never written anything. They make only marginal appearances, so to speak, and play only secondary roles. They founded a market town called Maméhni, but it was not until another people had occupied and embellished it that it became famous, under another name: Tula. Very few villages or hamlets still go by their Otomi names; the Nahuatl tide submerged everything from Toluca (Zeu-mi) to Jilotepec (Deuïnshi). Clinging to their village life in a country where other peoples built cities and empires, the Otomi did

2. *Historia Chichimeca*, Chap. XXVI.
3. Ramos de Cardenas, *Descripción de Querétaro*, 1582.

not leave any trace; there are no Otomi monuments, statues, or books. The only really remarkable aptitude they have displayed is for surviving as an ethnic group, complete with language; as a result there are over 300,000 of them living in the heart of the Mexican Republic today.

When all that is known of a given population is other people's judgments of it, and when it has never pleaded its own cause, we can expect that population to be unjustly belittled. This is certainly true of the Otomi. I lived with them for a long time. I found some very intelligent men among them, especially my first informer, Bonifacio, who taught me the rudiments of the language. On the whole they are more

Fig. 6. Woman's garment called *quesquemel* (from the Atzec *quexquemitl*), a sort of wool and cotton blouse, made of two rectangular bands sewn together in such a way as to leave room for the head. The small side of one band is sown to the end of the large side of the second band. The women make this garment on the traditional type of loom.

The *quesquemel* can be worn two ways: either with one point in front and the other in back, or with both points at the sides. Otomi Indians. Village of San Batrolo Morelos. State of Mexico.

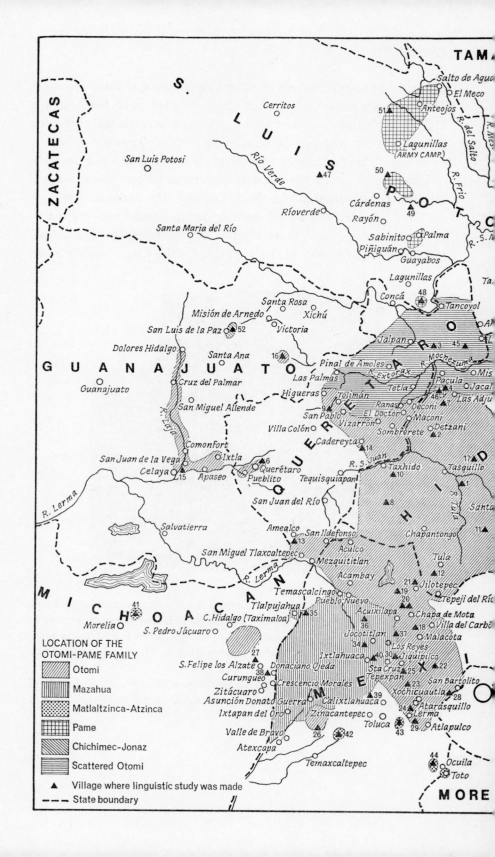

LOCATION OF THE
OTOMI-PAME FAMILY

- ▨ Otomi
- ▥ Mazahua
- ▦ Matlaltzinca-Atzinca
- ▦ Pame
- ▧ Chichimec-Jonaz
- ▤ Scattered Otomi
- ▲ Village where linguistic study was made
- – – State boundary

TAMA

ZACATECAS

S. L U I S   P O T O S I

Cerritos

San Luis Potosí

Santa María del Río

Río Verde

Ríoverde

Santa Ana

Dolores Hidalgo

Misión de Arnedo
San Luis de la Paz ▲ 52

Santa Rosa
Xichú
Victoria

Salto de Agua

El Meco

51 ▲   Anteojos

Lagunillas
(ARMY CAMP)

50 ▲
47 ▲

Cárdenas
Rayón
49 ▲

Sabinito   Palma
Piñiguán
Guayabos

Conca   48 ▲   Tancoyol

Lagunillas

Pinal de Amoles

16 ▧

Las Palmas

Higueras

Jalpan

Toliman

3 ▲   45 ▲

Tetla   Pacula
4   Jacal
Las Adju

Ranas
El Doctor   Deconi
San Pablo   Vizarrón   Maconi
9 ▲   Sombrerete
Detzani
Cadereyta   2

14 ▲

R. S. Juan   Taxhido
10 ▲   Tasquillo

17 ▲
1 ▲

Santa

GUANAJUATO

Guanajuato

Cruz del Palmar

San Miguel Allende

Villa Colón

Comonfort
San Juan de la Vega   Ixtla
Celaya ▲   Apaseo   6 ▲
15   Querétaro
Pueblito
San Juan del Río

Salvatierra

Amealco
San Ildefonso
13 ▲

Tequisquiapan

8 ▲

Chapantongo   11 ▲

Q U E R E T A R O

H I D

San Miguel Tlaxcaltepec

Aculco
Mezquititlan
Acambay

Tula
12 ▲

21 ▲   Jilotepec
19 ▲
20

Tepeji del Río

M I C H O A C A N

41 ▧

Morelia

C. Hidalgo (Taximaloa)

S. Pedro Jácuaro

27 ▧

S. Felipe los Alzate   Donaciano Ojeda
38 ▲
Curungueo
Zitácuaro
Asunción Donato Guerra
Ixtapan del Oro

Valle de Bravo

Atexcapa

Temaxcaltepec

Temascalcingo
Tlalpujahua   Pueblo Nuevo
17 ▲ 35
Acuixtlapa
36
Jocotitlan
34

Ixtlahuaca

Crescencio Morales

Calixtlahuaca
Zinacantepec
26 ▲   42 ▧
Toluca

Chapa de Mota
18 ▲   Villa del Carbó
Malacota
Los Reyes
40 30   Jiquipilco
25 ▲   22 ▲
Sta. Cruz
Tepexpan   23 ▲   San Bartolito
39 ▲   Xochicuautla
28
24 ▲   Atarasquillo
29   Lerma
43   Atlapulco

44 ▧   Ocuila
Toto

M E X I

MORE

1. Ixmiquilpan
2. Zimapán
3. Landa
4. Jiliapan (*cf.* 46)
5. Sta. Catarina
6. La Cañada
7. Mojonera
8. Huichapan
9. San Miguel
10. Tecozautla
11. S. Salvador
12. S. Ildefonso
13. S. Juan Dehedó
14. Tetillas
15. S. Miguel Octopan
16. Tierra Blanca
17. El Cardonal
18. S. Bartolo Morelos
19. Timilpan
20. S. Juan Tuxtepec (*on the left*)
    S. Felipe Coamango
21. Agua Escondida
22. Sta. Ana Jilotzingo
23. S. Bartolo Otzolotepec
24. Ameyalco
25. Temoaya
26. Amanalco
27. Siráhuato
28. Huixquilucan
29. Ocoyoacac
30. El Sitio
31. Texcatepec
32. Ixtenco
33. Sta. Ana Hueytlápam (*north*)
    S. Pedro Tlachichilco
34. S. Pedro de los Baños
35. El Oro
36. Atlacomulco
37. Yeche
38. Fco. Serrato
39. Almoloya
40. S. Bartolo del Llano
41. Charo
42. S. Fco. Oztotilpan
43. Mexicaltzingo
44. S. Juan Acingo
45. Tilaco
46. Jiliapan (*like 4*)
47. Pastora
48. Sta. María Acapulco
49. Tierras Coloradas
50. Alaquines
51. Cd. del Maíz
52. Misión de Chichimecas

distrustful and secretive, it is true, than other natives, because for so many centuries they have been under the thumb of the other Indians, the Spanish, and the mestizos; they have lived on the coldest and least productive lands, and have usually been reduced to complete poverty. Drunkards they are, unfortunately, but in their defense it should be added that this is the common lot of rural Mexico. Like their ancestors, the Otomi women excel at using the pre-Columbian loom, identical to that shown in the ancient manuscripts (and to that of the Lacandones).

Fig. 7. Maize granary. Otomi Indians. San José del Sitio. State of Mexico.

They weave belts, skirts, and those graceful diamond-shaped capes called *quexquemel* (in the Otomi language, *mohwi*), as well as very pretty woolen bags called *reuzan*. All of these items are decorated with geometrical patterns and stylized animals (particularly the two-headed eagle of the House of Austria, taken from coins used at the time of Spanish rule). The work is done with irreproachable taste and astonishing skill.

The men have borrowed the archaic European loom with pedal-driven harness. They make it themselves out of wood and weave magnificent blankets (*sarapes* or *dhantous*) with geometrical patterns of black and white, the natural colors of the wool. They also know how to make extraordinarily delicate cloth from agave fibers and decorate it with embroidery.

But once all that is said and done, there is no denying that this is an extremely limited culture. The "average" Otomi is a very small peasant

Fig. 8. Platform for straw, almost bare. In the foreground, the barley harvest. San José del Sitio. State of Mexico.

Fig. 9. Farm implement, with iron blade and wooden handle. It is used to cut away agave leaves which hinder the collection of sap from the heart of the plant for making pulque. Otomi Indians. Village of San José del Sitio. State of Mexico.

Fig. 10. Farm implement made of iron and used in extracting sap from the agave plant for making pulque. Once the leaves in the center have been taken off, the heart of the plant is hollowed out and scraped with this "spoon" so as to make a sort of bowl where the sap will form a deposit. Otomi Indians. Village of San José del Sitio. State of Mexico.

whose property amounts to a few stony, unirrigated scraps of land, a donkey, a few sheep, and a few turkeys and chickens. His rectangular cabin, built of sun-dried brick or of stones which have barely been dressed, is covered by a double-slope roof of small boards, thatch, or agave leaves. The only agricultural instrument he has is the wooden *coa*, a sort of spade; one end is broadened to scratch the surface of the soil—to "sweep" the ground, as the native expression puts it—and the sharpened handle is used as a drilling stick to make the holes where the peasant's wife deposits the kernels of maize. The Indian's diet is monotonous—from one year's end to the next, he lives on maize tortillas (*hmê*), black beans, and a little pimento; he rarely eats meat and does not drink milk. Pulque, if drunk in moderate quantities, is not unhealthful; the vitamins it contains help to make up for the deficiency of this diet. All in all the Otomi Indian, who for centuries, was sucked into the orbit of great civilizations and now follows that of a modern nation, is not as well fed as the Lacandon who wrests his living singlehanded from the forest. It is true that his natural environment, although less stifling and hostile than the tropical jungle, is terribly poor and arid, hard as metal. His culture, on the whole, resembles the steppes and the mountains he lives in: it is as gray as the dust which the thirsty wind pushes along the desolate streets of the little villages, sad and forbidding as the plains bristling with cactus.

It comes as a pleasant surprise, therefore, like finding flowers growing among the rocks, to discover one gay and colorful aspect in this desert-like cultural landscape: the Otomi poems which have been handed down by what must be a very old oral tradition. Many Indians, both men and women, throughout the region with a high density of native population that stretches from Zimapán to Actopan in the State of Hidalgo, around Ixmiquilpán, Tasquillo, and El Cardonal, know these poems. They will be bold enough to hum them if they feel sufficiently trusting, when the atmosphere of a market or a feast day or a few earthenware jars of *sêy* have helped to make them less timid and suspicious.

Usually these poems, which are recited in a sort of singsong, are very short—only two to six lines. They are genuine lines, separated by a longer pause in the recitation. Instead of rhyming, they are usually rhythmic. Each line is built on a series of internal assonances. The Otomi language has many suffixes and prefixes to indicate grammatical categories, such as singular or plural, the tense and mood of verbs, and

Fig. 11. Calabash for extracting sap from the agave plant; the Mexican name for it is the *acocote*. A hole is made at each end; the smaller end is placed in the heart of the plant, which has already been hollowed out, and sap is then sucked up through the *acocote* until it is full. Otomi and Mazahua Indians. Village of Atlacomulco. State of Mexico.

so forth. Structurally, the poems are based on a subtle use of phonetic correspondences, parallelisms, echoes, and even antitheses within each line and from one line to another. Sometimes, this interplay is so conceived as to maintain an equilibrium from beginning to end of the brief poem; at other times the balance is deliberately upset. Two closely parallel lines, for instance, may be followed by one or two lines with an altogether different beat. This creates a sort of shock, which gives the poem its rather fragile charm.

Fig. 12. Wooden scraper with an iron blade, used by the women. An agave leaf is first roasted, then moistened and placed flat on an inclined board. Holding the scraper in both hands, the woman scrapes the leaf from back to front to extract the fibers from it. Otomi Indians. Village of San José del Sitio. State of Mexico.

We might compare these two little poems.[4]

I

Noumândê enndeunitho
Nourapaya inntheundritho:
"Yesterday she was in blossom.
Today she is wilting."

4. The author's original (French) transcription of the Otomi words has been maintained throughout, as English does not come as close to the nasal and certain other sounds involved. *Translator's note.*

2

Bênngui rida, gramêhwini
Bênngui rida, grabweushwini
Yashtabâ rinana
Yashtamahêni:

"Look away, we will go away over there
Look away, we will go away up there.
Before your mother knows it
We will be far away."

The exacting parallelism of the first poem reappears in the two lines that begin the second poem but, in the latter case, the rhythm is then broken by a shorter third line and a still shorter fourth.[5] It should also be noted that the first two lines and the fourth line rhyme with each other. Doesn't the break in rhythm and rhyme correspond to the subject of the poem itself, the girl breaking away from her family?

Love is the theme of most Otomi poems in this region. Sometimes it is a blossoming young girl who wistfully calls to the unknown man to whom she will give herself:

"Little flower, little flower, here I am in bloom.
Let, let whoever wants to pick me, pick me.
Let him come, let him come, let him pick me."

Sometimes a husband whose wife has deserted him consoles himself, somewhat cynically:

"She went away yesterday, she left me.
Bah, let her go, I'll look for another.
She can die. I'll go get her sister.
Let her die, I'll still have her sister."

5. The poems quoted in this chapter are borrowed from R. J. Weitlaner, and J. Soustelle, "Canciones otomies," in *Journal de la Société des Américanistes*, N.S., Vol. XXVII, Paris, 1935.

Or boy meets girl on the mountain path:

> "Where are you going?" "I'm going to get wood."
> "Who is with you?" "I'm alone."
> "If I had known, I'd have gone with you. Let's go!
> Look away, let's both go up there.
> Before your mother knows it,
> You will be back home in your white house."

Fig. 13. Wooden spindle, terra-cotta balance; made by the men, used by the women. The right hand, with the little finger and the ring finger braced against the rounded part of the balance, holds the spindle, point upward. The thumb and index finger move clockwise, while the left hand holds and twists the agave fibers. Otomi Indians. Village of San José del Sitio. State of Mexico.

A young man speaks in these terms to the girl he wants to marry:

> "I love you, I love you but you do not love me.
> If your father sees us, he will be angry.
> I don't want him to beat you, because I love you.
> And I will make you my wife,
> No matter who gets angry."

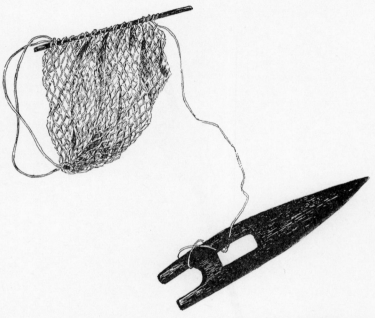

Fig. 14. A net being made out of cotton thread. The nets are used for fishing in the lagoons. Otomi Indians. Village of San José del Sitio. State of Mexico.

Other poems have to do with the holidays which provide the only interval of gaiety in the joyless, monotonous life of these Indians. This little poem, for instance, begins on a joyful, skipping rhythm:

> *Pê-i. pê-i, rizibida tt'eu:*
> "Play, play on your little fiddle, my boy;
> Here's my young sister who's coming to dance."

Fig. 15. Two ways of wearing the traditional *quesquemel*.

Still others, touched with melancholy, describe the incidents and
the dramas of daily life:

"I am going away. Forget me.
When I come back, you will find me on the mountain. . . ."

"Yesterday I went to the market.
From the market I came back to the house.
From the house I was sent out to get wood.
While I was looking for wood, the night came. . . ."

"I have buried my husband and my sons, they are living no longer.
I am going to share the land and the agave plants."

None of this, of course, could be called great poetry or be compared
to the admirable Aztec religious and philosophical poems which,
brilliantly cloaked in a style that avails itself of all the resources of a
flexible and harmonious language, express an intense inner life, a profound awareness of the mystery of existence and the dread of death.
Otomi poetry, on the contrary, is modest and down to earth; it sings in
a minor key, as befits a rustic people. But there is no denying that it is
poetry, in the full sense of the word. Not only does it reveal a genuine
sensitivity but it is shaped in regular, traditional forms, and the use of
rhythms and sounds is governed in very specific ways.

Even the Aztecs, who had so little esteem for the Otomi, made no
mistake about this. They included the *otoncuicatl* ("Otomi poem")
among the "types" to which the poets of Mexico City devoted their
skill. Although the Otomi tongue and the Aztec language have nothing
in common, and the harsh and nasal phonetics of the one are far from
the fluid sounds of the other, the literatures of both languages use
parallelisms and correspondences in analogous ways. Some of the little
Otomi poems remind us of Japanese *haiku*; some Aztec hymns are
reminiscent of Biblical psalms. Poetry can take on a great many
different aspects, but the number of possible forms is not unlimited.

Outside the Zimapán-Actopan region, a certain Otomi poetic tradition, of a totally different sort, has survived in two villages called San

Fig. 16. Brown-and-white bag of woven wool and cotton, made by the women on the traditional type of loom. This is a very old model, which the natives use when they go to market. Otomi Indians. Village of Santa Maria. State of Hidalgo.

Pedro and Santa Ana, at the easternmost end of the State of Hidalgo,
between the large mestizo market town of Tulancingo and the Sierra
where Nahuatl is spoken. The women of these villages wear simple,
graceful garments made by the weavers of Santa Ana: brown wool
skirts held at the waist by a red and blue belt; a small triangular white
and red cape; and, under the cape, a very beautifully embroidered white
blouse bought from the "Tepehua," mountain Indians. With their long
black hair, which they are constantly combing and smoothing as they
sit in front of their houses, their way of drawing themselves up straight
as they stretch their looms, their methodical gestures, and their light
copper skin, these strong and healthy women are impressive. They
become dry and leathery as they grow old, but their authority remains

Fig. 17. Wool-and-cotton belt with a pattern of animals and geometrical
figures. Worn by both men and women. Otomi Indians. Village of San
Bartolo Morelos. State of Mexico.

intact and so, unfortunately, does their taste for sugar-cane brandy.
Here on the rim of the plateau, within reach of the Hot Lands, pulque
is less common than alcohol. Two things characterize the songs heard
at Santa Ana and San Pedro: they are drinking songs, and only women
sing them. They are not about love, or about going away, or about
happy or unsuccessful marriages—they are about drinking bouts.
Whereas in Ixmiquilpan or Zimapán what matters is the words, and
not the singsong in which they are rendered, here it is the melody that
catches the ear. It is delicate as crystal and melancholic—as inappro-
priate as possible to a trivial, incoherent "libretto" of genuine drunkard's

drivel. Upon closer examination of the words, you can find some traces of the poetic technique noted farther north; here, too, there is a certain sway, a certain amount of parallelism and echo. But the exacting form of those little poems half a dozen lines long has been drowned out in a sort of gabbiness, particularly since the women will not consent to display their talent as singers until they have warmed themselves to it by tossing off a good many glasses of *aguardiente*. The surprising thing is that despite their Bacchic incoherence, these Indian women do not deviate one whit from the purity of the melodic line and hold it as surely as they weave fine thread on their looms.

For anyone observing this culture, the Otomi poetry is like a door opening onto a new vista: there is more to the life of these Indians than the gray monotony and precarious equilibrium of work endlessly begun

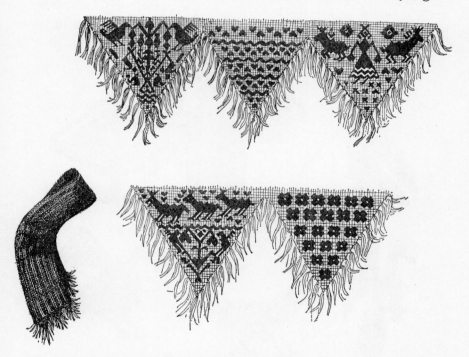

Figs. 18 and 19. Wool-and-cotton shawl with woven triangular patterns at both ends. It takes several months to make this exceptionally luxurious model. Otomi Indians. Village of San Bartolo Morelos. State of Mexico.

over and over. There is also a world of dreams and holidays, ritual and the sacred.

Next to each Otomi house on the Toluca plateau there is a cleaner and better-built cabin with whitewashed walls. Inside, a holy image, usually a picture of the Virgin of Guadalupe, is hung on the wall. A table holds crowns of flowers and sometimes some old bottles. In Spanish this place is called an *oratorio*; in Otomi, it is a *tsinikhâ* ("little temple"). The head of every family has one. My friend Bonifacio tells me that not much more than half a century ago the old people kept terra-cotta idols in these family temples and gave them offerings of maize and meat. Every year a feast was celebrated in their honor; then the idols were hidden in the rocks or the forests that cover the mountain slopes and new figurines were installed in their place. This idolatry —very similar, incidentally, to the way in which the Lacandones worship their incense-burner idols—has disappeared, at least in the

Figs. 20 *and* 21. Decorative animal figures from various examples of Otomi weaving.

overtly pagan form it took such a short time ago. The Virgin of Guadalupe has supplanted the clay idols. Like all the Indians who have been Christianized, the Otomi hold this brown-skinned Virgin, patron saint of Mexico, in special veneration. They call her *Tsinâñâ* ("honorable mother"), which is also their name for the moon. The words *"Shindoû Tsinâñâ Zânâ,"* which mean, literally, "honorable mother moon is dead," simply refer to an eclipse of the moon. But the old ritual theme has not changed. Every year, or every two years—probably because the Indians are too poor to be able to afford this ceremony any more frequently—the old temple is taken down and a new one is put up. This is a community affair; the head of the family concerned is helped by other Indians from the same village and rejoicing takes the form of meals of turkey cooked with pimento and *sêy*-drinking sessions. The Otomi feels bound, by a ceremonial relationship stronger than blood ties, to those who come to help him and whom he should help when the time comes. In this way, the entire village is linked in an invisible network of mutual obligations that creates a much more compelling type of social solidarity than the ties of natural and family solidarity, which appear to be very slack.

The highland neighbors of the Otomi are the Mazahua. Their hamlets, snug in the hollow of fairly well-watered valleys, are often wealthier, or at least less poor. In Aztec, the word "Mazahua" refers to the Mexican stag or roebuck, *mazatl*, and could designate "the people who hunt the roebuck," just as the name of the natives of Michoacán designates "those who have, or who catch, fish." The Otomi dislike the Mazahua and call them *Nyâmphani*, "those who speak roebuck" or "who speak like roebucks." Actually, the Mazahua and the Otomi are comparable in the way that the Spanish and the Portuguese are, and these two neighboring peoples may be considered close cousins.

The Mazahua have elaborated the system of worship in small family temples to a point where it is almost a luxury. They have expanded the *intsimi* (*oratorio*) into a spacious and very carefully built house which has a tiled roof; it is often preceded by a small patio like the *atrio* of Spanish churches. Most remarkable are the outside walls. After being whitewashed, they are covered with a number of pictures painted in lively

5

contrasting colors that stand out sharply from the light background of the walls and the green hedges of prickly pear that enclose each house with its temple. Whereas the Indians and their families continue to live in graceless, dusty cabins made of crude, unplastered bricks, the *oratorios* are well kept, clean, and gay.

The drawing and painting are the work of a Mazahua artist. One of the most common themes is a rabbit, either seated or "galloping" with his belly close the ground and the four paws arranged in pairs superimposed on the same plane. This reminds us that, in ancient times, the

Fig. 22. Varnished terra-cotta incense burner. The Indians buy these incense burners at the market and burn copal in them, in front of the pictures of saints which are found in every house. Otomi Indians. Village of Chapantongo. State of Hidalgo.

rabbit symbolized abundant harvests, village feasts, and, of course, drunkenness. The Aztecs grouped all the little country gods of harvest and drink in a sort of divine guild called the "four hundred rabbits" ("four hundred" was meant to convey "countless"), and the verb *"tochtilia"* ("to become rabbit") meant "to get drunk."

In further support of the comparison is the fact that worship of the little peasant deities certainly goes back to the most ancient times, long before the Aztec era. Moreover, the Mazahua, as I know from having frequented them for several months, are inveterate drinkers.

However that may be, other themes used to decorate the *intsimi*; in addition to the rabbits are birds, flowers, stars, and crescent moons. The painter first draws the outlines of these figures and then divides the area within the outline into a number of irregular zones. Finally, he paints in his colors zone by zone. The result is animals, plants, or stars made of red, yellow, blue, or white patches like the pieces of a jigsaw puzzle—figurative but totally unrealistic art, reminiscent of certain children's drawings or perhaps of experiments by certain modern painters.

So far I have mentioned only the traditional decorative themes. Unfortunately, there are other influences as well—popular imagery, commercial calendars, billboards, and the perforated-paper stenciling sheets sold in the shops of the big mestizo village of Ixtlahuaca. These have gradually introduced such themes as an eagle devouring a snake (the arms of Mexico), the green, white, and red flag of Mexico, and even Venetian *palazzi* and gondolas that clash, in a way that is somewhat burlesque, with the rabbits and birds romping among the flowers and the stars.

When a new *oratorio* is put up, this is the occasion for a whole series of ceremonies and feasts. Every step of the way—making the bricks, laying the foundations, finishing the walls, putting up the roof—is marked by a banquet and drinking bouts, where great quantities of *parê* (alcohol) and *ttaphi* (pulque) are downed. The heads of families involved in the building exchange toasts. The master of the house provides the drink, and his guests return the compliment by draining their glasses and shouting "*Po Kheu!*" The painter is always invited to these sprees, and the women take part enthusiastically. To close the cycle of rites and feasting there is a final banquet. This time it is not held in the home of the Indian whose *intsimi* has just been built but instead in that of the Indian who helped him the most and who makes it a point of honor to outdo his friend in generosity and splendor.

There can be no doubt that what we see here is a very old and deeply rooted set of social practices. This partially accounts for the fact that among the pre-Conquest Mexicans, as I have said, the Otomi were reputed to be great wasters of food and intrepid drinkers. I find two points especially noteworthy: first, the enormous amount of work and expense which so poor a society devotes to these ceremonial activities; and, second, the system of mutual aid which goes into effect on such occasions and forms the backbone of every village. From all appearances, family and matrimonial ties in the Otomi-Mazahua society are not very strong. Households are formed and disbanded very casually; there is no trace of complex regulations such as form the structure of other ethnic groups and of which we find vestiges among the Lacandones, for instance. Yet every seemingly amorphous village[6] does have a sturdy skeleton in the form of these cyclical exchanges of help, food, and drink among the heads of families on the occasion—on the pretext, one might almost say—of building and renewing the temples. Although there is an economic aspect to this phenomenon, it is essentially antieconomic since it causes a bout of waste and of emulation through consumption which this society tolerates and even encourages, despite its meager resources, as if, through some unexpressed collective awareness, it knew that this is the price it must pay in order to survive as a society.

So, in this case, it is not the economic factor which determines the social but, instead, the social imperative which overrules the economic.

If we transpose this system to a culture which is immeasurably

6. For administrative purposes, the Otomi and Mazahua hamlets and villages of this region are placed under such local seats as the Hispano-Mexican market town of Ixtlahuaca. The Indians actually have very little contact with the government and go to some lengths to avoid having any. Local matters—the few that ever come up—are handled by a *dzoya* (the Otomi term for chief) and the advisers who assist him. All are appointed by the married men and their authority is extremely limited.

richer, with an abundance of provisions and man-made objects such as the Otomi and Mazahua cannot even begin to dream of, we have the potlatch,[7] as practiced among those extraordinary Indians of British Columbia. Not only do they give and receive but, in a frenzy of ostentation and rivalry, they destroy whole quantities of food, canoes, blankets, and etched sheets of copper.

Far on the other side of the Otomi territory, in the villages where the women sing their Bacchic verses, there is also an *oratorio* cult, but here it has taken the shape of an institution found throughout Indo-Iberian Mexico: the brotherhood. To celebrate the name day of a given saint every year or to organize dances on certain dates, the Indian family heads form a sort of association. The leaders, sometimes called *mayordomos*, must bear the often considerable cost of preparing for each feast, buying costumes, providing meals and drinking bouts and the deafening *cohetes* ("firecrackers") that are part of any rejoicing. Here again expense is a matter of trying to outshine one's neighbor and prove one's lavishness, and the Indians will spend the little they have and even go into debt in order to keep up appearances. Here again the members of each brotherhood are bound by special ties. This structure is both Indian and Spanish, and the missionaries tolerated it even if they did not actually encourage it. The Catholic clergy takes part to a greater or lesser degree, depending on the place,[8] but its participation is always limited and the old Indians, who uphold respect of tradition, are watchful. Generally, the priest does no more than give his blessing.

Among the Otomi of San Pedro, there are half a dozen brotherhoods attached to as many sanctuaries. Their members, called *Behtoni*, change every year; for the duration of their period of duty, they must keep up the brotherhood's temple, place offerings in it regularly, and organize feasts. This responsibility is so absorbing and costly that it is easy to understand why it is rotated yearly. It is a point of honor for

---

7. "Potlatch" is a Chinook word meaning "to feed" and "to consume." It is used in reference to the exchanges of services, feasts, and accompanying ritual practiced among the Tlingit and the Haida of Northwestern America. See Mauss, *The Gift*.

8. Concerning the Nahuatl-speaking Indians of the Sierra d'Orizaba, see Georgette Soustelle, *Tequila, un village nahuatl du Mexique oriental*, Paris, Institut d'Ethnologie, 1958.

the *Behtoni* to be at least as zealous as their predecessors in the rebuilding or maintenance of the sanctuaries and as lavish in holding feasts.

The most important temple is that of Tsitânhmou, "the venerable great Lord." Although we do not know much about the pre-Columbian religion of the Otomi, we do know that the supreme gods in their pantheon were a couple: a god identified with fire and the sun, and a goddess who was the moon mother and earth mother. The Tsitânhmou was probably the husband of the Tsinânâ. His sanctuary is a large adobe house, very handsome compared with the rest of the village. The entire façade is decorated with pieces of *sotol*, a milky-white thick-leaved plant, arranged to form very stylized stars or birds. Inside there is first a rather narrow antechamber, then a step up into a large dark room, lit by the flickering ruddy flames of two candles. The walls are hung with garlands of flowers, painted calabashes, and ears of maize. Both a terra-cotta bowl suspended from the roof and a hole dug in the ground beneath that bowl are filled with the wax from burned tapers, and a strong odor of wax and incense pervades the room.

Against the back wall stands an altar table with offerings on it— packs of cigarettes and coins. Two wooden doors cover a niche in the same wall. And that is all. Yet this bare earth-colored shadowy room where the *Behtoni* stand silent and still while a woman comes to kiss the shutters that close the niche is charged with a certain emotive quality we cannot help respecting.

What does the niche hold? The *Behtoni* maintain that it houses a statue that must never be seen by anyone except the members of the brotherhood. Once a year it is carefully wrapped in several layers of cloth and carried to the church, where the curate blesses the statue although he is not allowed to look at it—the Indians make absolutely sure of this.

But the *Behtoni* who explained this to me seemed embarrassed, and I am not fully convinced that the occupant of the niche is actually a statue. It may simply be a stone, such as a piece of jade, or some other sacred object. The Aztecs, in their sanctuaries, also kept *tlaquimilolli*, or packages of a sort, which were entrusted to the priests. They remind me of the medicine bundles kept by medicine men among the North

American Indians. A chronicler named Pomar reported that the *tlaquimilolli* of Uitzilopochtli, the great sun god, contained agave thorns, while that of the night god Tezcatlipoca held an obsidian mirror.

However that may be, the *Behtoni* carry their sacred package to the church, the priest blesses it—and so much for post-Columbian religion.

As you walk around the temple, you notice a stone set among the bricks of the back wall a little more than two feet above the ground, exactly in line with the niche inside. Since the house is placed on an east-west axis, this stone faces the rising sun. A closer look reveals that it is a carved human face, but wind and rain have eroded it to such an extent that all that can be made out are the lips, worn thin, a nose reduced to a narrow ridge, and two patches of shadow for eyes under the still-jutting eyebrows.

For years, possibly for centuries, the Indians have preserved this idol. To hide it from the iconoclastic rage of the Spanish monks, they must have buried it underground or tucked it away in a cave and moved it from one sanctuary to another. In all its movements it was guarded by pious members of the Otomi tribe, just as it is entrusted today to the *Behtoni*. "Yes," say the *Behtoni*, "this is the place where the Tsitânhmou appeared." And it is certainly more than mere coincidence that the stone face is turned toward the sun, if it really does represent, as I believe it does, the male and solar member of that very ancient divine couple.

Clearly the brotherhoods were and continue to be one of the most active forms of the Hispano-Indian and Christiano-pagan syncretism which, to varying degrees, has become the religion of the natives of Mexico. Without going any farther afield than the Otomi and Mazahua country between Toluca and Jocotitlán, we can see just how such organizations cover the full range of a religion which combines, at one extreme, beliefs and rites of native antiquity and, at the other, ceremonies and an ideology imported four centuries ago.

Above the little village of Santa Cruz Tepexpán, not far from Ixtlahuaca, rises a steep cone-shaped slope crowned by a church and a market. The church, dedicated to the Virgin of the *Cerrito* ("the little mountain"), is the common sanctuary for all the Otomi and Mazahua throughout the region. Twice yearly, in May and again in October, several thousand Indians climb the long, winding path to the summit. Since there is no source of water on the little mountain, the women carry heavy water jars on their backs, with headbands to keep them in place. Although the air is thin at this altitude, they climb steadily, merely stopping now and again for a second or two, just long enough to empty their lungs with a sort of raucous cry and then inhale deeply.

From the top of the *Cerrito*, there is an extensive view over the whole broad plateau to the blue-green dome of the mountain of Jocotitlán; the plateau is studded with villages and with ponds or small lagoons that grow bigger or smaller, depending on the season. But the real spectacle is up on the mountaintop itself, for this is where the brotherhoods from all over the surrounding plain come together to dance. Starting at dawn, they perform their dances, half ballet and half dramatic mime, all day long to the high-pitched throbbing of guitars made of armadillo shells. They are surrounded by a solid mass of Indians, a silent but very attentive audience.

For three months I was a member of the brotherhood of San Bartolo del Llano, a fairly prosperous Mazahua village where a prodigious consumption of *parê* and *ttaphi* created a rather singular atmosphere. I was on cordial terms with the chief of the brotherhood and his brother, both of whom went around in a perpetual alcoholic daze. This did not lessen the chief's personality or his undeniable authority, although he was a somewhat disturbing figure, acting absent-mindedly at some times and excitedly at others, laughing suddenly, talking loudly and jerkily. In many ways he was different from the other Indians, who were very calm and reserved even when they had drunk, and his abnormal behavior both set him apart from the others and made him the natural choice to fill the role of what the North American tribes called the shaman and the Eskimos the *angakok*. In many societies in northeastern Asia and in America, the person whom we would consider as more or less mentally ill, as a neurotic requiring medical care, is used—precisely because he is an exceptional being—to make contact with the invisible world.[9] In this case, the brotherhood chief was halfway between the impresario of a small provincial theater and the leader of a religious sect. For him, putting on a good show and paying tribute to the Tsinânâ of the little mountain were twin goals, and he invested all his prestige in reaching them with an ardor which was no less real for being aswim in alcohol.

The brotherhood of which he was "captain" belonged to the category of groups of religious dancers which, in Mexico, is often named "Los Apaches," after the famous warring tribe to the north. In almost every Indian village, no matter what language the peasants speak or where they come from, there is a similar brotherhood. From all the country around they come, on the major feasts, especially, in December, to the basilica of the Virgin of Guadalupe in Tepeyac, to hail the goddess the Aztecs called Tonantzin and the Otomi call Tsinânâ. I have even seen brotherhoods which, on June 30, celebrated the anniversary of the defeat of Cortés during the celebrated *Noche Triste* by dancing near the tree of Popotla. Tradition has it that the defeated conquistador sank down at the foot of this tree and cried.

The uniform of the "Apaches" is the same everywhere: a skirt and a cape of variegated cloth and a feather headdress, with gold braid, spangles, and mirrors to enhance the whole. Each dancer uses a guitar that looks more like a mandolin; because its sound box is made of an armadillo shell, these musicians are sometimes called *concheros*, from the Spanish *concha*, "shell" or "carapace." Of course, there is no limit to the variations on this theme. The brotherhoods vie with one another to see who will wear the most luxurious costumes—the most stunning clothes, the brightest colors, and the shiniest ornaments. At San Bartolo, our captain and his colleagues could scarcely manage more than an averagely decent show, since the materials that went into making a fine costume cost at least one hundred pesos—a considerable

9. In 1930 or 1931, I wrote a short essay which has never been published—and probably does not deserve to be—on the ecstatic phenomena of Siberian and Eskimo shamanism compared with certain facts studied by modern psychiatry. My information was only secondhand, of course. But from it I have retained the idea that certain cultures find a place within themselves for the abnormal personality, create a setting for it, and put to use what we would call its pathological traits, "socializing" it as it were, instead of isolating it the way we do.

5*

sum when you think that at that time the official minimum wage in
Mexico was one peso a day. Each member of the brotherhood has to
provide or pay for his cloth, braid, spangles, feathers, and so on, and
it is the chief himself who makes the costumes, which he keeps, along
with the guitars, in his personal sanctuary.

Some pages back I described the *intsimi* of the Mazahua villages.
The *intsimi* of the "Apache" captain was the biggest in the entire
village. It formed one side of a quadrilateral enclosing a central court-
yard filled with a number of active children and several women. The
sanctuary was whitewashed and decorated with paintings, including
many-colored stars like a burst of fireworks, and inside there was a
niche, with a cross above it, that housed the costumes and guitars. This
was where the chief called meetings of the brotherhood, taught his men
the songs and the dance steps and held rehearsals.

It goes without saying that neither the dancers nor their chief knows
how to read music. The musical themes and the six or seven dance steps
in their repertory are passed on by tradition and imitation. The men
learn by heart how to place the fingers of the left hand on the strings,
high up on the neck of the guitar, while the right hand strums all the
strings at once in a rapid to-and-fro motion. The captain indicates
which theme he has chosen; then, with a harsh cry, he gives the signal
for all to lift their knees high and then raise and lower their legs to the
rhythm of the guitars, stamping on the ground with their sandaled feet.
Some of the figures call for the dancers to swivel around or to cross
their legs and strike the ground with the edge of their soles. Each
theme is only a few measures long, and is repeated as long as the chief
wishes. When he decides that it is time to change, his right hand
strums the guitar more slowly; his fingers slacken, touch the strings
absently, and then stop. After a short pause, he begins another figure.
This goes on all day long (in fact for three days at the top of the
Cerrito), under the sun and the steady gaze of the hushed crowd. They
cannot take their eyes off these men, men like themselves yet dazzling,
hieratic, transfigured by their capes stiff with embroidery and their tall
many-colored headdresses. The performers take on the gravity and
dignity of officiating priests, for this is definitely a religious ceremony—

no doubt about it in the minds of the Indians themselves—in honor of the eternal goddess-mother. Christianity has not abolished but actually confirmed the veneration in which the Mexican peasants have held her for thousands of years.

Here we have a close look at three essential features of the Hispano-Indian religion as it has developed over the last four centuries: Spanish elements (cult of the Virgin, stringed instruments) coexist and are intimately bound up with native elements (feather headdresses, dances, worship of the earth and moon goddess); the social role of this religion and the accompanying ritual, in terms of emulation between villages, cohesion of the brotherhoods, and the personal prestige of the chiefs; lastly—and this is just as important—the psychological function of these feasts and ceremonies, which lift the people out of themselves and, for the space of a few hours or a few days, dispel the grayness and poverty of daily life.

The same three features are found in another "dance"—really a play—which I was able to witness in Atlacomulco, a big village in the foothills of the mountain of Jocotitlán. Once a year, for two or three days, several thousand Otomi and Mazahua come from all over the plain and the Sierra to camp in this town. They hold the inevitable market, displaying their pitiful wares—a few little heaps of tomatoes, some pimentos, kernels of maize. But, above all, they form a dense throng in front of the church and watch the brotherhoods dance. In 1933, when I was there, there was no priest in Atlacomulco. The Indians could do as they liked with the church. A crowd, holding lighted tapers, filled the nave. From time to time, amidst the heat and the odor of wax, the procession formed by one brotherhood or another made its way through the mass of people with flags flying and guitars, flutes, violins, and drums echoing beneath the vaulted ceiling, while Indians perched in the belfry made the heavy bells peal, and countless firecrackers went off in a terrific din.

Outside, in front of the church and among the trees of the market place, the "Apaches," the "*Moros y Cristianos*," and perhaps twenty other groups had been dancing tirelessly since dawn.

The "dance" of the *torito* ("little bull") was performed by a small

Mazahua brotherhood from Santa Cruz Tepexpán. It was called a *cuadrilla* (the Spanish word), with a cast of eleven: the *mayor*, chief of the brotherhood; the *señor amo* ("the Master"), playing the role of the owner of a hacienda or large landed estate; the *mayordomo*, foreman of

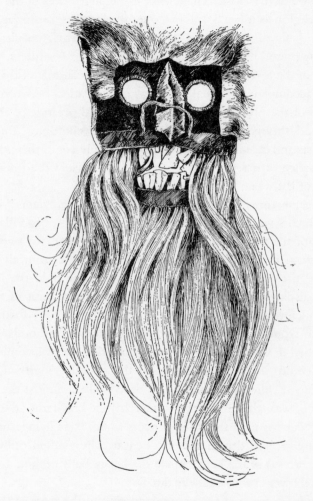

Fig. 23. Human mask made of skin, mica, donkey's and dog's teeth, cow's tail, cotton. Worn by the King of the Moors in the "*Moros y Cristianos*" dance performed by the Otomi and the Mazahua during pilgrimages. Otomi Indians. Village of San José del Sitio. State of Mexico.

the estate; three *peones*, or farmhands; two comic figures concealed behind bearded masks; a young man who carried on his head a small bull made of wood and leather, with bottle-glass eyes; a little boy of about ten, whose huge straw hat made him look like a mushroom and who clutched a picture of the Virgin of Guadalupe in both hands; and, last of all, a musician, a blind fiddler rolling leucoma-white eyes and scratching away at his instrument to produce the same thin melody again and again. The actors performed inside a rectangle that was only vaguely outlined, so that sometimes they had to elbow aside a spectator whom the pressure of the crowd had pushed too far forward. The atmosphere was both serious and good-natured; what was going on was halfway between ritual and theater, or even farce. The purpose was partly to pay tribute to Tsinânâ, partly to go through a traditional series of songs and gestures, and partly just to have fun—and although we may find all these things incompatible, our own ancestors did not, when they performed mystery plays in front of the cathedrals.

There is nothing sacred about the theme of the play. A little bull has run away and fled to the mountains. The hacienda master demands that it be found and lassoed and brought back. This the *mayordomo* and the *peones* try to do with the help—or, rather, the hindrance—of the two masked clowns who keep up a running stream of jokes, insist on being given something to drink, and pretend to be drunk. Yet the play begins solemnly enough. The *señor amo* and the *vaqueros* exchange elaborate greetings. Then the *peones* who have been instructed to bring the bull back from the brush brandish their banners (colored bandannas tied on sticks) and, equipped with ropes, they go off in pursuit of the animal.

Although the actors speak Mazahua among themselves, they sing in Spanish, but it is often a corrupted form of Spanish uttered with a strong Mazahua accent and full of unintelligible expressions. Roughly, the poem they sing as they pursue the bull could be translated like this:

"Let us go, in the name of God *at this, they all lift their
    broad hats or, rather, tip them with their thumbs*
Very holy Mary, Virgin of Guadalupe,

Lord Saint Isidor,
Lord Saint Luke,
Let me be successful!
I am going to go into the wilds,
I am going to look for my little red bull,
Son of the brown cow.
I have my good horse
With his silver saddle
And his reins of gold,
And my lasso of *lechuguilla*.
This is what the Master told me,
This is where I will find him:
Over there, on top of the red hill.
If I do not find him on top of the red hill,
I will go around to the other side.
Over there on the mountainside
Over there he must be tied
With a lasso of *lechuguilla*
To a cactus trunk.
Now I have found you, bull,
Where the Master said I would.
I have found you, now I am going to catch you in my lasso.
I will take you to the hacienda
And you will see what *banderilla* is waiting for you there."

While this is being sung, the bull carried by the Indian moves forward; the others pursue it and throw their lassos. The bull resists, throws off the ropes and aims his horns at his pursuers, most of all, of course, at the two clowns, who do outlandish somersaults. At this point the audience comes to life, siding for the animal and laughing— it is no ordinary sight to see Otomi and Mazahua laughing—and jeering at the two clowning scapegoats.

This comic interlude is followed by a series of single combats between the bull and each of the *vaqueros*. The two antagonists face each other and dance, while the actor waves his banner and sings:

"Follow me, bull.
I am waiting for you here, I am on the lookout for you here,
With my banner in one hand
And my *banderilla* in the other.
Follow me, bull.
Maybe I will die tomorrow or the day after.
I am not afraid of dying.
My only regret is a pretty girl
I left in the market place at Salvatierra.
She cried when I went away to my country.
So I must go back there
So that she will come to my country,
So that she will come to sit at the watchtower door,
So that she will come to see the *vueltecita*[10]
That I am going to do for her.
. . . No, I am not afraid of dying.
And you already know,
Gentlemen, my dear comrades,
Where I want my sepulture to be.
I don't want to be put away in consecrated ground.
I want to be buried in the country where my herds live.
There I have had a stone engraved
With four or five inscriptions
And there, every time my pretty girl goes by,
She will say, 'God help me! Here is where
They buried my departed *caporal mayor*.' "

By the time each actor has reached this point in his recitation, the atmosphere has become as grave and rapt as it was gay before. The crowd hushes and the *vaquero* ends his speech majestically:

"I have my fine hat
Which will be my crown.
I have my good shirt

10. Literally, "little turn or little dance."

Which will be my shroud.
I have my fine belt
Which will be my rope [?]
I have my golden spurs,
Which will be the bells to toll the knell[?]."[11]

When he has finished, the actor turns toward his fellow actors, takes off his hat with a sweeping gesture and asks them ceremoniously, "What do you think, gentlemen and dear comrades, of the *vueltecita* I have just done for you here? Do you find it good or do you find it bad?"

And they answer in unison,

"Just fine [?], sir, that is just the way the *vaqueros* in my country do the *vueltecita*."

Then comes the last act. The bull "dies"—that is, the young man who was carrying it places it on the ground with its hoofs in the air. The Master of the hacienda orders the animal carved up and the meat shared. This is the signal for some indescribable clowning. The two masked comedians, armed with an axe and a wooden cutlass, outdo one another in awkwardness, call each other names, and pun repeatedly. And again the miracle happens: the Indians are drawn into the fun and enter into the joking; there are word play and hooting from all sides, the spectators laugh uproariously, and the rectangle which is the scene of this tragi-comedy is virtually overrun by the hilarious crowd. But calm is gradually restored when the actors all gather before the picture of the Virgin of Guadalupe, who gazes down on the crowd as they pretend to share the meat, according to a list on a bit of paper. By then night has begun to fall. The whole brotherhood, bull and all, forms a procession and, to the sound of the fiddle, it enters the church. The actors kneel before the altar and make the sign of the cross, then back out of the church with many more signs of the cross. The show is

11. The last four lines are obviously deformed. The "Spanish" text goes like this:
Traigo mi buen cenidor
Que me sirva de cordon.
Traigo mis espuela di oro
Que me sirven doble de campana.

over—it has lasted all day long and will begin again at dawn the next day.

I have talked with the *mayor* of the brotherhood and several of its members. There is no doubt in their minds that their "dance" is a tribute to the Virgin of Guadalupe, who is present throughout the entire show and before whom the bull is immolated. But where did this rite come from? Why these Spanish songs, whereas the Indians who sing them and who come from one of the poorest villages of the whole plateau speak almost nothing but Mazahua? Here we come up against the usual explanation: "It was the custom of our fathers and our grandfathers before us." The rite has certainly been passed on from generation to generation for many years. But what strikes me most about it all is that the real life of these Indians is worlds away from the life their play and their songs talk about. They have never had cattle or horses. Even before the 1910–1918 revolution, there were never any cattle-breeding haciendas in that area. For the Mazahua, silver saddles and golden spurs are as fabulous, marvelous, and unattainable as a flying carpet in an Arabian tale. What the actors are mimicking and singing about is the life of the Mexican *charros*—mestizos whose harness, suits, and hats are indeed embroidered with gold and silver— and the *jaripeo*, where those daring riders pursue wild bulls and lasso them. The heroic concept of existence, the love of a pretty girl who will miss her *vaquero*, the disdain of death, the tomb in the midst of the herds and the grazing lands—all of this is lifted straight out of Hispano-Mexican folklore, especially that of the plain of Bajío, where the little city of Salvatierra, mentioned in one of the songs, is situated. The theme of the struggle between man and bull came from Spain; for many thousands of years it has been a Mediterranean theme, since it goes back to at least 2000 B.C. on Crete.[12] What a series of sequences, from the Minotaur to Mithra, from Spanish bull-fighting to the Mexican *jaripeo*, and from there to a rustic dance by Indians before a

12. *See:* R. W. Hutchinson, *Prehistoric Crete*, London, 1962. The author notes the analogy between the Cretan games with bulls and a dance which Aldous Huxley observed at Chichicastenango (Guatemala).

holy image, which in turn corresponds to the recent phase of a cult, of the goddess-mother, which again goes back thousands of years!

However that may be, the Mazahua of Santa Cruz Tepexpán are very attached to their *torito* dance, and this is no mere coincidence, because the need for compensation has full sway in this ritual. Here they are, the poorest of the poor, who own nothing more than a few sheep, who have never ridden anything but their donkeys or used anything but a piece of agave cloth for a saddle, who from one year's end to the next have only worn and often ragged clothing to wear—and, suddenly, for a few days, they can imagine themselves sporting handsome hats and sumptuous clothing, riding horses harnessed with gold and silver, going out into the country in pursuit of their cattle, leading the kind of life they have never had more than a distant glimpse of, the life of the horseback-riding herdsman, instead of the peasant pedestrian. So, in a waking dream, they hoist themselves to the level of an admired and envied culture. This is why they willingly make such an effort to learn long passages in a language they can scarcely understand and to organize these shows. The lowest of the low for so many centuries, they manage in this way to believe that they are climbing one step higher toward a freer and more brilliant life.

Whereas we have just seen a case of a group of natives taking over a set of themes and images borrowed from nonnatives, we can also find —again at Atlacomulco—a striking instance of the preservation of a rite whose origins go very far back in time. A brotherhood moves across the main market place toward the church. Except for the fiddler and the drummer who lead the way, the "brotherhood" is made up exclusively of Mazahua women, small and stocky, the skin a dark copper and the face Mongoloid, with prominent cheekbones and slightly slanting eyes. Their braids of shiny brown-black hair, interwoven with red wool cords, fall to their shoulders beneath broad hats of white straw, one side of which is raised and held in place by a mirror. Bows of different-colored ribbons on their hats, red earrings, glass-bead necklaces, the bright and clashing colors of the skirts and blouses covered with braid and more ribbons and spangles—everything gives the garb of these robust peasant women an air of ceremony. Usually they wear dark, sober blues and grays. But here exuberant reds and yellows stand out, reminiscent of the red feathers that the Otomi and Mazahua women used to stick on their arms and legs in pre-Columbian times—a fashion the Aztecs made fun of, calling it barbaric and ridiculous. But the whole point, on this occasion, is to do what contrasts most with the everyday, ordinary way. These women, released for a day from the dull life of their little hamlets, and dressed in dazzling luxury (what does it matter if their costumes are made of the poorest quality cottons and their jewelry of glass?), cease to be mere peasants and become priestesses officiating at a rite.

For this is definitely a rite. Each of the women holds a stick, the typical digging stick that the native farmers use; it has a leather handle with little bells sewn to it. The two musicians squat on the bare stone floor of the church, near the altar, and the dancing women arrange themselves by fives in the nave, where the crowd has drawn back to leave them room. Their faces impassive and their bodies stiff under the ribbons and the many-colored jackets, the women strike the floor hard with their sticks to the beat of the drum and the fiddle. The constant ringing whisper of the little bells sounds like a hard rain falling. From time to time, the women stop striking the stone flags and turn around several times as rigidly as large mechanical dolls. Then the obsessive pounding of the sticks and the trembling of the little bells begin again, punctuated by the thudding drum as it echoes under the vaulted ceiling. For hours and hours this goes on, until night falls.

It is easy to understand what the basic gesture here means: striking the floor with the digging stick imitates the sowing of maize, while the little bells are calling to the rain. At all times, the farming peoples of Mexico have relied upon the magic of sound to obtain water from the sky.

Among the Aztec religious chants that Sahagún took down from dictation by his native informers was the "*Ciuacontl Icuic*" ("Hymn of the Female Serpent"), which was sung during the ceremonies dedicated to the goddess of the earth, mother of the great sun god Uitzilopochtli. In several stanzas this phrase recurs: "In the field of the gods, she leans on her ringing stick." Now, the ringing stick or the rattle stick, *chicauaztli*, is exactly that instrument—both farming implement and magical device—that we have seen used in Atlacomulco. The Aztec annotator who commented on these hymns actually explained, "With the ringing stick I dig in the ground," and Eduard Seler notes, "We can assume that, at sowing season, a picture or a figure representing the goddess was carried through the fields with the ringing stick in its hand, and presumably the stick was used as a hoe or a digging stick to make holes in the ground in which to place the kernels of maize."[13]

So the Mazahua women in Atlacomulco are doing nothing other than imitating the eternal gesture of the goddess-mother, symbolizing the fertility of the soil. Sahagún's Aztec informers had heard about the women of that tribe. "The old women," they said, "paint their faces with red or yellow ocher, they even stick feathers to their arms and legs, and they carry a rattle in their hands and shake it as they dance."[14] Thus the rite we have witnessed was well established and was considered, in the pre-Hispanic period, as characteristic of that tribe.

The rattles or the little bells, whose whispering sound recalls the sound of rain falling from the skies, were used to call the rain or even "to make rain"—this we know from, among other evidence, the religious chant dedicated to Tlaloc, the rain god, where we find passages such as this:

> All day long we have made rain
>   in the courtyard of the temple.
> With the little mist rattles we have
>   called to the water in the paradise of Tlaloc.[15]

It is no mere chance, of course, that the magic rattle is manipulated by the women. The woman is the image of the earth goddess and guards the secret of the mystery of fertility. Only the woman is qualified to relive, year after year, that divine undertaking which is to restore fertility to the fields and call down the blessing of rain upon them. It is significant that the sowing season is the one time when the Otomi and

13. Sahagún. Robredo, Ed., Vol. V, p. 130.
14. *Florentine Codex*, Vol. X, p. 183.
15. *Tlaloc icuic. Florentine Codex*, Vol. II, p. 208.

Mazahua women take part in the farming work. The woman follows the man as he makes holes in the ground with his digging stick; then it is she who places the seeds in those holes, covers them over, and tamps down the soil with her heels. Since the woman is the outstanding conservative element in the Indian societies and speaks no other language than her native dialect, it is only natural that she "officiate" in the agrarian cult that goes back four or five thousand years. The dance of the women in Atlacomulco is like a fossil preserved intact throughout conquests, wars, periods of migration and domination, and all the cataclysmic historical events of which central Mexico has been the scene. Whereas the *torito* shows that the Indians can adopt themes and images foreign to their own culture, the women's ritual is an example of stubborn survival, of the deepest-lying roots of a rural people whose entire life, for tens of centuries, has simply been the reflection of the advancing seasons and the mysterious interplay of the cosmic forces, the forces of the earth and the rain.

Situations of this sort can be found almost everywhere in Mexico. From them we are forced to conclude that, because of actual historical developments, there can be such things as mixed religions, just as there are populations of mixed blood. The Spanish missionaries—including such first-rate figures as Sahagún, Motolinía, and Pedro de Gante—did not question the reality of the Mexican gods. They believed that those gods were demons who had seized the Indians' souls. Sahagún, for instance, spoke to his neophytes in these terms: "The false gods are nothing but lies invented by the father of all lies, who is the devil . . . Uitzilopochtli is not a god, nor is Tlaloc nor Quetzalcoatl. Neither is Ciuacoatl a goddess, nor Chicomecoatl nor Teteoinnan. . . . Nor is any of the others you adore a god. All are demons. . . . The devils deceived your ancestors and laughed at them."[16] Consequently, no compromise or conciliation was possible between the Christian religion—absolute truth and absolute good—and the religion of the Indians—absolute evil and absolute falsehood. The missionaries were acting in accordance with their own logic when they took it upon themselves systematically to destroy not only the temples, the statues, the objects of veneration,

16. *Historia general de las Cosas de Nueva España.* Robredo, Ed. Vol. I pp. 63 ff.

and the sacred books but in fact anything in the Indian customs and usages that in any way, remotely or intimately, referred to the native religion—such as proper names derived from the names of the gods.[17]

But at the same time, because the missionaries were led by their praiseworthy desire to protect the Indian from the too often corrupting influence of the Spaniard who had emigrated to Mexico in order to amass a fortune, they tried to put up barriers between the natives and the newcomers. The first such barrier was language. Rather than make knowledge of Castilian more widespread, they preferred to learn the more commonly used native tongues—Nahuatl, Otomi, and Maya in particular—themselves. In order to teach their catechumens the truths of their religion, they translated "God" into Otomi as "*Okhã*" and "the Holy Virgin" into Nahuatl as "Tonantzin"—that is, they availed themselves of names already used to designate gods or goddesses of pre-Christian antiquity. Tonantzin, "our venerated mother" (Tsinânâ in Otomi), was the great earth and moon goddess who was worshipped on Tepeyac Mountain. In 1531, an Indian, Juan Diego, described to the archbishop of Mexico City, Juan de Zumarraga, the apparition that had come to him on that mountainside. In proof of it he showed his *tilma*, a cloak of rough agave cloth, miraculously imprinted with the features of the good Indian Virgin. Both the bishop and the Indians had cause to be pleased: the bishop because this apparition definitely placed the stamp of Christianity upon Mexico (the Virgin of Guadalupe was proclaimed patron saint of the country in 1737, Queen of Mexico in 1895, and Empress of the Americas in 1945), and the Indians because they called the Virgin Tonantzin or Tsinânâ, as they still do today, so that the thread of continuity, after a momentary rupture, remained intact. It is a fact that the sites which drew the most pilgrims before the Conquest—sites such as Chalma—continued to do so as Christian sanctuaries. Toward 1540, at that site, an image of Tezcatlipoca Oztoteotl ("god of the cavern") was succeeded by the Señor de Chalma.

17. Sahagún, *op. cit.*, p. 73, notes that some Indians from good families still bore "diabolical names" such as Yauhtecatl, Acolhoa, etc., which are the names of the gods of abundance and drunkenness.

It would be a mistake to suspect either the Indians or the missionaries of duplicity. There is no lack of testimony to the ardor with which the natives embraced the new religion and the sometimes excessive lengths to which it was carried; Motolinía reported that recent converts had to be restrained from scourging themselves nearly to death. But these converts were not so much renouncing their old beliefs as incorporating them into a new body of faith and ritual. The Spanish priests, in turn, imagined that they had uprooted the tree, whereas they had merely grafted it onto another. Subjectively, the Indian who dances in front of the basilica of the Virgin of Guadalupe in Tepeyac is aware of performing a Christian ceremony and, at the same time, of perpetuating a tradition that goes back over one thousand years. If there is a contradiction here, the Indian does not feel it as such; it is we who pick it out.

The Indians' religion is *not* that of their ancestors, covered over with a superficial gloss, any more than it is the Christianity of Latin Europe. It is an original synthesis. Two streams from distant sources—one coming from Asia Minor by way of the Mediterranean world and the other springing out of the soil of Mexico itself—have mingled their waters to give rise to a river which is no longer either the one or the other.

Chapter Five

Frontiers

THE SIERRA GORDA COVERS THE NORTHERN portions of the states of Hidalgo and Querétaro and the southern part of the State of San Luis Potosí. Deep, narrow canyons wind between the barren mountains of this vast and chaotic range. The only river that cuts through, at mid-Sierra, is the Extorax, which generally has little more to show than a broad sandy bed with a thin trickle of water. To the north, the range grows lower and lower until it becomes the dry plateau of Rioverde, bristling with thorny growth. Cut off from the rest of the country and divided again and again by ravines, this land is a world in itself, and it has a wild and sorrowful beauty. You can travel all day long in these mineral wastes without meeting a single human being; even the motionless leaves of the *soyates* seem to be cut out of metal. Under the midday sun, the organ-pipe cacti and the acacias with their twisted shapes fill the heavy air with gusts of aromatic scent.

It is strange to think that in this rocky desert used to live people capable of building villages and even small cities, as we know from the ruins of Toluquilla and Ranas. There I have found fragments of hard, chiseled stone and shards of pottery showing that between roughly the third and the eighth centuries, in the classical era, these human settlements were subject to two influences: that of the great theocratic city of Teotihuacán, which dominated the central plateau, and that of the Gulf Coast civilization. The most complete remains of that civilization are found at El Tajín, in the State of Veracruz.

Doubtless these were only outposts, which must have been overcome by aridity and isolation. The Aztecs considered this extensive region as an area in which barbarians roamed, and it seems that, although the Aztecs did not hesitate to organize expeditions of several years' duration far to the south of their valley, they did not venture into this area to the north. But, as if by osmosis, the agricultural and sedentary way of life seeped beyond the limits of the Aztec Empire, so that gradually some of the nomadic tribes that wandered over the Sierra became maize-growers. Among them were the Pame—whose language is close to that of the Otomi—whereas the Jonaz tribe, of the same family, remained warlike hunters and clung to their wandering existence.

That situation remained almost unchanged until the end of the eighteenth century. In Mexico City I was able to examine an unpublished manuscript written between 1764 and 1780 by Father Juan Guadalupe Soriano, a Franciscan missionary who lived in these mountains for many years. The good priest seems to have had genuine sympathy for the Indians and although, on the whole, his manuscript is one big hodgepodge of history and theology, it provides some valuable items of information. From the vocabularies he gives it is possible to conclude without any doubt whatever that the Pame of his day were indeed the direct ancestors of those who still speak the language today. In the second half of the eighteenth century, there were about 1,700 Pame families in the southern part of the Sierra, from Jiliapan to Tancoyol, and a large number—though no exact figure is given—of those Indians in the northern half as well, that is, in the province of Rioverde.

"The huts of these Indians," writes Father Soriano, "are made of grass, *soyate*, and palm leaves. They go barefoot, their clothing is little more than nudity [*poco menos que desnudez*]. . . . They live on roasted maize."

The missionary goes on to say that

for the most part, they are still inclined to idolatry. They still have a great many evil customs and nearly all still believe in witches and quacks. In the old days, some of these Pames worshipped Moctezuma . . . whom they venerated as a god, and all worshipped the Sun. Others had their special divinities, like dolls of wood or stone. And this is true even in our day: in 1764 I took away two idols from them. One, in the hamlet of Cerro Prieto, was in the form of a fish and the other, in the hamlet of Zipatla, was in the form of a man bent over. They call these stones *Cuddo Cajoo*.[1] In July of the same year I took another, decorated with several green stones. . . . The Indians are very intimidated by these stones which, they believe, have the power to make them die. In order to appease them, they bring them a ration of tamales, so that the stones can eat.

If we leave aside the professional antipathy of the missionary toward the native priest, whom he terms a "quack" (farther on he calls the Pame priests "low scoundrels"), and his hatred of idols, and concentrate on the information he gives us, we find that it is slight but accurate enough to give us an idea of what the Pame religion was like, including offerings of food to their little idols—like the religion of the Lacandones, like that of the Otomi fifty years ago.

It would seem that agricultural rites had a very important place among the Pame. Father Soriano gives us this description:

They also have dances which, in Spanish, are called *mitotes* [here our good missionary is mistaken, as *mitote* is a slightly Hispanicized Aztec word], and they call their house of dances *Satoiz manchi* which, in our language, means the virgin house. They perform this dance in the sowing season, again when the ears of maize appear, and again at harvest time. [In the latter case] the field is said to be virgin, *manzegui*. They dance to the sound of flutes and of a little round drum which begin to play sad and melancholy airs with a very slow rhythm. The witch, or *Cajoo*, sits in the middle, holding his drum in his hands, grimacing in a myriad ways, and staring at the audience. Very slowly he reaches a standing position and then dances for several hours. After this he sits down on a small bench, pricks his calf with a thorn, and sprinkles his blood over the field as if giving it his blessing. Until this ceremony was performed, no one dared to pick a single ear of maize, because the fields were said to be virgin.

This set of harvest rites must have been brought into the Sierra Gorda along with the practice of farming itself. The priest's self-scarification is typical of the religions on the central plateau. The

1. Meaning "magic stones." In modern Pame, spoken at Jiliapan, *Kōdo* means "stone" and *kuhu*, "witch."

"virgin field" ceremony may have been passed on to the Pame by their Otomi "cousins" and neighbors. Unfortunately, the only known Otomi codex, the Huichapan Codex, which Alfonso Caso and I have studied, is posterior to the era of Cortés and reveals strong Aztec and Spanish influences. It does indicate, however, that the Otomi dedicated the fifteenth month of the ritual year, in which the Aztecs observed the feasts of Uitzilopochtli, to the feast of *Anthâxmê* ("the *tortilla* of white maize")—in other words, to the new maize, which announced the harvest to come. This is certainly a very ancient ceremony, common to agricultural peoples.

Consistent with the rule that applies throughout Latin America, the only Indians to survive were those of the Sierra Gorda who had taken up the sedentary way of life before the Spaniards arrived or at some time thereafter. There are some four to five thousand Pame, centered chiefly in Jiliapan, Santa Maria Acapulco, Alaquines, and Villa de San José (near Ciudad del Maíz), and a few hundred Jonaz Indians (452 of them in 1934) grouped at Misión de Chichimecas near San Luis de la Paz, in the north of Guanajuato. It is significant that the Jonaz have nearly disappeared, for theirs was the "bellicose, brutal, and barbaric" nation that Soriano mentions and which almost always refused to settle in villages and work the land.

There were a few fruitless attempts to establish Franciscan and Dominican missions in the seventeenth century, but they did not really appear in the Sierra until about 1750. In almost every instance they failed. The padres were caught in the middle, as it were, between the Indians who deserted the villages repeatedly and fled to the mountains and the Spanish troops to whom the viceregal government distributed pasture land. As a result, the missions were either emptied when the Indians deserted or broken up by the Spaniards. Worst of all, those Indians who were *bravos* or *infieles* even attacked their own fellow Indians who had settled in villages. The village of Vizarrón, for instance, was laid waste in 1691, founded again in 1717, destroyed completely shortly afterward, and built again in 1748. The chronicles of the time talk of Indians who had learned to ride horseback and, like the redskins farther north, attacked the mule trains that tried to trudge across the Sierra. Some of the attackers even scalped their victims, but in a curiously different way: instead of taking the scalp, they took the beard and the skin of the chin!

The description of the times, as culled from mission documents, reminds us of the patience of Penelope: again and again the same missions were founded at the same places, lasted a few years, and then collapsed. "If they are pressed too strongly [to go to Mass], the Indians desert the Mission, disappear and join their infidel brothers. . . . They become irritated and flee to the mountains with their families, and all is lost." Comments of this sort recur monotonously in the historical narratives of the times.

In 1724 the Spanish authorities began distributing the lands at the southernmost limit of the Sierra to their soldiers, and in October, 1748, the Jonaz Indians were defeated near Half Moon Mountain, which overlooks the Extorax. A *"presidio,"* with a population of Spaniards and some Otomi, was created in the valley of that river, "bordering on the land where the barbaric Chichimec Indians live"; this is the village of Peñamiller today.

Soriano describes the tragic end of the Dominican mission of La Nopalera. "One night the colonel and his soldiers fell on the Mission like wild beasts. They seized all the families who were there at the time, hanged some Indians, shot others, took away a great many of them to work [in the mines] and also led away many women and girls to serve them. This barbarous act was too much for Friar Juan, the monk who directed the mission. He placed a crown of thorns on his head, a rope about his neck, and a chain around his hands and, scourging himself as he walked, asked mercy for that multitude of innocents. But neither his blood nor his tears could soften their barbaric determination." The pretext for this attack had been the Indians' theft of a few head of cattle.

By an irony of fate, military colonization was no more successful than the missions it had so brutally opposed. The violence and aridity of both land and climate defeated the Spaniards' attempts to build up large herds and prosperous estates. In the depths of a torrid canyon, I once stumbled on a hut of palm leaves and branches where a woman clothed in the Indian way but with thoroughly Spanish features was weaving a belt on a pre-Columbian loom. Shy and beautiful, with her long dark hair and very light skin, she spoke only Pame, not a word of Castilian. Yet she was clearly a descendant of the soldiers who had driven the Indians out of the mountains in order to take their land: the physical features had remained and may even have been accentuated in this case by a quirk of heredity, but the imported culture had been swallowed up completely.

Today the Pame and the Jonaz Indians are becoming assimilated and gradually diluted in Indian-mestizo Mexico. I remember a very poor little village, Pastora, in the Rioverde region, which, when the missionaries founded it in 1722, had three hundred families of Pame Indians. In 1934 I could find no more than a handful of families, including five old men. Although all five were very willing, and spurred each other on, together they managed to recall only forty-eight words of the native language.

Possibly some of the larger centers, like Alaquines, where over a thousand Indians (including some who were relatively educated) spoke Pame at the time I visited them, will be able to hold out longer. But, on the whole, it appears that the northern branch of the Otomi family is doomed to disappear as an ethnic and linguistic entity. This is what has happened or is happening to the other, peripheral branches of that family: there is no trace by now of the Pirinda of Michoacán, while the Matlaltzinca of the southern Toluca region and their neighbors the Ocuiltecs are reduced to a few hundreds. On the other hand, the vitality of the compact nucleus of Otomi and Mazahua, in the center of the geographical area that that ethnic group has occupied for a very long time, is comparable to that of such other native groups as the Aztecs, the Zapotecs, the Mixtecs, and the Maya.

The marginal case of groups which are in the process of disappearing, in contrast with that of the many remaining ethnic groups, raises problems which give us food for thought: first, the problem of the survival and the future of the Indian in Mexico, and, beyond that problem, another one—the nature and future of Hispano-Indian civilization in America.

What is an Indian? Although for thirty years I have been studying, making contacts, doing research in libraries and museums, and living among the natives, I am still in the irritating position of being unable to give a scientifically accurate answer to that question. What about the young Aztec I knew when he was a child, who spoke only Nahuatl and whose face seemed to be copied from a stone mask? Some time later I came across him again. He was an engineer in Mexico City, spoke Spanish and English, and was at the start of a promising career. Is he still an Indian? Yes, if we consider his physical features and the language he still speaks when he goes back to see his mother and his sisters in his natal village. No, insofar as his way of living, his integration into Europeanized or North Americanized society, the books he reads, the music he listens to, his clothing, everything irrevocably draws him away from the small, traditional community where he was born. Or, to take the opposite extreme, what about that very Spanish-looking woman I came across in a ravine in the Sierra Gorda, where she was weaving a belt on a pre-Columbian loom? Is she an Indian? No, judging from the color of her skin, the bone structure of her face, and the texture of her hair. Yes, if I consider the material and spiritual world in which she lives and from which she has probably never emerged and never will.

Juárez, the reformer president, who triumphed over Napoleon III in the person of the unfortunate Maximilian, was undeniably a Zapotec Indian, but his political ideas and his conduct while in office marked him as a man cast in the mold of the liberal Europe of his century.

All told, I am inclined to attach little importance to the physical factors, i.e., to "race," if I must use a word which it is difficult to define. A person is Indian if he lives in the Indian way, in an Indian community where an indigenous language is spoken, and if he feels bound to that community by a network of traditions, beliefs, customs, and obligations whose roots go back deep into the Indian past. Here I am in agreement with Alfonso Caso, the Mexican master of archaeology and ethnology, and his *definición del Indio y lo indio*. It is the native community which makes the Indian an Indian, and even a community

6

whose physical make-up is only slightly indigenous is no less Indian if it feels Indian, if it considers itself distinct from the neighboring Mexican communities.

On two occasions I visited the little village of San Juan Acingo, in the Ocuila Mountains, between the Toluca plateau and the region of Taxco. It is a high-altitude hamlet of wood cabins in the midst of pine forests—the greenery and the thin air of a sort of Mexican Switzerland. Here, and also in a still-smaller hamlet some distance away, the old Ocuiltec dialect is spoken. It is a branch of Matlaltzinca and so is an offshoot of the Otomi family, but is characterized by a devilishly difficult system of phonetics. Now, from looking at the inhabitants of Acingo and from listening to the stories they tell of their past, it is clear that most of them are not Indians. Many of them have pale complexions with light eyes and blond or light-brown hair; as for the others, who do have Indian traits, they, or their parents before them, came from other areas of central Mexico. The fact is that because of its isolated position, this village lost in the mountains and the forests served as a place of refuge during the bloody years of the civil war, when the bitter struggle between partisans of Carranza, Zapata, and Villa rent the country from Sonora to Morelos. These woods and clearings provided asylum for whites, mestizos, and Indians of different ethnic traditions, and from this melting pot a new community emerged, with two basic and contradictory features: physical heterogeneity and cultural homogeneity. Regardless of whether they are blond or dark, Galician, Otomi, or Nahuatl in type, the people of Acingo stubbornly cling to their hermetic tongue which they alone can speak and which protects them, like a fortress wall, against the outside world. Zealously —as I found out at my expense—they guard the two-tone wooden pre-Columbian gong, the *teponaztli*, which they keep under lock and key in their little church and refuse to show to whoever is not one of them. They maintain that this *teponaztli* was miraculously born of another gong which was also a magical animal and had flown away to the pyramid of Tepoztlán. The entire ceremonial life of the village gravitates around this extraordinary object.

San Juan Acingo, as we have seen, is a case of a community which is not Indian by race but is Indian by language and culture. At the opposite extreme is nearby Mexicaltzingo, an example of a village where most of the inhabitants are native as far as their physical appearance is concerned but who have almost completely forgotten their own language, speak only Spanish (in its vulgar form), and have adopted the customs and beliefs of Catholicism as it is practiced in rural Mexico. Examples, side by side, of Indianized non-Indians and de-Indianized Indians.

Contrary to what one might expect, the Indian as such took only a small part in the social and political struggles which rocked Mexico from the beginning of the last century to the 1930's. Independence was sought and gained by the Creoles (Mexican-born whites of Spanish origin) or the mestizos (priests like Hidalgo or Morelos or officers like Iturbide). Their quarrel was not so much with Spain as with the "metropolitan" Spaniards in Mexico, who relegated the rising classes of the population to a subordinate rank. It was not against the imported, European form of civilization that the insurgents brandished banners bearing the Virgin of Guadalupe but rather against the rigidity of administrative machinery, the arrogance of civil servants, and their own economic dependence. What they were upholding was not native tradition, pre-Columbian religions, or ancestral customs, but the democratic ideas of Europe and North America.

Throughout the nineteenth century and into the twentieth, from Santa Anna to Juárez and Porfirio Díaz, everything that happened— revolutions, *coups d'état*, civil and foreign wars, bloody conflicts between conservatives and reformers, centralists and federalists, successive periods of anarchy and dictatorship—happened on the level of the higher social classes, over the heads, so to speak, of the rural Indians. Positivism and other ideologies brought over from Europe and either combined with or opposed to Catholicism were predominant; as a result, the Indian heritage, far from re-emerging, retreated still farther into obscurity. Not only did the native peasant derive no benefit at all from his country's chaotic development but in fact he was often the first to suffer from it. Rival armies plundered his village or forced him to join their ranks. In addition, there was an ironic twist of fate: whereas the liberal laws were aimed against the large landowners and the property of the Church in mortmain, at the same time they broke up the collective village landholdings and exposed the helpless Indian to financial and legal maneuvering which, in the end, stripped him more completely than colonialism had done.

Francisco Madero, a generous and idealistic bourgeois, was the apostle of the 1910 revolution against Díaz's paternalistic dictatorship. Following Madero's assassination, the important leaders were non-Indians from the north: Senator Venustiano Carranza, with the flowing white beard, Pancho Villa, the "bandit of honor," Obregón the farmer. The only exception was Emiliano Zapata; in the tropical state of Morelos, he led the rebellion of the peasants (mostly Nahuatl) with cries of "Land and liberty!" But it can be safely stated that aside from the warlike Yaqui Indians of the Sonora, no native tribe, no Indian ethnic group took part as such in the conflicts that shook Mexico from the downfall of Porfirio Díaz in 1910 until General Plutarco Elías Calles retired in 1934.

The 1917 constitution and the laws that sprang from it improved the Indian's lot, not as a member of native ethnic groups but as a peasant, through measures providing for distribution of the lands belonging to the *latifundia* and for the reconstitution of the *ejidos*, the collective village landholdings. But important though these measures are, they apply to the Indian in economic terms only, and leave the problem of a native culture or cultures unsolved.

Mexico is fortunate to have acquired its independence over a century ago, at a time when "decolonization"—which boils down to creating states willy-nilly, without any real basis—had not yet been thought of. Otherwise Mexico would have been carved up like Africa or "Balkanized," i.e., split into a couple of dozen impoverished and mutually hostile republics, instead of becoming one of the foremost nations on the continent. But, like revolutionary Mexico, postrevolutionary Mexico is still faced with the question, What is to become of the Indian, as bearer of a certain culture, within the civilization to which his country belongs? It is a terribly difficult question, one that has persisted since the Spanish Conquest, and it plunges any man of good faith into perplexity and contradictions.

On the 30th of June one year, I watched the celebration marking the anniversary of the *Noche Triste*, when Cortés was defeated. Standing before the statue of the emperor Cuauhtemotzin, the speaker addressed the crowd in Aztec and the crowd applauded, but how many of his listeners really understood a word of what he was saying? And, for that matter, when the speaker himself went home, didn't he speak to his wife and children in the language of the conqueror whose defeat he had just commemorated?

Because I am an ethnographer, and because I love the Indians, and because I know and respect the lofty civilizations of former times, how I would like to hear the tongue of the heroic emperor spoken in Mexico City—in Tenochtitlán! Might not the gods of long ago, the Plumed Serpent, inventor of the arts and of writing; the Sun; the benevolent Tlaloc; the Earth—might they not be better suited to the country and its peoples, more profoundly in agreement with them than the religion which originated in Asia Minor, crossed Europe, and was brought over on the caravels of the conquistadores? Some of the law-makers and educators of the postrevolutionary period, like José Vasconcelos, abhorred the Indian heritage; sadly mistaken, they could see nothing more in it than bloodshed and barbarity. Others dreamed briefly of recalling the deities of old Mexico from exile. On this theme, D. H. Lawrence wrote his *Plumed Serpent*, an appealing book, a pathetic book, and a failure. But in fact the Indian cannot be annihilated any more than what is not Indian can be eliminated. It is impossible to create a non-Indian Mexico or, conversely, to re-create an Indian Mexico.

One reason for these moot questions, as it were, is that although the Spanish Conquest did not annihilate either the Indians themselves (there are undoubtedly more Indians living in Mexico today than at the time of Moctezuma) or certain aspects of their culture, it did completely wipe out other aspects. The surviving elements are the grass-roots elements relating to the field of maize, the little village, and the rural life. What disappeared was whatever was connected with the cities and city-states, the temples, the military and religious aristocracy, the theological speculation. Indigenous Mexico is like a monument struck by lightning: all that remains are the nearly invisible foundations, scarcely distinguishable from the earth itself, because the blaze of conquest irremediably consumed the superstructures that used to reach up to the heavens.

We can imagine what Mexico would be like today if it had succeeded, as modern Japan has succeeded, in preserving the essential elements of its original personality at the same time as it fitted itself into today's world. Helicopter-borne priests of Tlaloc would bless the harvest from above, and at the beginning of each session of Parliament, the emperor would call upon Quetzalcoatl to protect it. Mexican scholars would publish their treatises on physiology or nuclear physics in Aztec, a language which would lend itself perfectly to that purpose. But fate has decided otherwise. When two religions collided—the first open and syncretic, always prepared to welcome new rites and unknown gods, and the second absolutist, refusing to recognize any truth other than its own—it was the first that succumbed. Its defenders had only bows and arrows, obsidian blades, and padded cotton armor, as against their opponents' cannon, harquebuses, swords, and steel breastplates. Since that religion had been the framework of the indigenous societies for two thousand years, its destruction brought all the rest down in ruins. Architecture and the plastic arts, hierarchies, literature, everything collapsed and was swept away like the tattered mist that floated at dawn over the lagoon of Tenochtitlán.

These historical facts are what they are, and no one has it in his power to alter them. Once the great revolutionary struggle was ended and the dust had settled on the battlefields, the statesmen and intellectuals of Mexico had to come to grips with the problem of what was to be done with the Indian and for the Indian in a Mexico that was chiefly mestizo as to its physical traits and Hispanic as to its language and religion.

Since it was vital to start with what was most urgent, the first solution was education—rural schools and cultural missions. Because the Indian population was illiterate and divided into isolated fragments by the obstacle of language, it was easy prey. So it was decided to give the Indians a basic education, as the first tool they would need in order to begin at least to emerge from their poverty. "Those down below," to borrow the title of Mariano Azuela's fine novel, had to be able to climb at least one step in order to move back up into the light. After years of living in Mexico, I am filled with admiration for the people who organized, directed, and carried through the first educational programs among the country-dwelling natives. Just try to imagine what it must have been like for a young schoolteacher fresh out of training college who found herself in a village in the middle of nowhere, alone among a people whose language she did not speak and to whom she was supposed to teach a language they did not speak!

The Indians of San José del Sitio, the first Otomi hamlet I worked in, on the high Ixtlahuaca plateau, had built their school with a will, but it was as desperately poor and stark as their own homes. The small room with adobe walls held a platform, a blackboard, and some benches. A young mestizo woman, about twenty, "taught" several dozen boys and girls. Being Indian children, they were very well-behaved, but "I do not speak a word of Otomi," she told me, "and they do not speak a word of Spanish." On the blackboard she would draw a flower or a house and then she would say "*flor*," "*casa*," repeating it over and over again so that these words of the *lengua nacional* would penetrate those young heads.

On orders from the Education Department, she had organized an "Arbor Week," during which some little trees were planted in front of the school and the advantages of reforesting this desert-like country were explained to the children and the grownups. But, alas! there wasn't any water, and the trees died in the parched ground.

In a hundred different villages I saw the same efforts being made amidst the same solitude and the same obstacles, some of them insurmountable. I especially remember the rural school at Misión de Chichimecas, the hamlet of Jonaz Indians that stands on a hillside near San Luis de la Paz. The teacher was an elderly woman who had devoted her entire life to these Indians. So poor, isolated, and ignorant were they that in the beginning, she told me, they hurt themselves by trying to get out through the windows because they did not know what glass was and leaped through the panes. But her labors had not been in vain, and I am moved every time I recall a little Chichimeca girl with tear-filled eyes who pointed to the teacher and told me, "*Ella nos ha hecho gente*"—"She has made us human beings."

Naturally enough, another idea was born. Why not train Indians to be teachers themselves, as they would be able to go back to their village and teach more effectively, thanks to their knowledge of the native tongue. For this purpose the *Casa del estudiante indígena* was created in Mexico City, but it did not produce the expected result because once the Aztec or Zapotec students had lived in the capital, they were not at all anxious to return to the rural areas they had come from. Very quickly, and with that flair for assimilation which, even centuries ago, filled the first Spaniards with surprise and admiration, these peasants had become city-dwellers. Only a very small fraction of them ever went home to their native villages.

Then it was decided to set up boarding colleges right in the heart of the rural area itself, so that the most apt of the young men and women could be trained without being uprooted. I saw this system in operation at the native college of Quitiyé (State of Querétaro), in Otomi country. The young people learned the rudiments that they would have to teach and at the same time worked in the fields, so that they were not abruptly taken out of the environment in which they would have to live. This method provides the villages with schoolmasters and schoolmistresses who are naturally on an equal footing with the people they teach, know both languages, and do not take themselves for city-dwellers who, by definition, are superior to any peasants.

Yet it was at Quitiyé that, as I observed the boarding students and talked with their teachers, I gradually became aware of the difficulty underlying every step of the way: just exactly what is the goal? To help the Indian to live and progress in modern Mexico, of course—but is he to do so by remaining Indian or by ceasing to be Indian?

It was my impression, and also the topic of absorbing conversation and discussion, that things were being carried too far toward a negation of the Indian as such. For instance, why teach the pupils (especially since the idea has no basis in scientific fact) that bread made from wheat flour is a better food than the traditional *tortilla*? In a maize-producing country, why try to introduce dietary habits based on wheat? Why should the girls be induced to give up their local style of dress, which is becoming, convenient, and suited to the climate, and which they can make at home on their own looms with the wool from the family sheep, and instead wear ugly cotton goods that are too thin for the icy air at this altitude and too expensive, shoddy though they are, for the small budget of a peasant household?

And as for the language, of course the Indian must learn Spanish since it is his unreplaceable link with all other Mexicans and his window opening onto all the rest of Latin America. But does this mean he must be taught to shun his mother tongue and feel ashamed about the heritage that he shares with hundreds of thousands of Otomi, Maya, and Aztecs and that foregoing generations have carefully handed down to him like a treasure?

At the time I am speaking of, the official doctrine of the federal government was "to incorporate the Indian into national life." The Indian was to be made into a Mexican "like the others," both in economic terms—by supplying him with the means by which to improve his lot (land, tools, irrigation, and credit)—and in cultural terms —by teaching him the language of the majority and even by persuading him to adopt the clothing, food, and way of life of that majority.

In other words, assimilation. No one who knows the Indians and their terrible poverty can deny that if this solution were feasible, it would certainly be an advance over their present situation. But is complete assimilation possible? Is it even desirable? That would seem doubtful. The real problem is to open wide the doors of Mexican society to the Indians but without requiring them to commit cultural suicide.

The itinerant cultural missions had already tried to work along those lines. These were groups of teachers, doctors, and skilled craftsmen who went from village to village for the sole purpose of bringing

6*

the native peasants the know-how and practical methods which would allow them to defend themselves better against their natural habitat, take better care of themselves, and live a little better. But the trouble was that their efforts were only transitory. All too often, once the mission had left, routine and the sad monotony of the days and the seasons took over once again. The myth of Sisyphus.

I am almost ashamed of taking so few sentences to sum up years of selfless effort. It has borne fruit in spite of everything. In the two decades that followed the revolution, the country schoolmasters, the members of the cultural missions, the enthusiastic young teachers who launched the campaign against ignorance and for the "incorporation" of the Indian accomplished something huge and admirable. Thanks to them, the Indian has ceased to be perpetually overlooked and all too easily "put in parentheses."

So far as I know, Mexico is the only country in the world[2] where the authorities have gone to the trouble of calling on specialists—ethnologists, to be exact—to deal with the problems raised by the existence of large masses of native population. The development of archaeology and ethnology (which are two sides of the same coin, in a country as rich as Mexico is in the remains of yesterday and in native populations today) strengthened and expanded what the educators had begun. The knowledge contributed by Alfonso Caso and the school that formed around him was a valuable addition. In areas with a high percentage of Indian population, the Native Institute, with Caso as director, set up centers that cover an entire region, training instructors and schoolmasters from among the natives themselves, striving to make schooling widespread and to improve living conditions at the same time as they respect the originality of the Indians, thanks to an accurate appraisal of their cultural characteristics. As a result, the doctrine of "incorporation" has given way to the more flexible and rational notion of "integration." The aim is no longer to make the Indians more or less carbon copies of the mestizos—in other words, to de-Indianize them—but, instead, to make sure that they actually

2. I am told that Iran is having ethnologists study the problems involved in integrating the nomads.

enjoy the same rights and opportunities. The aim is to unite, not to standardize. This idea was very clearly expounded in May, 1959, at the fourth *Congreso indigenista interamericano*, held in Guatemala City. Without doubt, it corresponds to what is both feasible and desirable in all the Latin American countries having a high percentage of native population. A motion adopted by the Congress states, among other things, that

> the social integration of a country does not mean that all of its inhabitants must become culturally uniform. . . . Nor does it mean that all the inhabitants of a national territory must be turned into non-natives. . . . Rather, it requires that the rights which are theoretically guaranteed to all actually be available to all and not just to some [and] . . . that the natives can expect those advantages without the non-natives challenging their right to do so. . . . It is not necessary to eliminate the cultural differences that distinguish one ethnic group from another; what is necessary is simply that the social discrimination founded on those ethnic variations cease to exist in practice.

And the motion stated in conclusion:

> This is precisely the way in which social integration would seem to have the advantage over earlier attempts [such as assimilation or incorporation] to find a solution: integration does not require the natives to turn into non-natives. Ethnic diversity is not an obstacle to integration . . . which aims for understanding, reciprocal adjustment—in short, for balanced coexistence.

This clear and generous doctrine, based on scientific knowledge, is certainly the most positive contribution which ethnology in America has made toward solving the enormous problems that the events of the past have bequeathed to the generations of the present. Unfortunately, it is a rare government which accepts or seeks out the advice of scholars in matters of this sort. No matter how much it may cost everyone (including the native populations themselves) in the long run, governments usually prefer to let fashionable slogans guide them and when taking decisions they turn a deaf ear to all but the fanatics and the ignorant. It is characteristic of our civilization and of our time that such an irrational line of conduct, which no one would stand for when it came to economics, for instance, is approved of when it comes to relations between ethnic groups. We seem to be much more concerned about things than we are about people.

However that may be, if the situation in Mexico continues to evolve along the lines laid down by the educators and the ethnologists, we can expect that, in future, the country's national unity will coexist with cultural plurality. Everything points to such an outcome: the university approach to the Indian languages and civilizations, as well as archaeological advances, ethnographic research, and the public's own, sometimes impassioned, interest in the Indian portion of its cultural heritage. So many times in the past Mexico has achieved a successful synthesis of several native cultures; surely Mexico can now complete the successful synthesis of an Indo-Latin civilization with two sets of links: to the builders of Rome and the builders of Tenochtitlán.

Along with the other countries of Spanish America, which are moving or will be moving in the same direction, Mexico is like an original province within the whole that we call our civilization. Or, to take a still broader view, we can look on the American continent as the extreme western edge of that civilization, and on Russia and its Asian territories as the extreme eastern edge. The old Mediterranean and ocean world is flanked on the one side by an America with linguistic roots in Latin or Anglo-Saxon and, on the other, by an Asia rooted in the Slavic tongues.

We often hear that a civilization loses in depth and originality what it gains in area. It is also a matter for observation that in the later phases of a civilization, power, wealth, and brilliance shift from the center to the periphery. These two statements are not contradictory. In the Greek and Latin world, Athens, as a center of meditation and research, had to give way to Alexandria; and Rome, as a nucleus of power, had to give way to Nicomedia, Milan, and Trier (Augusta Treverorum). From the third century on, Rome was merely a magnificent setting from which the jewel of power had been removed and Athens had become a small provincial city that echoed to the arguments of its rhetors, while at the same time vitality had fled to the two extremities of the Empire. One extremity was formed by Asia Minor and Egypt—Constantinople, Antioch, Alexandria—facing Persia and touching the Oriental world. The other was Gaul, where, since the time of Caesar, Latins and Celts had begun to stand together against the threat from the Germanic peoples. Italy was depopulated and Greece impoverished; it was as if both had been exhausted by the effort of giving birth to an entire universe. In striking contrast were the Asiatic cities that overflowed with people and wealth, and the obstinate Gallo-Roman resistance to the chaos of barbaric hordes. Significantly, from the second century on, the great emperors were no longer Romans or even Italians but instead Spaniards, North Africans, Illyrians, and Syrians, and, amidst disaster, the Roman order of things was preserved at the outposts of the Empire by Gauls like Postumus and Arabs like Queen Zenobia of Palmyra.

At the same time, neither the brilliance of public and private life nor the glow of the intellectual and artistic activity of Byzantium, Pergamum, Milan, or Lyons should make us forget that the quality and authenticity of Greco-Roman civilization were becoming more and more profoundly modified. I am not making any value judgment, and I am not saying that the art, the philosophy, the scientific and religious thought of Alexandria or Constantinople were *inferior* to those of Athens or Rome. I am saying that they had become *different*.

Spengler forcefully developed the "pseudomorphosis" theory, to the effect that first Greek and then Greco-Roman civilization, which were imposed upon Asia Minor and Egypt first by Alexander and his successors and then by the Caesars, covered over the Asiatic civilization that he calls "Arabian" the way a layer of lava covers the ground. Crushed under the weight of a foreign world, that same civilization took two forms of revenge: first, with the eruption of the religions of salvation and the triumph of Christianity; second, by blossoming into Islam. Thus, according to this theory, the rationalistic and static "classic" vision that characterized the Greek city-states and Rome was replaced by a "magian" vision of the world.

At first glance, it seems there is much to be said in support of this theory. In Asia Minor, Syria, and Egypt, Hellenism certainly did not reach beyond city limits; the people who lived in the country and even in the outskirts or certain districts of the larger cities clung stubbornly to the Semitic languages and customs. Hellenic and Roman civilizations were essentially urban; they did not "take" among peasants and still less among nomads. In North Africa as well, Berber shepherds continued to live as they always had, just a stone's throw from the forums and colonnades of Constantine, Tebessa, and Timgad. At the same time, as the official religion of the Empire gradually withered and shriveled until it was no more than a set of rites that did not awaken any profound response in the human heart, and as the upper classes oscillated between skepticism and stoicism or other philosophical doctrines that were meaningless to the masses, the appeal of religions that promised their faithful a direct link with a savior and personal immortality became increasingly irresistible.

The affinity among the preaching of Zoroaster, the solar cult of Mithras, and nascent Christianity was certainly greater than that between all these religions of salvation and the altogether external cult of the old Greco-Roman deities. Above all, the messages of salvation spoke to the individual and opened up to him an afterlife that was a marvelous contrast with a real world which crushed him between the overwhelmingly static, measureless weight of imperial authority and the attendant disasters, wars, and invasions. It is too often believed that only the oppressed masses and the slaves (what Toynbee calls the "internal proletariat") wished to penetrate the deceiving veil of appearances to attain mystical knowledge of a Supreme Being. That the upper classes had the same desire is more than amply proved by a number of phenomena: the rise of the neo-Platonic and neo-Pythagorean philosophies; the spread of the cult of Isis as magnificently described by the African, Apuleius, in his *Metamorphoses*; the success of the Mithraic religion which the army carried, along with the Roman eagles, from Asia to the heart of Gaul; and, finally, the attempts of successive emperors, from Alexander Severus to Julian, to restore some life to the traditional religion by injecting large doses of Oriental mysticism into it.

But this picture of things does call for some corrections. It is inaccurate to place Hellenism in radical opposition to the Asiatic-

Egyptian complex that Spengler wrongly looks upon as an Arabian civilization stifled and paralyzed by the civilization of Greece and Rome. There is a false vision of classical antiquity—governed by serene and rational thought (too serene and too rational in the face of the mysteries of life and of the world), symbolized by the narrow-minded Pallas Athene of Renan's "Prayer I Said upon the Acropolis. . . ." Nietzsche notwithstanding, we are too often prone to single out the Apollonian aspect of Greek civilization and overlook the Dionysian aspect. Yet the Orphic and Eleusinian mysteries and the cult of Dionysus, with their initiation rites, their revelations about the hereafter, and their paroxysms of emotion were just as much a part of Hellenism as the myths and rites relating to the gods of Olympus. After all, didn't the Greeks of the second millennium B.C., who were still barbarians, receive many ideas and beliefs from the high civilization of Minoan Crete? And hadn't Crete itself borrowed a part of its religion and of its vision of the world from nearby Asia? Most of the elements in the story of Zeus, as Hesiod tells that myth in the eighth century B.C., can be found in Hittite texts dating from the second millennium B.C.

For that matter, isn't Pallas Athene herself, patroness of the city of Pericles, with her typically Cretan attributes (a pillar, an owl, and a snake), the classic reincarnation of the Minoan serpent goddess?

When it comes to the Romans, how could we understand anything about their religious beliefs if we left out their Etruscan heritage dating from the time when Clusium and Tarquiniis stood out in a landscape where Rome was a poor little market town? Obscure though the origins of the Etruscans may be, there is no denying the importance of the Asian element in their culture. One proof is that the way in which they practiced divination by the entrails of sacrificial animals was identical, in every detail, to the rite which the Babylonian priests invented shortly after 2000 B.C.

So it would be illusory to imagine, as Spengler does, a classical Greco-Roman civilization, free of any trace of Asian influence, that oppressed the civilization of Asia and was finally rejected by it. The civilization of Mediterranean Europe and those of Asia Minor were never out of contact with one another; in fact, their common roots go

back to the Neolithic Age, since the plants grown, the animals domesti-
cated, and the metal techniques used east of the Mediterranean are the
same as those west of it. Coming back to ideas concerning the supernatural world, there can be no doubt that Asia and Egypt contributed
to the ideas expounded by Pythagoras or Plato. In the *Republic*, Plato
describes the judgment of souls: those "fierce men, and fiery to look on,
standing by . . . [who] thrust down [the tyrant] Aridaeus and flayed
[him] and then dragged him to an outer road, tearing [him] on thorns,"[3]
and the mouth of the opening in the heavens that bellows to announce
the punishment of the wicked, and the chasm in the earth in which the
condemned souls are punished for a thousand years. Isn't that Dante's
Inferno, and his Purgatory, his demons and tortures? It cannot be
denied that Greece and Asia shared a whole set of beliefs and representations which were perpetuated as long as the Hellenic and Roman
civilizations lasted. An optical illusion, as it were, makes us believe that
what occurred was a radical innovation or even the involuntary leap of a
stifled civilization when the religions of salvation took hold of the
whole Mediterranean world and when one such religion was finally
triumphant, through Constantine and his Christian successors.

There was a change, of course, but it was a matter of dosage, of
emphasis placed upon certain aspects of thought in the midst of growing confusion. At that point, the springs of mysticism—for which the
most favorable terrain had been the eastern extremity of the Mediterranean—overflowed, but in fact they had always been flowing
throughout Hellenism itself.

At opposite poles of our modern civilization, North America and
Soviet Russia also represent two aspects of the European complex of
which they were born. America is the conjunction of Christianity, in
its Protestant form, with the pioneer spirit, free enterprise, and the
democratic ideas of the eighteenth century. On the Russian side, we
find the Byzantine heritage—still very apparent in the way the temporal
and the spiritual are constantly mingled—associated with Marxist

3. *The Republic and The Statesman*, Book X, Ch. XIV, Washington and London, M. Walter
Dunne, Publisher, 1901, pp. 342–44.

dogmatism, which in turn is the legitimate descendant of nineteenth-century German philosophy. Whether we like it or not, the might of these two political and economic giants dominates our world today, and de Tocqueville had the genius to realize what separates them and what brings them together. What I wish to emphasize here is that, despite their antagonisms (which remind us of the way the Greco-Syrians of the Eastern Empire and the Gallo-Romans or Romanized Franks of the Western Empire hated one another), both the civilization of North America and that of the Soviet Union correspond to two late and marginal versions of the civilization to which we belong.

From that standpoint, the Latino-American variant which is still taking shape seems to have a rich future ahead of it, provided that its development is not prematurely stunted. Its future is promising thanks to the physical and cultural amalgam of Spain and the indigenous peoples. Two things, however, could compromise that future. Either the amalgam may fail or, like Europe itself, Latin America could be crushed in the event of a merciless duel between the two extremes. It is not impossible that our civilization, in new and different forms, may flourish again in the tropical countries of the American continent if it incorporates the heritage of the Indian civilizations, just as Hellenism was brilliantly perpetuated in Asia and Egypt. But will the Indian really be called upon to make a genuine contribution to the new edifice or will he be left out, as the Syrian peasant and the Egyptian fellah were left out of Antioch and Alexandria?

I said earlier that all the known civilizations have been limited in time. It is equally clear, of course, that every civilization is limited in space. The classical civilization of antiquity and our own civilization are examples of how, given a certain phase of development, it is possible to make out marginal variants that tend to surpass the former centers by their mass, their vitality, and their power. Within such variants, although on the whole they represent an extension of the entire civilization, there can be notable differences as to political organization and ideology. These give rise to subjective judgments, such as those which the inhabitants of fourth century Rome or Athens

may have made about the inhabitants of Lyons or Alexandria, or those
which Europeans today so often make about the inhabitants of New
York or Moscow. It is hardly necessary to point out that the only real
thing such judgments reflect is the gap which evolution has created
between the central forms of a civilization and its peripheral variants,
and sometimes the resentment which someone else's wealth or power
arouses.

But it remains for us to consider just what constitutes the boundaries
of a civilization. The ancient world stopped at Hadrian's Wall, at the
Rhine and the Danube, at the limits of the Persian Empire in Mesopotamia, and at the desert belt that stretches from Syria to Morocco.
Alexander had led that world a giant step toward the east, but this
proved to be only a marvelous adventure which was never followed up.
When the tide ebbed, it left only scattered traces behind, like the
Greco-Buddhistic art of Afghanistan and the Hellenic provinces of
Bactria and Sogdiana. It is tempting to dream about what the history
of mankind might have been if Europe and Asia had consistently joined
hands over the past twenty-three centuries, instead of being repeatedly
confronted, first by Persian and then by Arabian empires. Who knows
what synthesis of the arts, of knowledge, and of wisdom might have
been born if Mediterranean intelligence had wed Buddhist sensitivity?
Instead, the fusion of East and West which may have been Alexander's
great design, as symbolized by the Greco-Persian weddings at Susa in
324 B.C., was an abortive enterprise. The encounter of two philosophies,
symbolized by the conversations between the Macedonian king and the
Indian sage, Calanos, was likewise abortive. The ancient world stayed
within its barriers. Yet, even so, the influence of that world's civilization was felt outside its political and military framework. Goods and
currencies circulated toward India, Ceylon, China, and the depths of
Germany. At times the Bedouin principalities, the Berber tribes, and
the little Scythian or Frankish kingdoms entered into the "Romans'"
allegiance; at others they gravitated toward desert, steppe, or forest,
fluttering around the Empire and its fabulous cities like moths around
a lamp. At various times, and in certain areas, the satellite states, like
Armenia, acted as buffer zones between the power that governed the

Mediterranean and that which held the plateaus of Persia. Although the means of transport in the ancient world were poor in technique, people then traveled much more and much farther than we generally suppose. During the reign of Ptolemy Soter in Egypt, the periodicity of monsoons in the Indian Ocean was discovered, and from then on the route toward India was open to the Greco-Roman vessels. Every year they set sail in July and returned in December.

In this way, a sort of halo spreads around the territory occupied by a given civilization, a halo of political and ideological influences, economic weight, artistic themes and techniques. The installation of Nestorian Christianity in China and Mongolia, and of Monophysite Christianity in Ethiopia, the evangelization of the Slavs and the invention of the Cyrillic alphabet by the Byzantines are only some examples of the extent to which a cultural nucleus can emit its rays beyond the geographical limits of its political power.

It is not very difficult to recall the things which Islamic civilization succeeded in spreading beyond its own borders. The Christian troubadours of Aquitaine drew their inspiration from the poetry of Moslem Spain when embroidering on the theme of chivalrous love. In the year 976, Mohammed ibn Ahmed revealed the use of the zero, borrowed from the mathematicians of India. Algebra, alchemy (the mother of scientific chemistry), the trigonometry of Al-Barani, the medicine of Avicenna, and the philosophy of Averroës—all these Islam contributed to European civilization in its formative phase, even though, on the battlefield, the Europeans repulsed Moslem domination.

Today, geographically speaking, the region where political power is held by countries deriving from the classical civilization of the ancient world or from one of its variants, covers the former *Oikoumenê* of that civilization with the exception of the countries conquered by Islam and of vast additional areas in Soviet Asia, America, and Oceania. Yet our civilization is far from being universal, as we like to think it is. The fact that our techniques, our way of dressing, and certain external forms of our political life have been adopted in a great many countries— although often by a very limited portion of the population—should not by any means be interpreted as an extension of our civilization itself.

It is simply the "halo" phenomenon all over again, but a more striking and widespread instance of it because of the extraordinary way in which means of communication have developed in our day. Japan seems to be in a category by itself. Although throughout the upheavals it began to experience a century ago Japan has kept most of its religious and artistic culture and its language intact, it has assimilated the European and American technique and way of life more thoroughly than any other non-Western country. But in all other cases, and even where the "halo" appears particularly bright, we are deluding ourselves if we speak of a "universal civilization." The people of India and the Arab countries, for instance, may drive cars and elect their parliaments, but they do not belong to our civilization. In saying this, I am not passing judgment but merely observing. Since a civilization can be defined only by the convergence or simultaneous presence of a certain number of technical, ideological, and institutional traits, so the absence of some of those traits obliges us to set a limit.

Not only is our civilization not universal—as in fact no civilization ever has been; significantly, Christianity aimed to be universal, i.e., "catholic," and so did Islam, but neither succeeded—but it actually seems to have entered a phase of regression or contraction. For the historian or the ethnologist, this is a familiar phenomenon, since expansion and regression usually follow one another like the throbbing rhythm of the heart; Kroeber in fact uses the term "pulse." This late phase appears to be characterized by a shrinking of the civilization's geographical surface. The Roman Empire abandoned Dacia, the Decumates Agri, and England; the Moslems lost Spain; China fell back to the continent after dominating the Indo-Chinese peninsula. It is pointless to imagine that our civilization can maintain a durable presence in those vast reaches of Africa, Asia, and Indonesia from which it has withdrawn its political apparatus over the past two decades. No one can say as yet whether its "halo" will continue to glow in such places, but it appears doubtful. For a civilization, such a withdrawal is like the earliest sign—the first wrinkles—of old age.

Now let's come back to our starting point. On the basis of what we have said above, we can accurately determine what phase Mexican civilization, under the leadership of the Aztecs and their city of Tenochtitlán, had reached by the beginning of the sixteenth century, when it was suddenly struck down and demolished. Its political power, shaped in the crucible of the central plateau, covered an area bounded on the north by the steppes and the sierras where the nomadic hunters roamed, and on the south by the Maya states of Yucatán and Guatemala. Its "halo" radiated over part of the steppes and the northern mountains (according to Father Soriano, the Pame "adored Moctezuma"), over such independent states wedged inside the Aztec Empire as the Republic of Tlaxcala and Yopico, over Xicalanco (now called Tabasco) on the border, and even extended as far as Central America.

In most instances, territorial annexation was a recent matter. Expansion had begun only in the fourteenth century and may have been virtually ended by 1520, but nowhere had the Mexican civilization lost ground. From this we can deduce that it was then in a period of transition: the expansion phase was at an end, or nearly so, but the phase of probable regression was still very far off. We can be certain, therefore, that it was a young and still vigorous civilization which suddenly fell victim to an accident of history, a dramatic one, but with no more intrinsic meaning than the death of a jungle beast in the fangs and the claws of a jaguar.

Chapter Six

A Look at Tenochtitlán

I AM NOT AN ARCHAEOLOGIST BUT, IN MEXICO, HOW can anyone help but feel the continuity of past and present more strongly than anywhere else? After all, the Indian of today is the direct descendant of the Indian of yesterday. He speaks the same tongues. His daily behavior, his reactions to the world and to his fellow men, his beliefs and rites are derived, to an often striking extent, from what has been described in Spanish or native literature.

Although the Otomi of long ago clung stubbornly to their village way of life, leaving neither monuments, carvings, nor writings, the same does not apply to most of the other ethnic groups, especially the Maya, the Zapotecs, and the Aztecs. When I studied the Lacandones, I was obliged to work back to their ancestors, the Maya. Later on, I was drawn to the Aztec civilization by the fascination of its art, its language, its social and political organization, its mythological and theological concepts. Despite the destruction that has been wrought at various times, remains and documents are unbelievably abundant. I began doing research even before the Second World War. The vicissitudes of public life, which at first hampered but did not interrupt me, eventually gave my work renewed impetus.[1] I can think of few other types of research which bring the researcher as much satisfaction, especially if he takes the trouble of doing what reality itself incites him to do, namely, look at that civilization, which was a form of belated synthesis, as one part, the final manifestation, of a whole.

1. *The Daily Life of the Aztecs on the Eve of the Spanish Conquest*, Harmondsworth, 1964; *La pensée cosmologique des anciens Mexicains*, Paris, 1940; *Arts of Ancient Mexico*, London and New York, 1967.

What were the Aztecs to begin with? Merely one of the "Chichimec" (barbarian) tribes, as the chronicler Tezozomoc tells us: "For a long time the Chichimecs-Aztecs remained over in Aztlán: for twice four hundred years, plus ten times twenty years, plus fourteen years, according to the reckoning of the Ancients." The same author, as well as the other traditional histories, states that the tribe left Aztlán (somewhere in what is New Mexico today) in the year *Ce-Tecpatl*, "One-Flint," or what we call the year 1168, date of the fall of Tula. So we can calculate that the tribe had settled in Aztlán by the second century A.D. The term that Tezozomoc uses, *"Chichimeca Azteca,"* the "barbarians of Aztlán," suggests that these first Aztecs probably did little or no farming and lived chiefly on what they could pick and hunt.

The several stages of the Aztecs' migration are described in the figurative manuscript Codex Azcatitlán and in other manuscripts, such as the Codex de 1576, also known as the "Histoire de la nation mexicaine," in the Aubin Collection at the Bibliothèque Nationale in Paris. In the year *Ome-Acatl*, "Two-Reed" (1325), the migration ended in the founding of a sanctuary and a village on a small island in the middle of a lake in the swamplands of the Valley of Mexico. Two things are worth noting. First, the movements of the tribe were guided by Uitzilopochtli, its god; his idol, or more likely a sort of bundle of cloth decorated with hummingbird feathers which represented him, was carried on a litter by soldier-priests called the "bearers of god." At night the god spoke to his people and gave them instructions. Second, in the course of the migration period, the custom grew up of lighting the New Fire every fifty-two years, to mark the beginning of an era. In the Codex Azcatitlán we find the hieroglyph for the mountain; serpents are issuing from it, on its top stands a pyramid, and on the top of the pyramid stands Uitzilopochtli, wearing armor made of hummingbird feathers and carrying sword and shield. At the foot of the mountain is a temple, the glyphs of the serpent and the turquoise surmounted by a banner of feathers and the inscription *"xiuhcoatl oncatemoc"* ("the serpent of turquoise was born here"). This serpent of turquoise—or of fire, since the word *"xiuitl"* ("turquoise") is the equivalent of the word *"tletl"* ("fire") in the theological language—is the weapon of the sun god, Uitzilopochtli. And according to the myth which Sahagún noted down, it was on Coatepec, the "mountain of the serpent," that the earth goddess Coatlicue, having seen hummingbird feathers fall from the sky and placed them in her bosom, became miraculously pregnant and gave birth to Uitzilopochtli. Armed with his *xiuhcoatl*, he exterminated the "Four hundred southern bodies"; in other words, the southern stars.

The Codex Azcatitlán situates the event between 1186 and 1194. Without insisting on perfect accuracy, we can assume that it was toward the end of the twelfth century that this tribe which, with its rudimentary culture, had already reached the center of Mexico began to incorporate more complex beliefs and ritual into its own religion, probably after coming into contact with what remained of the Toltec civilization. At that point, it may have seen the oracle that guided it in a new light. It is odd that Sahagún's Aztec informers, speaking of Uitzilopochtli, should have stated: "*çan maceoalli, çan tlacatl catca, naualli, tetzauitl*" ("He was only an ordinary man, just a man, a sorcerer, an apparition"). They did not talk about any other god in similar terms. From this we can infer that the deity who was later to become foremost among the gods of Mexico, incarnation of the Sun and protector of the Empire, had had more humble beginnings, as the little god of a small uncultured tribe or, rather, a sort of familiar jinni who spoke through the voice of the shaman. It is possible that the Aztecs eventually turned him into an important god, miraculously born of an important goddess, in imitation of the more elaborate religions that they observed all about them as they penetrated into the region of the high civilizations.

In all events, there can be no doubt that even in very ancient times the Aztecs looked upon themselves as "the people of the Sun" and that "the hummingbird on the left side" (the translation of the name "Uitzilopochtli") was a solar deity. In the ancient theological manuscripts, showing the universe in the form of a sort of Maltese cross, the south is the left side of the world. Uitzilopochtli is the god of the southern sun. Why the hummingbird? Because the hummingbird seems to go to sleep and die in the winter, only to be reborn in the spring, and so symbolized the resurrection of the warrior who had been killed in battle or sacrificed. This explains the myth of Coatepec, the mountain: those feathers that fell from the sky and which the earth goddess gathered to herself were the soul of a dead warrior, and the birth of Uitzilopochtli was resurrection.

All the northern peoples of Mexico, including the Aztecs, worshipped astral deities: Mixcoatl (the Milky Way), Tezcatlipoca (Ursa Major), and the Morning Star, which they embodied in the old god of Teotihuacán, the Plumed Serpent. But the Aztecs are certainly the only ones to have taken the astral, warrior *Weltanschauung* to its most cruel and exacting extreme. The regular return of the Sun is indispensable to the salvation of the universe. The Sun needs blood to give him energy. This blood is provided for him through holy war and sacrifice. In exchange, the warriors enjoy a blissful immortality: first they are the companions of the Sun, whom they escort to empyrean; then, after four years, they become hummingbirds fluttering joyously among the flowers. This is the sequence of cosmological and mythological representations which, as the power of the Aztecs grew, were gradually reflected in the monstrous increase in the practice of human sacrifice.

Of course, the Aztecs are not the only people in the world to have sacrificed human victims. The Incas of Peru practiced that bloody rite. Traces of it remained in the Semitic religion and in that of the Greeks; Moloch, like Uitzilopochtli, demanded human victims. Similarly, the notion of holy war and of the blissful immortality promised to warriors is easy to find in other civilizations, too; the Koran, for instance, states that heroes fallen on the field of battle go up to heaven. But there is no denying that no other people was so obstinate or so horribly courageous as the Aztecs in offering the hearts and blood of human beings to the sun god. What is even more remarkable is that at the same time as this terrible ritual became increasingly important both within the Aztec Empire and even beyond its borders, the intellectual and artistic civilization of the Aztecs was developing, manners and morals were growing more refined, and the taste for poetry, the fine arts, and luxury was becoming more widespread. It is a striking fact that human sacrifice, which was connected at first with sun worship, invaded agrarian rites and the cult of the rain god. Not only was the victim's chest opened so that the heart could be ripped out and offered to the Sun but also women dressed and bedecked like the earth goddesses were made to dance in their honor and were then decapitated with one rapid blow, as a peasant breaks off an ear of maize. And then, there were the victims who were thrown into the lagoon to appease Tlaloc, and the victims who were burned in honor of the god of fire, and the victims who were first killed, then flayed during the ceremony of tribute to Xipe Totec, god of goldsmiths and of spring. Not to mention the young man who was perfect in every respect (the list of physical defects which he must *not* have would take up two or three pages) and who was raised amidst the most refined luxury for a year before being sacrificed to Tezcatlipoca or the young courtesans who were killed as an offering to Xochiquetzal, their gracious patron. Suffice it to add that, of the eighteen feasts celebrated yearly in Mexico City, one every twenty days, there were only four, according to the Florentine Codex, at which the blood of sacrificed men or women did not flow.

Mexico City was not the only place where such permanent massacre was the custom. Even the philosopher-king of Texcoco, Nezaualcoyotl, who was remembered for his wisdom and humanity and who adored a faceless god superior to all other gods, did not prevent human sacrifice from being practiced in his own city. Although the Tarascans of Michoacán had withstood the Aztec invasion in the fourteenth century and preserved their independence, they, too, later adopted the same terrible rites. In Yucatán, the Maya in turn, going against their thousand-year-old tradition, also gave themselves over to human sacrifice. In fact, they took to the practice so fanatically that they continued clandestinely even after the Spanish Conquest; the Inquisition brought a number of cases to light in the sixteenth century. Sometimes, under the influence of Christianity, the victims were crucified. A sixteenth-century account, for instance, reports that in 1562

another sacrifice was made, at the foot of a cross in the cemetery of the church, to some idols and demons that were there. A boy named

Ah Tuz was killed, and for the sacrifice, he was crucified on a large cross; his hands were nailed down and the cross was erected. After which, the cross was placed on the ground again. While the boy on the cross was still alive, Luis Nauat opened his chest, ripped out his heart and gave it to the *Ah-Kin* Francisco Balam, who offered it to the demons and the idols.

Here, as we can see, the Christian crucifixion was mingled with the rite of ripping out the heart and the whole act was done by two baptized Indians, one with a name of Nahuatl origin and the other with the typically Maya name of Balam ("tiger") and the title of *Ah-Kin* ("sun-lord"). As late as 1868, in the State of Chiapas, the Chamula, who were convinced that, in ancient times, the *ladinos* (Spaniards) "had chosen one of their own people to nail him on the cross and call him their Lord," decided to do the same. For the purpose they chose a ten- or eleven-year-old boy named Domingo Gómez Checheb, from the village of Chamula. They led him to a place called *Tzajal-hemel* and there nailed his feet and his hands to the cross. The poor boy cried out in pain while the Indian women, exalted to the highest degree, gathered the blood from his wounds and burned incense around him. He died shortly afterward, before the eyes of thousands of natives who had come from all over the region.[2]

So the practice of human sacrifice, completely or generally unknown during the great classical age when the agrarian religion was dominant, and forbidden by Quetzalcoatl but introduced into Mexico by the northern star-worshippers, had succeeded in becoming an unbelievably tenacious part of the way of thinking, greatly overlapping both the geographical limits of the Aztec territory and the period when Tenochtitlán exercised its hegemony.

How are we to interpret such a phenomenon? Should we, like Lévi-Strauss in *Tristes Tropiques*, take it to be the result of "a maniacal obsession with blood and torture," in other words, an innate psychological tendency toward cruelty?

First of all, we should note that the very notion of cruelty differs

2. The account of Yucatec sacrifice is found in Landa, *Relación de las Cosas de Yucatán*, Tozzer, ed., p. 116. The Chamula crucifixion was described by Vicente Pineda, *Historia de la sublevaciones . . . y gramatica de la lengua Tzel-tal*, Chiapas, 1888, p. 77.

greatly from one place or one era to another. Generally speaking, man has found pleasure in destroying, killing, and causing suffering. Voltaire wrote that "we can scarcely read history without conceiving horror at mankind."[3] An encyclopedia of human cruelty would take up a great many volumes and would have, unfortunately, a wealth of riches from which to choose, so refined and ingenious have our fellow men been, from antiquity down to and including our own times. The path of history is bristling with landmarks—massacres, tortures, cities razed and whole populations put to the sword, heretics burned and prisoners tormented in a hundred ways. From one age to the next, war, justice, and religion have never ceased to exact fearful and bloody tribute. Entire ethnic groups have been wiped out. Although certain peoples or certain states, such as the Assyrians or the Mongols, deserve a prize in this macabre competition, I don't believe there is any people or any state that could stand blameless before an imaginary court of conscience. Perhaps not all are equally guilty, but not one of them is innocent.

It would seem that extreme cruelty often goes along with the brilliance of a refined civilization. Byzantium is a convincing example; Byzantium with the marvelous art of its architecture and its mosaics, the unbridled luxury of its emperors and nobles, the elaborateness of dress, food, and perfumes, the proverbial intricacy of theological and metaphysical arguments, the undeniable vigor of religious feeling—and, at the same time, the systematic use of torture, mutilations, and the most atrocious types of punishment. For eighteenth-century French society, elegant though it was, and intelligent, and receptive to all human problems, the horrifying spectacle of condemned men being quartered, burned alive, or broken on the wheel was an amusement.

The Spaniards in Mexico were horrorstruck at their first sight of the temples dripping with blood, human hearts offered to the Sun in the *quauhxicalli*, and grimacing skulls piled up on the *tzompantli*. But the Spaniards themselves, and Cortés not least among them, considered it perfectly natural to mutilate, flog to death, burn, or cut the throats not only of the Indians who opposed them but of their own compatriots

3. *Philosophical Dictionary, op. cit.,* Vol. VI, article on "Idol-idolater-idolatry," p. 135.

as well. Later, when the Inquisition was rampant in New Spain, the flames of autos-da-fé replaced the flint blades of the Aztec priests, but who is to say that this was progress?

Where the human sacrifices practiced in Mexico are concerned, can we attribute them to a taste for torture and cruelty, a deliberate wish to inflict suffering? In all honesty, I do not think so. The warrior who had been made prisoner and was to be placed on the stone of sacrifice stoically accepted his fate, a glorious one for him, and in fact he often begged for it. There are historical accounts that show the captors offering to spare their captives' lives and the captives refusing, voluntarily placing themselves under the knife of the *tlamacazqui*. A strange relationship grew up between the prisoner and the man who, having captured him, was to lead him to his death: the prisoner addressed his captor as "venerated father."

No effort was made to make the victims suffer or to increase their suffering more than was necessary and, in fact, they were given a drug called *ololiuhqui* to dull the pain. Usually the sacrificed victim personified the god who was being worshipped at that particular rite and wore his ornaments and his mask. The women embodied the goddesses of the earth and of vegetation while the warriors, covered in downy white feathers symbolizing the dawn, knew that they would rise into the eastern sky and join the sun god. Because such sacrifices were so extremely widespread throughout and beyond the Aztec Empire, there must have been a very real complicity between the victims and those who sacrificed them, as part of a system wherein everyone expected to play one or the other of those roles someday. "Today it is your turn, tomorrow it will be mine," the emperor Moctezuma said to a renowned Tlaxcaltec chief who had fallen into his hands. The complicity went so far that following the great famine of 1450 the sovereigns and lords of Mexico City, Texcoco, Tlacopan, Tlaxcala, Uexotzinco, and Cholula, who were convinced that the drought of preceding years had been brought on by the lack or the rarity of sacrifices due to the prevalence of peace during that period, decided deliberately to stage an artificial war, called the *xochiyaoyotl*, so that the captured warriors could be sacrificed to the gods of the sun and the rain. Early in the sixteenth century, Mexican garrisons at the outposts of the empire carried out raids in Tarascan or Huaxtec territory for the sole purpose of taking prisoners, and the demand for sacrifices was such that Aztec traders were even instructed to buy victims in the tropical provinces.

All this happened and developed at a time when Mexican society was undergoing a profound mutation. The monarchy was becoming stronger, at the expense of the old tribal democracy; the social status and prestige of merchants were on the increase; the people forsook the old rustic and military ideal of frugality and introduced luxury into their dress and finery, into the houses they lived in and the meals they ate; and such virtues as gentleness, moderation, and elegant manners gained popularity, while the impassioned violence of the last century's great adventurers was discredited.[4] This was also the time when an epicurean strain invaded poetry, where flowers, precious stones, a love of life were blended with gentle resignation to the brevity of existence and inevitable fate.

Thus, we cannot help noting that the increasing practice of sacrificial rites in Mexico, far from being caused by inborn and ever more pronounced cruelty, actually coincided, on the contrary, with a social and cultural evolution characterized by a new gentleness. This is a paradox, of course, but there is no getting around it, since it is shown by established facts. If we are to understand it, and we must, I believe the only way is to escape as far as possible from the field of gravity of our own civilization and put ourselves into the mental universe of Mexican antiquity.

The idea that dominates this universe and imbues its entire conception of things and men is that the machinery of the world, the movement of the sun, the succession of the seasons cannot continue and last unless they are nourished on the vital energy contained in "the precious water," *chalchiuatl*; in other words, human blood. The reality we see and touch is merely a fragile veil that may be torn at any minute and reveal the monsters of dusk and decline. Four worlds before our own,

---

4. J. Soustelle, "Apuntes sobre la psicologia y el sistema de vàlores en Mèxico antes de la conquista." In: *Estudios antropologicos publicados en homenaje en Dr. Manuel Gamio*. Mexico City, 1956, pp. 497 ff.

7

the Four Suns, have already perished amidst cataclysms, and the world we live in will succumb as well. As a result, all men and especially the people of the Sun, the Aztec tribe, have a cosmic mission to accomplish: fighting off the incursions of nothingness day after day. Every day that dawns, every new appearance of the Sun, is a miracle, and it will be renewed daily provided the warriors and priests have offered the Sun its "nourishment," *tlaxcaltiliztli*, the blood and the hearts of the sacrificed.

As we can see, this civilization, although its fundamental psychology was not any more inhuman or cruel than that of any other, was pushed to its paroxysm of bloody sacrifice by an idea. According to a perfectly coherent logic, that idea was carried to its very final and, for us, monstrous consequences. Although the link between the continuity of natural phenomena and the offering of blood must have been perfectly clear and unquestionable for the people of Mexico, our analysis is incapable of grasping it. We are obliged to consider that notion as a datum, an element like the form of house or the type of ornament or clothing which sets one culture apart from another, or the choice of phonemes used by this language and not by that. It has nothing whatever to do with necessity. It is merely one of the myriad ways in which man, faced with the mystery of his fate, can try to picture that mystery so as to derive a rule of conduct from his image of it. All we can say is that starting at a certain point in time, certain peoples selected this *Weltanschauung* from among all those open to it, whereas the peoples of the phase before that one, the people of Teotihuacán and Palenque, had selected another. Once the Mexicans had made their choice, they were locked within the universe it implied and within its own special logic (like the logic of a dream, obvious to the dreamer but incomprehensible to the same person once he has awakened), and they could not act in any other way. It would be absurd, of course, to try to give such "superstructures" a Marxist-type explanation in terms of economic and social "infrastructures."

I mentioned dreams just now. Don't we begin to suspect that what is reality for one civilization is dream for another? What seemed absolutely, undeniably real to a Mexican in the fourteenth century, to such an extent that it even provided stimulus for countless acts of self-denial and heroism, seems ὄνειρος χαὶ τῦφος to us, "dreams and mist," because we belong to two different civilizations, or two different planets. Do we come any closer to understanding how the Christians of the Byzantine Empire could actually come into heated conflict and even kill each other over such doctrines as Arianism, Monophysitism and Monotheletism? Of course we can analyze such doctrines in intellectual terms, just as we can analyze the cosmological concepts of the Aztecs, but neither of these makes us feel the sacred fury which drove so many men to kill and to die.

The later Mexican civilization, insofar as its features seem exaggerated to us and offend our sensibilities, makes us realize more clearly just how arbitrary and accidental human affairs can be. In Euclidean geometry, no triangle can ever, simply because it is a triangle, be an exception to the rule by which the sum of its angles is equal to that of two right angles. But each civilization is its own geometry.

The arbitrary aspect becomes still more striking when, as the result of historical accidents, a civilization forms the synthesis of different traditions and structures; the combination of two or more fundamental patterns then turns the triangle into a square, so to speak. When the Aztecs had ended their migrations and settled in the Valley of Mexico and, especially, one century later, when they had become the ruling power of a whole nebula of cities older than their own, they were plunged into a cultural and ideological environment most of whose essential features were derived from the distant classical past. They could have been proudly and dogmatically exclusive, sure of their truth and rejecting all else. But instead they eagerly adopted and absorbed the dynastic customs of their neighbors, the monumental architecture and the sculpture of Toltec tradition, the hieroglyphic writing and the chronology that had originated in the classical era, the goldsmithing of the Mixtecs, the pottery of Cholula. When it came to religion they were just as eclectic. Their pantheon and their rites made room for the old goddesses of the earth and the moon, of vegetation and water, for the young gods of maize, love, and music, and, of course, for the great god Tlaloc from the most venerable agricultural religion, as well as for the Huaxtec goddess of carnal love and confession, Tlazolteotl ("eater of sins"), for the little rural deities of drink and drunkenness, and for the "Otomi Lord," god of fire. The Aztecs' passion for the gods of all tribes and all countries was well known; Ixtlilxochitl reports that it was joked about in the more refined city of Texcoco. The Aztecs went so far as to build a special temple, *Coacalco*, to house the foreign deities. Certain rites were celebrated in a "barbaric" tongue and once every eight years, at a ceremony in honor of the planet Venus, Indians from far-away Oaxaca or Mexicans disguised to look like them pretended to devour live serpents, as in the Mazatec rite. It is more than likely that the Aztecs would willingly have placed the cross and images of the Virgin in their *Coacalco* if only the Spanish had allowed it. The Aztecs could not understand where the conflict lay between the religion of the newcomers, who looked on it as the one and only truth, and their own religion, which was open to all gods and all rites.

When we examine the Aztec beliefs, the way the Mexican "church" was organized and the young Indians were brought up, we cannot help but be struck by a certain duality. Ecclesiastical authority was shared by two grand priests, the two "Plumed Serpents," with equal powers. One was titled the priest of Tlaloc and the other the priest of Uitzilopochtli. Two equal sanctuaries stood side by side at the summit of *Teocalli*: the blue-and-white sanctuary of Tlaloc and the red-and-white sanctuary of Uitzilopochtli. Two sorts of paradise were promised: the luminous heaven in which warriors who had died in battle or as sacrifice victims accompanied the Sun from the east to the zenith and women who had died in childbirth escorted it from the zenith to the west; and the eternal verdure and humidity of *Tlalocan*, the warm and luxuriant garden of the rain god. There were two contrasting systems of education, whose mutual antipathy sometimes became outright hostility: on the one hand, the college-monasteries of the benevolent Plumed Serpent and, on the other, the "young men's houses," under the aegis of the bellicose Tezcatlipoca. Isn't it astonishing that this society, where war and battle played such an outstanding part, did not entrust the training of its elite to the schools of Tezcatlipoca but instead to the sacerdotal colleges of the peaceful Queztalcoatl?

When a civilization nourishes contradictory elements within it, a sort of social schizophrenia sets in. The groups that are guided by opposing ideologies are divided by tensions and antagonisms. The unfortunate Moctezuma II, more priest than warrior, was consumed by religious scruples; he handed over his city and himself to the conquerors and died at the hands of his own warriors, whose military virtues were embodied in the emperor Cuauhtemotzin.

Similar contradictions can be discovered in other civilizations having incorporated varying ethnic and cultural elements. The fact that the Mediterranean world became dislocated, giving way to a Latino-Celtic and Germanic West and a Greco-Semitic East, shows that the tensions I mentioned earlier can reach such a point that the civilization explodes, not only into a number of states but even into new civilizations. In fact, it was the complete rupture between the Eastern and Western parts of the ancient world which, starting in the sixth century, made possible the slow process that was to shape our Western civilization. Arabian civilization first went through a triumphal period of expansion, but then, torn between its several zones (Persian, Syriac, Egyptian, Maghrebian, and Hispano-Moorish) and submerged by the Seljuks and the Ottomans, it lost Spain and Turkey and became fossilized elsewhere.

When it comes to our own civilization, I still maintain that from Vladivostok westward to San Francisco it forms a whole. But already the Western, Anglo-Saxon variant is very different from the Slavic variant, and we cannot overlook the possibility of a deep-seated rupture which might either give rise to one or more new civilizations or cause the whole civilization to collapse.

And so we are led to extend and modify the notion of "pseudomorphosis" that Spengler used so brilliantly in connection with the relationship between Hellenism and the "Arabian" civilization. This is actually a much more general phenomenon than he was willing to admit. The reason is that he took each civilization as a living organism, strictly individualized and destined to go through a series of phases between its birth and its death. Accordingly, when two civilizations were superimposed and formed an amalgam, he felt that this was a regrettable exception. Yet it appears, on the contrary, that "pseudomorphosis" is

not the exception but the rule and constitutes one of the moving forces
of historical evolution, causing civilizations to become different from
one another, change, take on new forms, and even multiply by a
process of schizogenesis.

Mexico is a revealing example in this respect. Insofar as we are able
today to reconstruct the history of the civilizations of this part of
indigenous America, we find the first series of native civilizations,
breaking away from the rural substratum and stemming from a sub-
tropical center. Although these civilizations were certainly distinct
from one another as concerns the ethnic and linguistic groups belonging to them, they were obviously related and drew upon a common
ideological fund. Then came the long succession of "pseudomor-
phoses," from the Toltecs to the Aztecs, blending what remained of
the preceding phase with the characteristic themes and structures of the
northern peoples. The various Mexican civilizations, neither identical
nor completely dissimilar, came into being one after another and some
arose out of others as the result of those blendings. Again and again
the Maya have been compared to the Greeks, the Toltecs to the
Etruscans, and the Aztecs to the Romans. Even the unpolished Bernal
Díaz del Castillo, when he discovered the extent of Mexican power at
an early point in the Spanish Conquest, naturally compared it to Rome.
Although it goes without saying that these comparisons are not to be
taken literally, neither are they meaningless. They may be a way of
putting our finger on one general form of the process we know so
little about, leading to the crystallization of civilizations and to their
sequence in time.

We do not know enough about any civilization, from the Sumerian
down to our own, to formulate genuine laws. But we can have a general
impression, which is this: human phenomena are subject to rhythmic,
alternating oscillations. Now civilizations converge and now they
diverge, now they merge and now they separate. It follows that,
depending on the phase in which the observer finds himself, he may
fall prey to illusion and take what is merely a passing trend for an
ultimate direction, particularly since those pulses that we talked about

earlier, even though they are more rapid and brief than the pulses of climate or geological phenomena, are still very slow compared with the duration of our own lives and the passing of generations. It can happen, of course, that war or a revolution causes a sudden mutation or, as is more often the case, makes clear a process of change which was initiated long before and which some sudden shock or violent convulsion brings to completion. But in the last analysis, most of the *coups de théâtre* that narrative history describes to us are just like a surprise ending in the last act at the theater: they can be explained only by the concealed action of a hundred different levers, ropes, pulleys, and machines hidden from the spectator's sight. Any man who participates in the life of his country and his times and who keeps up with developments every day easily gets the impression that his own age is richer in events than any other and that the past, which he looks at from afar, was as smooth as a broad river interrupted only by the occasional cataract. But that is an illusion like the illusion of the air traveler who sees mountains gradually slip away under the wings of his airplane as it rises and can no longer make out the details on the surface of the ground.

When archaeology, in the broadest sense of "knowledge of the past," brings the traveler back down to earth again, he discovers that the landscape which, from high above, he had taken for a monotonous plain was really as uneven and as complex as his own here-and-now. In human history just as in nature, we find the infinitely large and the infinitely small. At one extreme is the metaphysician, who glides over the ages in such lofty flight that reality escapes him; at the other, is the historian of events, who is likely to be overwhelmed by the swarming presence of men and the labyrinth of accounts. Between these two is the ethnologist—an ethnographer when he observes, and an archaeologist when he reaches back into time. Although he does not always succeed, he attempts to grasp human phenomena halfway between the general and the singular, that is, at the level of cultures and civilizations, which in turn can be broken down into traits, themes, and structures.

Earlier I defined what I understand by "culture" and "civilization."

I call cultural "trait" any clearly individualized phenomenon, whether material or not, which can be observed in one or more cultures or civilizations—such as the stilt house or the igloo, the bow or the spear thrower, the bark canoe or the monoxylous dugout canoe, the pipes of Pan or the pottery drum, the use of bronze, the various types of divination, the types of burial or cremation and the attendant rites, sacrifices, the different sorts of marriage, forms of authority, and so on. For all of these elements we can draw up tables showing whether they are present in or absent from given societies, and in this way we can do descriptive "profiles" of those societies. The most valuable application of this method is in the comparison of two cultures—as, for instance, that of the Lacandones and that of their Maya-speaking neighbors, the Tzeltals of Tenango—by means of a table like the one below:

Cultural traits	Lacandones	Tzeltal
(+ means presence, —means absence)		
Agriculture, maize, clearing land by fire	+	+
Hunting with bows	+	—
Rectangular house	+	—
Square house	—	+
Pottery utensils	—	+
Pottery drum	+	—
Clothing: tunic	+	—
Clothing: European type	—	+
Hat	—	+
Polygamy	+	—
Incense burners, idols	+	—

The above table is merely a sample; actually, a comparison can take in a considerable number of traits. Such tables seem even more appropriate for purposes of analyzing and comparing complex civilizations, including their architecture, their art, their institutions, their rituals, their cosmological concepts. Finally, we can use such tables to demonstrate the presence or absence of certain traits in groups of civilizations, as in the northern half and the southern half of America, or ancient Mexico and Greek antiquity. This would produce, for instance:

I. *Cultural traits*	Mexico	Peru
Agriculture: maize	+	+
Agriculture: potatoes	—	+
Pack animals	—	+
Wheel	—	—
Bronze	+ (late)	+
Hieroglyphic writing	+	—
Authoritarian economy based on census of resources and needs	—	+
Etc.		

II. *Cultural traits*	Mexico	Classical antiquity
Agriculture: maize	+	—
Agriculture: wheat	—	+
Fermented beverages	+	+
Pack animals	—	+
Wheel	—	+
Bronze	+	+
Iron	—	+
Potter's wheel	—	+
Bow and arrows	+	+
Spear thrower	+	—
Metallic coins	—	+
Temples on pyramids	+	—
Statuary	+	+
Mural paintings	+	+
Hieroglyphic writing	+	—
Alphabet	—	+
Books	+	+
Education organized by the community	+	—
Poetry[5]	+	+

5. This should be taken to mean the recognized existence of poetic forms conceived as such. The inhabitants of ancient Mexico placed great importance on poetry, and divided it into several categories: religious, historic, lyrical, philosophic, and even dramatic. These poems were sung or recited against a background of musical accompaniment. The names of several poets, belonging to the aristocratic families, have come down to us, especially Nezaualcoyotl, fifteenth-century king of Texcoco. Women of the nobility rivaled the men in this field. Poetry and singing competitions were organized in Texcoco, where one of the four government councils was called "council of music." In Mexico City, the "house of song," "*cuicacalli*" (the word "*cuicatl*" means poem and song at the same time), was placed under the emperor's authority.

7*

II. *Cultural traits*	*Mexico*	*Classical antiquity*
Stringed musical instruments	−	+
Flutes	+	+
Two-toned gong	+	−
Arithmetic, with notation of the zero	+	−
Twelve-month year	−	+
Eighteen-month year	+	−
Observation of the stars	+	+
Divination: by victims' entrails	−	+
Divination: by calendar of omens	+	−
Divination: by dreams	+	+
Sacrifice by ripping out the heart	+	−
Sacrifice of animals	+	+
Ritual ball game	+	−
City-state as type of government	+	+
Slavery[6]	+	+
Polygamy	+	−
And so on . . .		

What I call themes are what the English-speaking anthropologists term "patterns." These are no longer relatively simple and isolable facts but, instead, complexes, attitudes to the world and to life. Each culture has its patterns and thereby its style.[7] Or we could speak in terms of "cultural outlines" and say that they determine the "cast" of the features of a particular culture, in contrast to or comparison with another. Every pattern is an aggregate of cultural traits, but it is more than that. It implies that man has, often unconsciously, taken a certain attitude to his fellow beings and to things. Thus, the pattern has a psychological aspect, since an element of value and orientation enters into it. Human sacrifice by ripping out the heart is an easily definable

6. Slavery in Mexico was much more gentle and humane than in Greek and Roman antiquity. The *tlacotli*, which we translate as "slave" for lack of a more accurate word, had extensive rights as to property, marriage, and family life, and his children were not in bondage. There were many possibilities of being freed. Slaves were placed under the protection of Tezcatlipoca, who punished bad masters. But the two institutions are comparable in that the *tlacotli*, like the slave in our classical times, ceased to be a citizen and became the property of another.
7. *See:* Kroeber, *Anthropology*, Harcourt, Brace, New York, 1948, Chap. VIII; Ruth Benedict, *Patterns of Culture*, Houghton Mifflin, New York, 1946; G. Soustelle, *Tequila, un village nahuatl du Mexique oriental*, Paris, 1958, Chap. X.

cultural trait; it is possible to situate this practice on a map of the American continent and state fairly accurately when it began and when it ended. But an enormous complex of rites, myths, beliefs, and moral and emotional attitudes forms the characteristic pattern of the late Mexican "style"—cosmic war, the feeding of the stars, the duty to offer human blood to the gods.

It is possible to compare the fundamental patterns of the Nahuatl civilization with those of the Maya civilization, and those of the Otomi culture with those of the Lacandones, so as to discover their points of resemblance and contrast. In this way the "physiognomy" of a civilization or a culture is revealed. It is often as striking and as difficult to define as the physiognomy of a person or the style of an age in painting or sculpture. This is where the ethnologist becomes more of an art critic and less of a scientist, in the usual sense of the word, since his task is one of evaluating qualitative variations which can be neither represented nor measured.

I am not willing to go as far as Ruth Benedict when she calls the Zuñi Indians of the southwestern United States "Apollonian," the hunter Indians of the prairies "Dionysian," the Kwakiutls of the Northwest "megalomaniacs," and the Dobuans of Melanesia "paranoid." Psychology and even pathopsychology play too large a part in such definitions and, anyhow, things are not that simple. A single feature, a single adjective is not enough. But it remains true, nonetheless, that every culture and every civilization has its own easily recognizable physiognomy, just as an archaeologist can tell a Nazca vase from a piece of Maya pottery at first glance.

Spengler, too, thought that each of the great civilizations could be defined in terms of a single, fundamental pattern: the civilization of classical antiquity by its attachment to the *hic et nunc*, the finite and static form; what he calls "Arabian culture" by its sense of cosmic and "magian" mystery; that of "Faustian" Western Europe by its insatiable desire to go further, its thrust toward the infinite. Certainly there is some truth in this "morphology." But by fixing on only one pattern, at the expense of others, Spengler overlooked, for example, all of the "magian," orgiastic, and impassioned aspect of Hellenic civilization;

everything "Faustian" about the impulse of Arab civilization; and all that our civilization has borrowed from the Roman concept of law and the Semitic vision of a single God, to mention only two items. Clearly, it is impossible to define the physiognomy of a culture or a civilization by a single pattern, if only because in certain civilizations, at least, the collective mentality is split between two antagonistic patterns, as I have showed in connection with the Aztecs.

Coming back to the Aztecs themselves, we can see that although the physiognomy of their civilization was strongly marked by the pattern of holy war, other patterns should be cited as well: predestination, since the fate of every individual was determined from his birth to his death by the impersonal mechanism of the signs and numbers of the *tonal-poualli*;[8] prestige, which was eagerly sought, whereas the accumulation of wealth was scorned; expansion, which led the city of Tenochtitlán to extend its authority over a huge portion of the continent. All of these patterns can be contrasted with those of the ancient Maya civilization. At Palenque or Yaxchilán, there was also a spiritual pre-occupation with predestination, and there is every indication that prestige was much more prized than wealth; but here the pattern of cosmic war was missing and each city led an independent life for centuries without carving out an empire for itself.

Finally, I call "structures" the institutional, legal, and mental relationships which surround cultural traits and patterns within a given society. In the concrete reality of the historical process of change, those traits and patterns that we encounter when we analyze a culture form an amalgam which is constantly moving, constantly varying, like the river of Heraclitus in which one cannot bathe twice. Structures correspond to the dynamics of each culture or civilization. It is within

8. "Account of days" and also "account of destinies," as the word "*tonalli*" has a double meaning. Every date is defined in relation to a series of thirteen numbers and a series of twenty names; moreover, it is placed under the influence of one of the thirteen gods of the days and the nine "lords of the night." Furthermore, the series of 260 days (13×20) which formed the divinatory "year" was divided into twenty "thirteen-day series," each of them dependent upon a certain god (or divinized star). The years themselves were given a number and a sign. All of these divisions of time could be catalogued as favorable, harmful, or indifferent, depending on their sign and their numerical coefficient. For this purpose, specialized divines called "counters of days" (or, "of destinies") consulted the "book of days" or "book of destinies," "*tonalamatl*," and they were called upon at all times.

the structures that traits and patterns become hierarchically established and play a more or less decisive role, depending on the phase. On the analogy of a building, traits and patterns are the stones, the elements of construction, whereas the structures are the plan—except that the structures of a society change, whereas the plan of a monument does not.

Considering these three types of phenomena makes us wonder about the *coherence* of a culture, still a very obscure question. Are the various parts of a culture necessarily linked together? Are the facts of material culture (way of producing food, dwelling, weapons, clothing), of intellectual culture (art, religion), and of legal or political institutions related to one another like the organs of a living body or the parts of a machine? Or, on the contrary, are they related in a purely accidental, historical, coincidental manner? In the last analysis, is a culture merely a "planless hodgepodge" (to use Lowie's term), an aggregate of phenomena flung together by the ebb and flow of events like jetsam washed up on the beach?

Marcel Mauss rightly poked fun at certain German and Austrian scholars of Father Schmidt's school—like Frobenius, for instance, who believed that from the shape of chipped stones discovered in Africa he was entitled to deduce what sort of institutions and beliefs the man who made them had had. The Schmidtian theory of *Kulturkreise* had the effect of establishing artificial relationships between such phenomena as the bow and arrow and the forms of family organization. Under this theory, it was possible to speak of a "culture of the bow," and its essential traits were assumed to be the same everywhere. Now, it is very clear that certain facts permit valid deductions and that others do not. It seems fairly safe to suppose that the prehistoric inhabitants of the cliffs of Grimaldi practiced funeral rites and had some ideas about an afterlife, since we have found burial places and skeletons coated with red ocher and still wearing shell ornaments. But we cannot deduce anything from the chipped stone blades, scrapers, and chisels about the social organization or mythology of Paleolithic man.

Marxist sociology is based on the claim that causal relations exist between the economic infrastructure and the ideology of every society. And of course it is quite true that, generally and roughly speaking, the way of living, which is largely determined by the way in which food is produced, contributes to shaping social and political structures and the collective consciousness. "Existence determines consciousness." Earlier, I showed that the introduction of agriculture, followed by the shift to urban living, were the conditions without which the Mexican civilizations would not have existed. But a condition is not a cause. There is nothing more doubtful than a causal relation, such as we can observe in the physical sciences, between economic facts and intellectual facts, with the former determining the latter. A tribe of nomadic animal breeders does not build temples because its way of life does not allow it to do so. But although the living conditions of the tribe of Abraham and those of the pre-Moslem Arab tribes were identical, the cosmological and theological concepts of the two groups were profoundly unlike. The Nahua became a sedentary people, farmers and builders of cities; yet they continued, with even greater enthusiasm than before, to perform the rites connected with the theme of cosmic war.

It would be absurd to deny that the means of production, the distribution of property, and the division of society into classes according to their economic role have a double function. First of all, they make certain forms of social organization possible, or impossible. Second, they color collective ways of envisioning things in a certain way. But this does not make it any the less false to say that they and they alone cause all social phenomena. What intelligible causal relationship can there be between the economy of the Kwakiutl, the Haida, and the Tlingit, based on salmon fishing, and the extraordinary importance of the potlatch in those tribes; or again, between the caravan economy of Medina and Mecca in the seventh century, and the preaching of Mohammed? Of course, there would be no potlatch in British Columbia if fishing did not provide the Indians with an abundant and regular source of food and they had to spend their time finding and picking wild fruit instead, like the Indians in California; and it is likely that the Prophet drew part of the ideas that he transposed in the Koran from the environment he lived in, especially from the Jews of Medina. Yet surely we can see that these are not causes but conditions and adjuvants instead. No amount of Marxist dialectic will ever explain why, starting with the Hegira, the Arabs, who had been polytheistic from the beginning of time, became fierce champions of absolute monotheism and spread it from the Indian to the Atlantic Ocean within a matter of decades.

In a like manner, we can note that important factors in the downfall of "Romania" were the permanent economic crisis which set in in the third century, the depreciation of the currency, the deterioration of the urban economy, and the inefficiency of slave labor. But it would still be ridiculous to claim that these factors account for the sudden blossoming of the mystical religions and the triumph of Christianity, in the way that one physical phenomenon can bring about another.

A more subtle way of linking the facts which, when taken together, make up a culture, is to consider, along with Bronislaw Malinowski, that each fact helps to form and maintain the total set of facts by virtue of relations which are functional rather than causal. This concept is actually very close to the organicism which Spengler carried to its most extreme consequences. A given phenomenon within a society is no more the cause of another phenomenon within the same society than the liver is the cause of the vertebrae or vice versa, but each organ performs a function which is essential to the whole. Here again, no one will deny the harmony which exists between one particular phenomenon and another in a given culture. Obviously, a society could not survive if certain functions were not performed within it. Relations between the two sexes, protection of children, production and distribution of food, defense against enemies—all of these presuppose institutions surrounded by a "halo" of beliefs. Accordingly, and step by step, collective needs give rise not only to the means by which to satisfy them but also to the intellectual images associated with them.

Yet the functional theory is far from taking everything into account.

It comes up against the obvious fact that certain cultural traits and patterns not only do not contribute in any intelligible way to the indispensable functions of a given society, but in fact go completely counter to that society's very survival. Thinkers of all schools have been demonstrating for thousands of years that war is a "great illusion," that the victors lose as much as the losers, and that everyone would be better off beating his sword into a plowshare; yet all human societies, and especially the most elevated civilizations, have continued to resort to war at the risk of committing genuine suicide. The eager obstinacy with which Hellenic civilization tore itself apart in the Peloponnesian War, and the way Europe went about destroying itself in the first half of this century are clear examples. To what function do such customs as "couvade" among the Indians of Brazil correspond?[9] Or the food taboos among the Semitic religions? Why have human beings built such a bewildering variety of matrimonial and family institutions around sexuality, which is based on an instinct common to man and animals and is essentially the same throughout the human species? What is the social need behind circumcision, excision, ablation of the phalanxes and other types of mutilating treatment which various peoples inflict or have inflicted upon themselves, not in obedience to some fleeting fancy but out of a profound sense of duty and over long periods of time? As a matter of fact, any theory that assumes everything is explicable in terms of functions, the necessity for which is more or less consciously or even unconsciously felt and which in turn correspond to such vital needs as nourishment, sexual instinct, or the desire of a collectivity to persist as a group, is overlooking the enormous portion of man and his behavior that is irrational.

9. Malinowski (*Sex and Repression in Savage Society*, Harcourt, Brace & Co., New York, 1927) attempts to explain this "apparently absurd" custom of couvade by claiming that it represents a "necessary function." According to him, the purpose of it is "to establish a social situation of close moral proximity between father and child. . . . It provides the necessary stimulus and expression for paternal tendencies. . . . [It serves to] accentuate the child's need of a father. . . ." The weakness of this explanation is obvious. If couvade really fulfils a function as necessary as creating a link between father and child, stimulating paternal tendencies, etc., why is it not practiced in all societies or at least in a good many cultures? For that matter, *who* feels the need to "stimulate paternal tendencies"? I don't think it is the father himself. Are we to assume, then, that a collective consciousness or subconsciousness invented this means, which certainly seems odd and roundabout?

What Spengler does amounts to diving headfirst into the ocean of irrationality and calling it "destiny." Every civilization (which he calls "culture," while what I call "culture" he considers merely primitiveness or degeneration and places out of bounds of his *Kulturmorphologie*) is an organism, he says, a living being equipped with a soul, governed by a destiny that determines its birth, growth, aging, and death. His description is poetic, often brilliant, even fascinating—but nothing more.

In an attempt to take a more objective approach to the problem, I would like to come back to the three types of facts I distinguished among a little while ago, that is: traits, patterns, and structures. The obvious characteristic of cultural traits is that they are mobile, easily dispersed and spread. We can demonstrate this by marking on the map of a continent or of the world those points where one such trait is known to be present. If we make these maps for successive periods, we obtain the distribution pattern for that trait in time as well as in space. I find that the often bitter quarrel which divides ethnologists—*genus irritabile*—into diffusionists and supporters of parallel invention is in vain, because both diffusion and parallelism are possible and both have been demonstrated. Certain inventions were made only once and their presence, wherever they are found, can be accounted for only by diffusion; all the known alphabets, for instance—Greek, Latin, Hebrew, Arab, Gothic, Cyrillic, Sanskrit, and so on—derive from one and the same Semitic source. Bronze, on the contrary, was discovered separately, first in Asia Minor in about 4000 B.C., then in Andean America shortly before A.D. 1000. From the first point of origin bronze metallurgy spread throughout the ancient world from Europe to China, and from the second it spread northward as far as Mexico.

Much of the cultural history of mankind is made of borrowing. Techniques, tools, clothing, and means of transport are borrowed, of course, but so are art forms, ideas, rites, and myths. Nothing travels farther than mythological themes, as in America, for instance, the theme of incest between the Sun and the Moon. A rain god with a monstrous mask was worshipped throughout Mexico, from the high plateau all the way to Yucatán. The plumed-serpent motif—that very peculiar association of features belonging to very different animals—is found in the art of every part of Mexico and even overflows northward to the Mississippi Valley and southward to Costa Rica. And as we have already pointed out, human sacrifice in the Nahuatl manner spread to ethnic groups of a totally different origin.

But the extent to which a cultural trait expands does have limits. The northern limit of the adoption of Olmec-Maya hieroglyphic writing was the southern edge of the steppes, and the southern limit was the border of the Maya country. The series of rites known as the Ghost Dance first appeared among the Paiute of Nevada in 1869, and although it quickly spread toward California and the prairie lands, it did not reach the Pueblo Indians. Divination through animal entrails was invented in Mesopotamia; it was then adopted in Asia Minor, in Greece, by the Etruscans and the Romans in Italy, and as far east as Malaysia. Another type of divination, using the shoulder bone of certain animals (sheep, deer, elk, reindeer), spread from China and Mongolia to Tibet, Arabia, the Maghreb, Siberia, and even to the Algonquin Indians in America, but remained unknown to the Egyptians, the Hebrews, the Greeks or the Romans.

People do not borrow just anything. Obviously, certain techniques or customs cannot be borrowed because they cannot be assimilated by a given culture; for a Moslem society, for instance, adopting the art of statuary would be to deny its own essence. Furthermore, alongside the tendency to borrow exists a tendency to reject whatever is new and foreign. Two ethnic groups can live side by side in the same climate and in analogous or identical conditions and yet never borrow from one another cultural traits which would clearly be useful. The Eskimos living on the arctic fringe of America have never borrowed the snowshoe from their neighbors the Indians, even though they would find it extremely helpful, nor have the Indians ever borrowed such inventions as the igloo or the kayak from the Eskimos.

Cultural patterns likewise travel, spread, and are borrowed—again, within limits formed by the resistance of certain societies to them. Theoretically, it seems easier for cultural traits, particularly technical ones, to spread than it is for bodies of complex ideological thought. Japan has borrowed the techniques and sciences of the West but has scarcely borrowed its religion at all. Cars are more common throughout the world than is the democratic form of government; radios, chemically produced medicines, and synthetic fabrics are more common than monotheism. Chinese writing, as an instrument or technique suited to expressing ideas in any language whatsoever, has spread beyond the area covered by its own civilization and even to Japan, which has a language fundamentally unlike the Chinese. So, we find that cultural traits and patterns are somewhat independent of one another, in that, as they travel, their content can change.

At any time, a people can abandon one technique in favor of another which is, or which it believes is, more effective; but it is much less willing to drop its traditional concepts as to family or religious ethics. Military technique abounds in the clearest examples of borrowing because the belligerents, driven by danger and necessity, quickly learn lessons from their adversaries, but the religious or political ideas they are fighting for are not altered by such borrowing. When the Romans realized that armor gave the Persian cavalrymen a definite superiority over themselves, they formed their own cavalry of cataphracts, but were not induced to convert to Mazdaism.

All in all, the farther we go from technique and the closer we come to ideology, the more we step out of the realm of limited and individualized cultural facts and the farther we enter into complex global concepts that involve intellectual activity and arouse feeling, the less change, diffusion, or borrowing we find. The general orientation of a culture, that is, the attitude of a given people to the world and to life, is less malleable, less subject to imitation and questions of fashion, less affected by short-term fluctuations and the demands of an immediate advantage than are clothing, arms, or dwellings. It is all the more remarkable, therefore, that at certain periods, enormous sets of ideological facts have been able to cover such vast areas of the globe with such astonishing vigor. This is the case with Judeo-Christian and Moslem monotheism, with Buddhism and with the Renaissance ideal of humanism.

What I call structures are the part of a civilization which are the least likely to change or to incorporate elements from the outside. In spite of historical upheavals, and amidst the most rapid mutations, structures tend to be perpetuated and even to become fossilized, like the Hindu caste system, even though the façade of a modern state was clapped onto that framework. The basic Chinese structures persisted from remotest antiquity to our own day, and it remains to be seen whether the present revolution in China will have succeeded in uprooting and, above all, in replacing them. It is about a thousand years since the Slavs of Russia received from Byzantium the structures upon which they built their variant of our civilization, and especially the idea of a seat of power (basileus, czar, or government) with jurisdiction not only over the bodies of its subjects but over their souls as well; and these structures the Russians have preserved throughout all their tribulations.

One comparison immediately comes to mind: the comparison between culture and language. The basic elements of a language are words, which in turn can be broken down into phonemes. The number of distinct sounds which the human vocal cords are able to produce is not infinite, of course, but it is very considerable. We need only compare the simplicity of Polynesian and the extraordinary richness of Arabic, the complex phonetics of Otomi and the far less elaborate phonetics of Aztec, the "glottalized" consonants of Maya and the nasalizations of Pame. All the possible phonemes are used or have been used by some population or another at one time or another, from the "tones" of Chinese to the "clicks" of Hottentot. It is as if each ethnic group had drawn on a fund which is common to all mankind (for the organs of speech are the same everywhere and any human being can learn to speak any language) and chosen from it arbitrarily, so as to build a system of meaning from the chosen sounds. These phonemes were used to build words, which are symbols that nothing other than the will of the person speaking links to what they are supposed to represent. Aside from the few onomatopoeic words which are attempts at imitation and the words taken from baby talk (papa, baby, *tatli* for father in Aztec, *dada* for father in Otomi, etc.), it is obvious that there is no such thing as an internal necessity binding a given group of sounds to a given image or idea.

If we situate sounds and words on a map, if we establish the cartography of a given area in terms of its phonetic systems and vocabularies, during one or more periods, we find that phonemes vary, change, disappear, or are replaced by others, although the people who use them are totally unconscious of the laws governing these movements, and that as words appear, die, are borrowed, and travel through space and time, they take on different meanings. The Old French *bougette*, meaning "small pocket," crossed the English Channel and became "budget." The Aztecs' *petlacalli*, or wickerwork chest, became "suitcase" in modern Mexico but "cigarette case" in Spain. Any culture which encounters another makes extensive use of the words designating the unfamiliar objects, institutions, and customs. Toward 2000 B.C., the Greeks who had left central Europe came in sight of the Aegean Sea and borrowed from languages which were neither Indo-European nor Semitic the name of the sea itself ("*thalassa*," the famous cry of Xenophon's soldiers) and the words for olive tree, wine, cypress, king ("*basileus*"), and lord ("*anax*"). The Europeans arriving in America incorporated the words for tobacco, hammock, canoe, tomato, and chocolate into their own languages. Modern Spanish, as spoken in Mexico, is full of Aztec terms, just as the Spanish spoken in Peru and Bolivia is sprinkled with Quichua words. French is a similar case; although the chauvinists and the purists periodically moan and wail, it has never ceased to embrace many words of German, English, Dutch, Italian, Spanish, Hungarian, Turkish, Arabic, and so on.

Now, the way words behave is very like the way cultural traits behave and, in fact, the words which travel and are borrowed the most frequently are those that symbolize the cultural traits that likewise travel and are borrowed. Just as cultural traits are absorbed into and assimilated by the culture that borrows them, so words are absorbed and assimilated by the language that takes them in. An Englishman doing algebra is no more aware of using an Arabic word (*al-djeber*) than a farmer who plants potatoes realizes he is appropriating a discovery made in ancient Peru.

Because of their complex nature, the tools which a language uses to express conceptual variations (number, gender, aspects and periods of action), the processes peculiar to each linguistic family, the morphology of a language can be quite accurately compared to cultural patterns. They vary and travel less than phonemes and words. A Nahuatl Indian today, when talking about his horses, uses the Castilian word "*caballo*" but adds the Aztec particles indicating possession and number; the result is *no-cauayo-me*. When my Otomi friend Bonifacio wanted to say that he had to hurry to "go away earlier," he combined the Spanish words "*pa(ra)*" ("for") and "*mas*" ("more") with the Otomi words "*nshudi to*" ("early") and "*ma*" ("to go away"), forming an expression whose structure was pure Otomi: *pamasnshuditodima*. French, of course, does just the same when it makes a feminine word, "*une redingote*," out of the English neuter, "riding coat," or when it adds an *s*, its own indication of the plural, to the Hebrew word "cherubim," which already has the Semitic plural ending, "*-im*."

Finally, the syntax of a language—that is, the system by which words and phrases are arranged and function properly—corresponds to what I have called structures. The syntax is actually the most permanent, stable nucleus of any language. It can incorporate sounds, words, and turns of phrases obtained either through internal evolution or through borrowing, but its fundamental articulation will change only very slowly and reluctantly. If we compare modern Greek with the Greek that Pericles spoke twenty-five centuries ago, we find that the phonetic system has undergone profound change, the vocabulary is now full of words borrowed from the Latin and Slavic languages and from Turkish, the form and meaning of many words have changed, and new words have been fashioned; but, on the other hand, nouns are declined and verbs conjugated in a way which, although simplified, is very close to that of the classical language, and there has been no basic change in the syntax. So, the three types of cultural and linguistic phonemes have this in common: traits, patterns, and structures, words, forms, and syntax are increasingly stable, in that order.

The above considerations may be useful in understanding why theories like that of Father Schmidt, Montandon's theory of "cycles" and "cultural areas," Spengler's theory, and even Toynbee's to a large extent are not convincing. They are not based on a sufficiently clear distinction among several categories of facts. The *Kulturkreise* school muddles together various sorts of phenomena, postulates rigid and highly debatable relationships among them, and all too often rests its case on metaphysical assumptions, like Father Schmidt's "primitive monotheism." Montandon chooses no more and no fewer than seventeen characteristics by which to define any culture, a most arbitrary way of proceeding which overlooks the complexity of the facts involved. Spengler goes astray in his historico-mythical description of the "souls" which, he claims, appear in the birth and decline of each civilization. Toynbee, it is true, with his prodigious erudition, does take a whole multitude of factors into account; but he confuses the political and military organization of the Spartans, for instance, which was an important cultural pattern but a limited one, with the structure of a civilization. He also characterizes the Maya civilization very summarily (and, judging from the known facts, inaccurately) as one of "abandoned sexualism," claiming that it occurred simultaneously with a contradictory and "exaggerated asceticism." Now, there is no denying that this scarcely coincides with what we know of Maya antiquity.

The truth is that we are still very far from being able to put such definite labels on things. We would like to make a systematic study of the traits, patterns, and structures of cultures and civilizations and of their position in time and space, and to compare these facts with one another; but we are hampered by the gaps in our knowledge. Moreover, many ethnic groups have disappeared completely, and the means available to researchers are meager. With respect to the science of man, we have reached approximately the same point as the great thinkers of Greek antiquity had reached concerning physics. But, in addition, the human phenomena differ from those of nature in that any culture, any civilization is both arbitrary and systematic—arbitrary in the choice of the material and nonmaterial elements making it up, systematic in the way it combines them.

Every culture, every civilization is a fortuitous assemblage of technical, legal, ethical, and religious phenomena which the group or groups concerned try but never entirely manage to integrate into a structured whole. At any point in time, a given culture emerges as a compromise between what is *received* from tradition and from external influences and what is *produced* by the society as it functions at that particular moment. Today's Western European speaks an Indo-European language which has been transmitted to him from very remote antiquity. The religion he practices, or which is practiced all around him, originated in Asia, was enriched and modified by Hellenistic philosophy, and uses the language of the Roman Empire for liturgical purposes. His law is "Roman" law, although it should be noted that such outstanding jurists of the Roman Empire as Papinian, Ulpian, and Paul were Asiatics with an Aramaic ethnic background, and that as the result of invasions a rather large portion of Germanic law was injected into European law. His official moral code arose out of Judaism and Christianity, mixed with strong strains of classical thought. His science, and the vision of the world which it produces, are distantly rooted in the atomism of antiquity and began to assume their modern form in the eighteenth century. For the most part, his social concepts stem from the democratic movement that began in England, North America, and France some two hundred years ago. In addition, either separately or simultaneously, the North American variant and the Russian variant of modern civilization influence both individuals and groups in a number of ways—research and technical progress as to consumer products, entertainment, gadgets, music, dancing, or authoritarian economic systems. At the same time, these various inherited or borrowed factors are constantly being modified by the action of the objective and subjective conditions that obtain in Europe or in a particular country. An Italian Catholic is not a Christian in quite the same way as is a Danish Lutheran. A French businessman does not run his business exactly as an American executive runs his. From country to country, the laws on property, legacies, and marriage differ. In short, each civilization—and, within it, each variant or province—is maintained by a process of constant adaptation in a state of perpetual imbalance which provides the driving force of its evolution.

Chapter Seven

The Human Adventure

THE GEOLOGICAL AND PALEONTOLOGICAL DIS-coveries and research of the past half century have continually broadened our vision of the history of life, especially human history, on our planet.

Although unicellular aquatic creatures, which were probably the first form of life, appeared on earth some five and a half billion years ago, the first mammals did not begin to exist until four and a half billion years later. Anthropoid monkeys are believed to have appeared during the Miocene period some forty million years ago, and it took another thirty-nine million years for the first hominoids, such as Pithecanthropus, to emerge. Men as such are considered to have been in existence for only five hundred thousand years; Neanderthal man goes back only one hundred and fifty or two hundred thousand years. The type of man who boastfully and wrongly calls himself *"sapiens"* is only fifty thousand years old. The first villages of farming peoples, in Asia Minor and Egypt, were Jericho (7000 B.C.), Çatal Hüyük (6500 B.C.), Jarmo (4700 B.C.), El Fayum (4500 to 4000 B.C.). The first civilization, Sumer in Mesopotamia, dates from 3500 B.C. In other words, the history of our own species covers only a very tiny period of time and the history of civilized life only an insignificant, even micro-scopic, instant. Suppose we compare the time that has passed since life first appeared on earth to a single day; then the period since the origins of man corresponds to roughly fifteen seconds, and the time since the beginning of civilization scarcely amounts to one tenth of a second.[1]

1. Scientists now tend to place the origins of hominoids, if not of man himself, farther and farther back in time. The Tanganyikan *Homo habilis*, the most recent discovery in this connection, dates from 1,800,000 years ago, according to Dr. L. S. B. Leakey of Nairobi.

The ancients were aware that a number of species had disappeared without leaving any descendants:

Multaque tum interiisse animantum saecla necessest
Nec potuisse propagando procudere prolem,

wrote Lucretius in the *De Natura Rerum*, V, 855–856. Prefiguring to some extent the theory of the struggle for life and the survival of the fittest, the wise Latin poet accounted for the defunct species with a theory that they had been neither clever, strong, nor mobile enough to survive. Perhaps the most striking example is the disappearance of the colossal reptiles that dominated the earth for five hundred million years, only to vanish without leaving any other traces than their enormous bony remains. We still have four hundred ninety-nine million years ahead of us before our existence will equal in longevity that of this totally extinct species.

Although all scholars accept the fact of the evolution of species, Darwinism, which has gone through some naïve versions in the popular sayings of our day, is far from accounting satisfactorily for the known facts. As Dr. Bruce C. Heezen maintains, it is possible that reversals in the terrestrial magnetic field, occurring at certain times, enable cosmic rays to "bombard" living beings and cause sudden mutations. However that may be, and confining ourselves to our own species, we can say that a process of "hominization" apparently got under way nearly two million years ago. It may have appeared first in Africa, with the Australopithecus of Tanganyika, and later appeared in Asia (Pithecanthropus and Sinanthropus). In the beginning, as a number of signs indicate, man was but one of many variations on a theme: he learned to stand erect, his thumb grew longer, his hand more skillful, his brain bigger. It was the passage from nature to culture, as techniques and social organization allowed him to multiply his strength and his capacity for survival to an enormous extent, which made him what we mean today by the word "man."

The minimum requirements for the passage from nature to culture are tools (including weapons), fire, language, and some sort of organization in groups.

With respect to tools and weapons, it has been found that apes, such as baboons, know how to make use of pebbles or bits of wood when the occasion requires it, for instance, to kill scorpions.[2] But they use a stone or a stick just as they find it, without either altering or keeping it. The Australopithecus of South Africa did make some very rough pebble tools, and they may have used long bones, such as the humerus of an antelope, to club their prey. Since Raymond A. Dart discovered the first Australopithecus in 1924, he has disagreed with other specialists over those bone "weapons" and no conclusion has been reached, although it does seem likely at least that, as Dart claims, this hominoid killed baboons for food with the help of antelope bones. As for Peking man, the Pithecanthropus, whom Teilhard de Chardin discovered in 1927 in Choukoutien, there is no doubt that he was carnivorous and a hunter, and that he carved up his victims by means of pebbles chipped or flaked for that purpose.

From this we may deduce that, already, creatures that were not yet really men knew how to fashion weapons to compensate for the fact that nature had given them such weak nails and teeth. Weapons existed before men did. The extraordinary fierceness that shows up so often in our species is rooted in a very remote past when carnivorous pre-human beings used their more developed brains to make up for the inferiority of their physical endowments. The art of killing may have been the very first technique of all.

There is no trace of any hearth in the Australopithecus shelters at Sterkfontein or Olduvai, any more than there is at Ternifine (Palikao) in Algeria where, in 1954, Arambourg discovered Atlanthropus, the five-hundred-thousand-year-old man who did, however, make stone tools. The use of fire in Asia, on the contrary, was demonstrated in 1930, when Teilhard de Chardin discovered a charred bit of deer antler in a hearth in Choukoutien. It is quite possible that the first users of fire did not yet know how to make fire but rather had discovered how to take advantage of fire produced by natural causes, such as lightning;

2. Kenneth P. Oakley, "On man's use of fire, with comments on tool-making and hunting," *Social Life of Early Man*, Chicago, 1961.

"*caelestibus insita flammis*," wrote Lucretius long ago. All the prehistoric peoples, beginning with Neanderthal man, kept fires burning, but we do not know whether they knew how to light them. In 1906, Radcliffe-Brown noted that the natives of the Andaman Islands did not know of any way to produce fire; each of their hearths was lighted with a stick taken from another. The Pygmies who lived along the Epilou River bought fire from their black neighbors in the Congo by barter. Such fire-lighting methods as striking a flint, or using fire sticks (like the Aztecs and the Lacandones) or the curious fire piston which is peculiar to certain parts of Southeast Asia and Indonesia may not have been invented until long after men had learned to "gather" fire caused by natural agents, just as wild plants were picked and gathered before it was known how to grow grain.

Language and life as a society are inextricably linked. Washburn and DeVore note that although baboons do form localized and endogamous troops, a large tribe composed of more or less exogamous groups is a phenomenon which is peculiar to man and that such organization probably could not exist without language. There is obviously a close relationship and a reciprocal effect between the existence of language and that of a social group within which that language provides the means of communication. Adolph Schultz[3] stresses the "surprising variety" of sounds emitted by hominids living in groups. "The amount and variety of information that can be exchanged by means of sounds in the highly social catarrhines," he writes, "surpasses that in any other mammals and culminates in human speech." Schultz points out that the anatomical speech apparatus is as good in an ape as in man. This observation merely lends greater pertinency to the question. If these animals have the necessary speech organs, and if life in a society favors the emergence of language, than why is man the only superior vertebrate to have invented language? The classical philosophers were keenly aware of this problem. Had language been invented by one or more "cultural heroes" who had

3. "Some factors influencing the social life of primates." In: *Social Life of Early Man*, Chicago, 1961.

given things their names by convention, or had it been a spontaneous creation? "Men, whose ideas and passions varied from one people to another, spontaneously formed these names by uttering the sounds produced by each passion or each idea, in different ways according to the country and the people."[4] Although the notion that language originated in conventions consciously invented by individuals is inadmissible, the contrasting theory of spontaneity amounts to confusing the raw materials of language with the language itself. Doesn't the "variety of information" that Adolph Schultz speaks of really amount to exclamations, for instance, or calls, or danger signals? Language, on the contrary, is a structured system of symbols, and nothing entitles us to claim that there were ever any rudimentary quasi-languages or protolanguages since, as I have already indicated, the most "primitive" languages are often the most complicated ones.

Furthermore, language not only expresses thought but also shapes thought. As soon as a notion goes beyond the limits of pure affectivity and image to become conceptual thought, it also becomes discourse, *logos*. Talking to other people means thinking for them, "thinking out loud"; conversely, thinking for oneself means talking to oneself. The first social structures and the first languages may have become crystallized simultaneously; rather, those two crystallizations were two aspects of one and the same mutation which was possible because of a certain degree of complexity of the nerve cells. Language and society are two sides of the same coin. The sounds uttered by the anthropoids and even the simplest language spoken by human beings are as far apart as a band of monkeys and the most rudimentary society.

Now, this does not mean that culture was created *ex nihilo*. First of all, a number of animals and, in all events, the anthropoids, possess the social instincts—cohesiveness of a group, the defense of a given territory, co-operation. Freud's mistake was to want to make the sexual instinct and the antagonisms it arouses the basis of everything; I do not believe that any ethnologist can accept the demonstration which the father of psychoanalysis attempts to make in *Totem and Taboo*. Moreover, the use of certain objects in their raw state as tools or

4. Epicurus, Letter to Herodotus.

8

temporary weapons, the use of vocal signs, and the hierarchical relationship which can be observed among the members of certain groups of anthropoids constitute the elements of a "protoculture," as it were. But even the poorest of human cultures is so much richer and so much more capable of changing that we can clearly see a difference not only of quantity but of quality as well.

Even assuming that progress came about through a slow process of accumulation—improved tools, mastery of fire, formation of sufficiently dense groups, conditions favorable to more orderly cooperation, recourse to certain sounds as signals—still, at one point or another, the decisive step had to be taken. A language and a social structure (as, for instance, the set of matrimonial regulations among a given people) have this in common: they cannot be made of bits and pieces. They either exist or they do not. What is involved in both cases is a system, and a system is valid only if it is coherent. There are a great many possible systems in both areas; a culture is characterized by the choice it has made among those possibilities. There is no denying that we are unable to picture just what that final "jump" from nature to culture must have been, nor to divine the initial choice by which a specific culture got under way. The mechanism of the nature-culture mutation is as much of a mystery to us as that of the mutation which, at certain periods and in certain areas of the world, caused the movement from culture to civilization.

The oldest human being whom we know relatively well is Neanderthal man. Over the last century, complete specimens, entire skeletons, and skulls in good condition have been found in France, Spain, Belgium, Italy, Croatia, and, of course, in the Neander Valley of Germany, not far from Düsseldorf, in 1856. "Neanderthaloids" with less pronounced features have been found elsewhere, especially in Palestine and Iraq. Southwestern France has been particularly rich in fossils of this variety of our species: Le Moustier, La Chapelle-aux-Saints, La Quina, La Ferrassie are some of the sites having yielded the greatest number of vestiges. These fossils, and those of Western Europe in general, were associated with the so-called "Mousterian" stone tools; geologically, they are linked to the last glacial period, the Würm period, an estimated 50,000 to 75,000 years ago. But discoveries of Neanderthal remains in central and eastern Europe indicate that those men lived in a remoter period, that is, in the third interglacial period, about 150,000 years ago.

Despite the fact that the physical features of Neanderthal man were different from our own—his enormous brow ridges, his long, low skull, his incurving thighs, his generally massive build and relatively small stature (between 5 feet 4 inches and 5 feet 6 inches)—we have no basis for assuming that he was any less intelligent than we.[5] His brain was actually bigger than ours, judging from the volume of the skull at Le Moustier (1,560 cc), and that at La Ferrassie (1,610 cc) as compared to our own average of 1,450 cc; for the African Australopithecus, Pithecanthropus, and Sinanthropus, the average cranial volume is about 600, 867–5, and 1,070 cc, respectively. Now, of course, the volume of the brain does not correspond to the intellectual level of that brain, as was the case with H. G. Wells's imaginary Selenites, the wisest of whom collapsed under the enormous weight of their own heads. The skull of Anatole France, for instance, measured little more than 1,000 cc. All we can say is that the larger the brain, the easier it is to achieve the combinations of billions of nerve cells governing memory and language. Judging from the age of the individuals whose skeletons have been found at the time of their death, 98 per cent of Neanderthal men did not live beyond the age of forty, and over half died before they reached the age of thirty. Such an extremely short life expectancy gives us an idea of how rigorous the climate and their general living conditions must have been.[6]

In any case, there is no doubt that our remote predecessor was very skilled in making pointed stones, that he used fire, and that he buried his dead and placed offerings alongside their bodies. Skull Number One in the cave of Monte Circeo, not far from Rome, would seem to be that of a man who was decapitated, since no trace of a skeleton was found anywhere in the cave. The cause of death was a hard blow on the right

5. "He was every bit as intelligent as we are today," states Ashley Montagu in *Man, the First Million Years*, New York, 1957.
6. H. V. Vallois, "The social life of early man: the evidence of skeletons." In: *Social Life of Early Man*, Chicago, 1961.

temple, after which the *foramen magnum* at the base of the skull had been carefully enlarged—a mutilation which bears a striking resemblance to that practiced by certain head-hunting peoples, in Borneo for instance, on the skulls of their victims, for the purpose of extracting the brain and eating it in ritual fashion. Dr. Vallois cites other cases, from Africa and Southeast Asia all the way to Europe, which point to murder, whether ritual or not, and cannibalism. Professor Alberto Blanc points out that the fossil skulls of Stenheim (pre-Neanderthal, about 300,000 years old) and Ehringsdorf (old Neanderthal, about 150,000 years old) underwent similar mutilations. He further remarks that the Monte Circeo skull had been placed inside a ring of stones on the floor of the cave, along with three groups of bones, from a wild pig, a deer, and an extinct form of ox called *bos primigenius*. Inevitably, this reminds us of the Roman sacrifice of a pig, a sheep, and a bull, the suovetaurilia of classical times, whose origins must have gone back tens of thousands of years. We also know that this triple sacrifice was practiced during the Chu dynasty of ancient China.

In all events, we cannot doubt that Neanderthal man practiced a certain form of ritual, as well as a certain form of cannibalism, probably linked to religious beliefs. Can we say that he spoke a language? We can say, at least, that his brain, judging from its volume, was probably not unsuited for that function. Furthermore, if there was no language, how can we account for the fact that for more than 100,000 years a culture which was constant and remarkably true to itself was transmitted from group to group, each member of which lived an average of only thirty years? Ritual itself—and ritual there was, judging from such discoveries as those at Monte Circeo—is difficult to imagine without spoken formulas and without a form of instruction by which to pass it from one generation to the next.

About 50,000 years B.C., Neanderthal man disappeared, not so much under the violent impact of invasions and battles, eventually causing his extermination, as because of interbreeding with the several varieties of *Homo sapiens*. The process may have begun very far in the past, as shown in 1931–1932 by McCown's discoveries in the caves of Mount Carmel, in Israel: the skeletons of men, women, and children who can be described as hybrids of Neanderthal and Cro-Magnon man. Archaic man was absorbed, rather than destroyed, by "neanthropus," new man, whose most stunning contribution to cultural history was his discovery of the way to draw three-dimensional beings on a flat surface. The cave drawings of Altamira and Lascaux were the result.

We are far from realizing just how many inventions that are still used today, and not only among exotic tribes but sometimes within our own civilization, come from the Paleolithic period, particularly from the last forty thousand years before the revolutionary discovery of crop-raising and animal-breeding. Among such inventions are the fashioning of tools from stone and bone, the needle, the harpoon, the spear thrower, the use of shell necklaces and animal teeth to decorate the body, mural painting, the carving of bone and ivory, and the ritual burial of the dead. The sacrifice of animals and even of human beings would also seem to be a very ancient practice. We are the continuation of prehistoric man, not only by blood but by the performance of such day-to-day acts as sewing, hunting, embellishment of our persons, and mourning. Certain forms of family and social organization, of art and of religion, still alive today, are rooted in the remotest past of the human species.

From this we can see that cultural traits and themes are capable of perpetuating themselves throughout very long periods and over very great distances, and that they do so altogether independently of the cultures and civilizations in which they took shape and onto which they graft themselves. Even the cultures that appear to be the simplest are actually composite, and this is still more true of civilizations. Every cultural phenomenon behaves as if it had an existence of its own, coming down through the centuries, crossing oceans, and becoming "naturalized" in the most divers times and places. Coins made of metal were invented in Lydia in about 700 B.C.; they have since gone around the world. Seven was a sacred number in Mesopotamia; hence the names of the seven planets given to the days of the week, transposed in antiquity and even in our own day in the form of their Latin or Germanic translation: Monday, moon day; Thursday, Thor's day;

Friday, day of the Germanic Venus, Frigg. To this common fund were added the Hebrew sabbath, which in turn was close to the Babylonian *shabattum*, and Sunday, day of the sun, proclaimed as such by Constantine. Thus the week as we know it today, which has withstood all attempts to change it (such as the "decade" of the French Revolutionary calendar), represents about two thousand years of blending of Babylonian, Jewish, Germanic, and Greco-Roman ideas and vocables. It has had a remarkable gift for implanting itself in various civilizations and staying there. Sometimes it has achieved this at the cost of a few changes. The Arabs, for instance, adopted the seven-day week but eliminated the references to the planets and the pagan gods which the Christian nations, with the exception of Portugal and modern Greece, have preserved. What has lasted, in all events, and persisted throughout the centuries is the basic idea of the number seven. In the New World, among the ancient Mexicans, thirteen was the number used to mark out the segments of time. Each series of thirteen days began with a sign to which a unit—"One-House," "One-Serpent," "One-Jaguar"— was assigned, and that unit extended its harmful, indifferent, or favorable influence over the entire thirteen-day period. This system, which was common to all the civilizations of Central America, arose out of the pre-Maya chronological inventions, made at some unknown date B.C. in a tropical country, but it did not spread beyond the Meso-American area.

Another instance of the extraordinary tenacity of cultural traits is present at every moment in our own civilization. We count the hours by series of twelve, and divide each hour into sixty minutes, each of which in turn is divided into sixty seconds. Over five thousand years ago, the Sumerians used this type of reckoning; the fruits of it today are not only the divisions of time but also the division of the circle into 360 degrees and the twelve pence in every English shilling.

We can see that cultural history is a twofold matter: the discontinuity of cultures and civilizations, yet the continuity of some of the traits which make them up. This is why we can argue both for and against the existence of progress, in that techniques are spread from one place to another and from one period to another, and, as a result, the achievements of one civilization are not lost, or at least not wholly lost, for the others and for mankind as a whole. Of course, the process is not always a smooth and regular one; there can be reversals, conquests can be abandoned and then won back. Not only did the Greco-Asian astronomers know that the earth moved about the sun and that our planet was spherical, but in fact their measurement of the earthly meridian was accurate to within thirty miles. But it was not until A.D. 1615 that Galileo rediscovered what was already known in Alexandria in the second century B.C., and we all remember what trouble his boldness brought him. The science of classical antiquity has been greatly underestimated, the science which—particularly in the Alexandria museum, that marvelous scientific research center!—had actually studied and understood many a phenomenon. But the results of that research were forgotten when the Greco-Roman civilization collapsed. As long ago as the third century B.C., for instance, Herophilus and Erasistratus were teaching the role of the heart in the circulation of the blood, the distinction between arteries and veins, and the existence and function of nerves.

In other instances, the principle of a given invention was laid down and some of its applications were found, but the invention was not fully developed until much later, by other civilizations. It is commonly agreed that the ancient Mexicans did not have the wheel, and that is true insofar as they did not make practical use of it. Yet excavations in the Pánuco region have brought to light some terra-cotta animals mounted on four discs. These must be toys. But the idea was never transposed to vehicles, possibly because the Indians did not have any animal capable of pulling a wagon. In a country with such uneven terrain, it would have been too costly to build roads merely for vehicles pulled by men. For that reason, all commercial transport operations were done by bearers, and messages were carried by runners. From accounts of the Conquest, we know with what surprising speed Moctezuma's messengers linked the Gulf Coast to the capital.

Between 150 and 100 B.C., the Alexandrian scholar Heron, a disciple of Ctesibius, who had been a disciple of Archimedes, invented the aeolipile, a steam engine based on the turbine principle. He even used it to operate automatons or to open and close doors. But vehicles continued to be drawn by horses, and ships to be propelled by oars. The Chinese used gunpowder to launch rockets and set off fireworks, but the Arabs were the first to use it in a cannon, at the siege of Algeciras in 1342.

Even during the so-called "Middle Ages," such inventions as the watermill and the mechanical clock were developed and became generally known.

All in all, and despite some regressions, technical progress has been made, because the cultural traits in the technical category travel, survive, shift from one civilization to another, and accumulate in the course of time.

But can the same be said of other areas of culture? Can we state that ever since civilizations have existed, up to and including our own, art and morality, for instance, have progressed? It seems to me the answer is no. Here we are no longer dealing with cultural traits and patterns but instead with the structure proper to each civilization. In other words, we have shifted from the continuous to the discontinuous.

Every civilization is an exceptional phenomenon in itself. It is limited in space and in time. Each one adopts a certain attitude to the world and the problems of man. It is impossible to make value judgments by which the various civilizations could be ranked above or below one another. We can say that an automobile is faster than a carriage drawn by horses, or that an atomic submarine is a more effective weapon than an Athenian trireme, or that a chronometer measures time more accurately than a water clock. But we are unable to state that our thinkers are superior to Plato, our monuments more beautiful than the Acropolis, we ourselves wiser or more humane than Pericles' contemporaries. Or, again, although it is possible to evaluate the progress made in the various technical branches from Vermeer's time up to Picasso's and to express it mathematically, it is not possible to establish a similar relationship between the works of the two painters. When it comes to producing and applying inventions, men's efforts add up, despite interruptions, pauses, and reversals; but where aesthetics and morals are concerned, efforts are begun anew, relapse, start again from scratch, and, at rare moments in history, reach dazzling summits, only to shrink down again almost immediately.

In the realm of ethics, no new idea representing any progress whatsoever seems to have been introduced since Buddha, Greek philosophy (particularly Stoicism), and the Bible. Even Christianity is not so much of an innovation as is commonly believed. The Old Testament had already commanded every man "to love thy neighbor as thyself" (Leviticus, 19:18) and to "love . . . the stranger" (Deuteronomy 10:19), and laid down rules for the protection of wage-earners (Leviticus, 19:13). Hillel, the Hebrew scholar who lived a little over two thousand years ago, summed up the entire Law in a single sentence: "Do not unto others what thou wouldst not have done unto thyself."

If there is one area where no appreciable progress has been made since the beginning of history, it is certainly in relations between governments. Wherever we look, in the remotest or most recent past, we find that diplomacy and war are motivated by the same ambitions, unleash the same passions and resort to the same means, the only difference being that the perfected techniques of our own day have made those means worse still. For six thousand years, the major themes of international politics have been cynicism, lies, and hypocrisy, an abusive use of force, and oppression of the weak. Machiavellism has been rife between all countries at all times and also, but for rare exceptions, within all nations; the struggle for power between individuals and groups has not fundamentally altered nor become substantially more moral since governments began.

The illusion that humanity has made over-all progress stems from several related errors. The (relative) continuity of techniques is confused with the discontinuity of civilizations. Cultural history is pictured as a single ascending line, and we flatter ourselves that we are in the vanguard, carrying that line onward and upward. And, lastly, we more or less consciously feel that *our* civilization is identical with civilization as a whole, and that ours will not meet the fate of the civilizations that

8*

have gone before it. In addition, we tend to believe, because language has anchored that tendency deep within our minds, that by giving a name to a set of phenomena, we are conferring reality upon what is actually a mere label. History, with a capital H, quickly becomes a personage and even a deity. We begin to talk about "the meaning of History," about what History wants or does not want, forbids or commands, about the "current of History," and we forget that the word "History" is no more than a *flatus vocis*, a convenient and conventional handle we put to a whole complex series of human actions and reactions. We forget that History cannot want, command, or forbid anything whatever.

Teilhard de Chardin is an eminent biologist—although challenged by Jean Rostand, among others—a first-class paleontologist, a metaphysician, and a poet. But even he has not been safe from the illusions and errors outlined above. One commentator[7] in sympathy with his thinking was bound to point out, nonetheless, that Teilhard "drops ... the dialectical process of the human advance of civilizations" and that he skips from prehistoric times to mankind today. Indeed, it is remarkable that Teilhard, who is brilliant and learned when it comes to the forms of life that preceded man and to anything concerning the times of our remotest origins, seems to be totally uninterested in the human phenomenon throughout the entire period between Sinanthropus and ourselves. His work contains very few allusions to cultural history, or to just plain history, for that matter, and those few are used to shore up his repeated claim of continuous ascension. In *The Phenomenon of Man*,[8] for example, he writes, "It is easy for the pessimist to discount this period, so extraordinary among the civilizations which have fallen into ruins one after the other. Is it not far more *scientific* [my italics, J.S.] to recognize, yet once again, beneath these successive oscillations, the great spiral of life: thrusting up, irreversibly, in relays ... Susa, Memphis and Athens can crumble. An ever more highly organized consciousness of the universe is passed on from hand to hand, and glows steadily brighter."

7. Emile Rideau, *Teilhard de Chardin, A Guide to His Thought*, London, Collins, 1967.
8. Harper & Brothers, New York, 1959, p. 211.

Another example, this time from *La grande Monade*: "Universal history shows us that always, following each revolution and each war, mankind has been a little more coherent, a little more united." Now, as a matter of fact, history does not show anything of the kind; quite the contrary. How can mankind be said to have been more coherent and united after the great barbarian invasions than when the Roman Empire was at its height, or after the First World War than at the start of the twentieth century? There is an alternation of gathering and dispersal, creation and destruction. The remains of dead civilizations, the deserts that man has made with iron and fire or simply through neglect, the ruins of monuments and the ashes of books litter the surface of our planet; they are there for anyone to see. Far from helping to bring our species closer together, the proliferation of the human population and the awakening of peripheral or backward peoples merely make the collisions more violent and the divisions deeper. Even the purest, most lofty ideologies tend to shatter into sects that are bitterly opposed to one another and to persecute heretics and infidels in the cruelest ways. The histories of Mazdaism and Christianity are there to prove it.

Two postulates crop up at every point in the development of Teilhard's thinking. The first is that man "occupies a key position in the world, a position as the principal axis, a polar position." The second is that "although mankind too often appears to us as a vast incoherent restless movement around the same spot . . . it is possible to see the confusions of detail in which we think we are lost merge into one vast organic guided operation."[9] Our civilization, in this metaphysical vision, is at the top of the "spiral." "There can be no longer any question of 'disappearing civilizations' . . . [there is] one definitely established planetary civilization, and this latter cannot perish without *ipso facto* the movement of hominization on earth being permanently halted."

Contrary to the scientific rule that facts are taken as a basis from which conclusions are drawn if it is possible to do so, Teilhard tries to force the facts to fit the intuitive idea he has of them from the outset.

9. *Man's Place in Nature*, Harper & Row, New York, 1966, pp. 14–15.

He readily admitted this as early as 1916, when he wrote, ". . . the sap of my thought and activity is sentient rather than intellectual . . . there are temperaments in which intuition is born from an excess of tension or vital ardor much more than from methodical effort: and probably it's to this type that I incline. I am much more enthusiast than scholar."[10] His essentially metaphysical passion rejects the findings of cultural history as "superficial" and makes him look for a "meaning" in what does not seem to have any. In his *Transformation et prolongement en l'homme du mécanisme de l'évolution*, he wrote, "Even for such powerful and penetrating minds as those of Spengler and Toynbee, history is reduced essentially to a periodical function, without either beginning or end; whereas what would be needed, in order to understand History, would be to treat it as an ocean, to dive beneath the cultural oscillations on its surface and discover the general drift at the bottom."

Any vigorous philosopher will manage to find in his world system what he has decided from the beginning to find there. It has never failed. Any metaphysical scheme is like the proverbial Spanish inn: all you find there is what you bring. Accordingly, Teilhard de Chardin looks on the unification of humanity as "the natural culmination of a cosmic process of organization which has not varied once since those distant ages when our planet was young" and maintains that "history is not agitation . . . but guided growth of beings toward the maximum of being."

It is remarkable that the author of these claims, which he repeats dozens of times with the greatest assurance, has never offered so much as the shadow of a proof. Honestly and deeply convinced, a poet-philosopher whose talent sometimes makes us think of the pre-Socratic "physicists," Teilhard has confined himself to imparting his vision of things to us. He has not offered a single fact in support of his theory, and yet there is abundant material to draw on in history, archaeology, and ethnology.

Maybe it is his training as a biologist which makes him refuse to see that the cultural evolution of man is a fundamentally different phenomenon from the biological evolution of living species. For him,

10. Letter published in *The Making of a Mind*, Harper & Row, New York, 1965, p. 106.

the history of mankind is only an extension of biology, and the cultural phenomenon is merely "educational heredity" which picks up where "chromosomic heredity" leaves off. This amounts to confusing two heterogeneous types of notions and phenomena. In short, there is nothing at all in between biology and metaphysics, and it is precisely to this gaping hole in Teilhard's work that ethnology, as the study and history of cultures, corresponds.

For him, the migrations, conflicts, and influences of the various cultures are merely the effect of "the ramification of living forms being continued in civilized environment," and this constitutes an "evolution the *guided* nature of which appears with utmost clarity."

"Guided nature." According to Teilhard, mankind has achieved the final and planetary civilization in the form of our own civilization and now—i.e., beginning about fifty years ago[11]—it is engaged in a process of unification or totalization. As early as 1918, in *La grande Monade*, he called this "solidification." He considered that all of mankind, squeezed by its own mass onto a globe that had become too narrow, was forced into unification. "We are strongly led to assume that the human molecules, shoved against one another by rapidly rising pressure, will finally succeed in overcoming the crucial obstacle of their mutual repulsion . . ." which "necessarily determines, at some finite distance in the future, a critical summit or point of encounter." This point of encounter is the "omega point" that symbolized the ultimate confluence of the world and God. "Mankind will come to an end when it has . . . reduced everything to a common idea and a common passion." "Happy the world which will end in ecstasy!" Thus, at the end of the human ages, when the "omega point" coincides with Christ, there will be the "extraordinary phenomenon of the whole world set aglow, through total *amorization*."

It is up to the theologians to decide whether this doctrine does or does not fit the dogma of Revelation. But I, speaking for myself, cannot agree that such a conclusion was reached "only through frank and illuminating reflection on scientific data," as Emile Rideau maintains it was. "Scientific data" does not prove anything of the kind, for

11. *Man's Place in Nature.*

the obvious reason that this grandiose vision of cosmic destiny cannot be proven. Insofar as the science of man—which is still so unadvanced, and cannot be made to advance further by means of metaphysical speculation—can lead to conclusions of a prudent and temporary nature, none of Teilhard's fundamental arguments appears to be justified. Nothing proves that man is the acme, the ultimate form of life. The history of civilizations does not point clearly in any specific direction. Our civilization does not seem at all destined to conquer the whole planet in anticipation of that "final glow." As for the convergence and ultimate identity of a biological-cosmic "omega point" with Christ as revealed by Scripture and defined in the earliest centuries of Christianity by the meditation of the Church Fathers and the Synods, I do not know what theological view can be taken of such finalism but, from a scientific standpoint, there is no denying that it is very unconvincing.

According to Saint Thomas, "it is possible to describe a complete, co-ordinated, coherent system of natural laws and actions on the level of nature, without ever encountering the action of God or having to refer to it. On the level of natural causes, everything happens as if those causes were the only ones that existed."[12] The same can be said of ethnology, the history of cultures and civilizations. Fervent and respectable though Teilhard's faith is, it is responsible for his dragging science into a field where it does not belong and into an adventure that has nothing to do with it. Possibly, in a sort of boomerang effect, he is even led by his faith to compromise that faith itself by making it depend on the brilliant but brittle edifice of a highly debatable metaphysical system.

The first and fundamental duty of any ethnologist, be he Christian, Moslem, Buddhist, or agnostic, is to observe the facts and compare them without any preconceived notion. In that way he remains entirely free to accept or reject a given dogma, believe in any given revelation, or open his soul to any given grace. Confusing the orders is as dangerous as mixing up the types of literature.

Suppose we lift the alluring veil in which Teilhard wraps up his

12. Abbé R. Lavocat, *L'Eglise et la communauté scientifique internationale*, Paris, 1965.

ideas; then the doctrine he has set out so eloquently boils down to the "search for final causes" which Descartes rightly wished to "exclude altogether from our philosophy." It is a biological-mystical finalism; but its biological basis seems uncertain and its mystical culmination, obviously accepted a priori, does not by any means follow from its premises. And, as I have already pointed out, when it comes to man as a bearer of cultures and to man's history, man's civilizations and everything that is the object of the science of man, all of that is quite simply put in parentheses in his work. Messianism, whether Marxist or Teilhardian, leaves aside what is most important from the scientific standpoint, namely, the characteristics and classification of cultures and civilizations in the same way that natural history characterizes and classifies plants or animals. Kroeber, the great American ethnologist, rightly states, in the posthumous work which sums up an entire life devoted to science, that this is the most urgent task facing ethnology,[13] in contrast to the dogmatisms that are offered as philosophies of history.

Ethnology is neither a branch of philosophy nor a branch of biology. The notion of "race," which lends itself to so much confusion and is so heavy with emotional implications, can have a biological meaning, in that it refers to the entire set of hereditary physical characteristics of certain men. The same notion does not have any ethnological meaning, since there is no discernible link between those physical characteristics—the *only* allowable subject of a racial study—and the various known cultures. It goes without saying that the hybridization of the varieties of the human species began very early (as shown by the example of the Mount Carmel caves I mentioned earlier) and that it has been going on continually for several thousand years, as a result of migrations, wars, conquests, and colonization. If by "race" is meant a "pure" group, harboring physical traits which have survived from remote antiquity, then "race" is a myth. Even more clearly still, it is impossible and even ridiculous to try to account for the cultural traits

13. "The problem of recognizing the world's cultures is essentially one of natural history, and involves dealing with all the phenomena and then building up their patterns or classes step by step." *A Roster of Civilizations and Culture*, Chicago, 1962. p. 16.

of a given people in terms of biological heredity. Thus, cultural history as Gobineau explained it in his *Essai sur l'inégalité des races humaines* is no more than a sort of chemical fantasy; supposedly all the varieties of political organization, of law, religion, and art in all the civilizations are determined solely by the proportion of white, yellow, or black "blood."

American Indians, on the whole, share a general "type" which is characterized by a few specific features such as a coppery yellow skin, high cheekbones, and a fairly common tendency to have slanting eyes; in other words, there is a sort of family resemblance among them. But, on closer examination, we find a disconcerting amount of variety. There are tall Indians (certain tribes of North America and Patagonia) and Indians who are of short or medium stature, like the Maya; there are long heads and round heads, light complexions and dark complexions, straight hair and wavy hair, not to mention "blond Indians" and Pygmies.[14] There is no doubt that a sizable Asiatic element played a dominant role in peopling the double continent of America. But the word "Asiatic" cannot be used to label "a race"; after all, a Chinese from Canton, a Tibetan, a Mongolian from the steppes, a Turk from central Asia, a Chukchi, a Kamchadal, and an Ainu are all "Asiatics" and all different. Moreover, we must not overlook Paul Rivet's theories on Melanesian and Polynesian contributions.

There is nothing to prove that the physical characteristics we find today among such and such tribe of Indians are identical with those of their ancestors when they first set foot on the American continent some 25,000 or 30,000 years B.C. There is every reason for thinking the opposite. Boas has demonstrated that the physical type of the children and descendants of Italian, Czech, and Jewish immigrants in the United States gradually, over the generations, grew more and more unlike that of their parents and ancestors. Similarly, it seems that as the Indian tribes gradually moved about in the New World, settled in certain regions and there underwent the influence of widely differing climates and ways of life (especially where food was concerned), they developed specific features, such as the characteristic facial type of the Maya or the

14. Paul Rivet, *Les origines de l'homme américaine, op. cit.*

tall stature of the Patagonians. As a result, we cannot talk about an Indo-American "race" or Maya, Nahuatl "races" or the like. The only thing we can observe, in reality, is an "ethnic group," and such groups change in the course of time, either because of physical factors or because of interbreeding. Even so, as I found where the Lacandones are concerned, these ethnic groups are seldom homogeneous.

Suppose we make three maps: one, of the principal physical characteristics of the Indians; another, of linguistic families; and the third, of cultures. If we superimpose these maps, we find that they do not coincide at all. The Pueblo Indians all share the same very distinctive culture and there is a physical resemblance among them, but they speak several quite different languages. The Aztec civilization extended to a whole group of peoples belonging to a number of linguistic families. At the opposite extreme, Indians of the Uto-Aztec family, such as the Huichols, preserved their archaic culture while others, sharing the same linguistic source, continued to be "Chichimec" hunters. The Otomi-Pame Indians, although very closely related to one another in terms of language, were divided into two groups on the cultural level, one group of sedentary farming people, the other of nomadic hunter-gatherers. Even the Maya family, so geographically compact, includes not only languages spoken by Maya whose physical appearance is strikingly reminiscent of the figures in bas-reliefs and frescoes, but also other languages spoken by Tzeltals or Tzotzils who differ widely from the classical Maya type.

To take an example from our own ancient world, the Greeks and the Persians never suspected that they belonged to the same linguistic family, nor did the Latins realize that in this respect they were close to the Celts.

The cultural fact is original and cannot be reduced to any other. The history of the Hungarians and the Finns, the influences to which they have been subjected and the religion they have adopted—all of these weigh more heavily and explain far more than the fact that their two languages have a common origin. The fact that they belong to European civilization is more important than the fact that their languages are related to the Turkish.

The known civilizations thus far have been the work of Orientals speaking Semitic or non-Semitic languages, such as the Akkadians or the Sumerians; of whites speaking Indo-European tongues, such as the Persians; of swarthy Egyptians who spoke a Hamitic language; of Greeks and Italiots, Chinese and Maya, Indians (from India), Arabs, Peruvians, Amerindians of the Nahuatl family, etc. etc. In other words, of peoples belonging to the most diverse physical and linguistic groups. Of course, it can be pointed out that, to date, the black peoples of Africa have not built up any civilization. But it is only fair to add that an Egyptian at the beginning of the second millennium B.C. could justifiably have said the same thing about the first Greeks who were beginning to move down toward the Balkan Peninsula, and that a Roman at the time of Caesar could legitimately have doubted the capacity of the Germanic peoples to develop a civilization worthy of the name. For a Maya from seventh-century Palenque, the Nahua of the north (assuming that he even knew such people existed) would have been no more than barbarians living on roots, wild fruit, and game, living in huts and absolutely incapable of rising to the level of a civilization. Just as the attempts of overzealous propagandists to prove that Egyptian civilization, for instance, grew out of the deep-lying roots of "negritude" or to uphold the notion of the "tall blond Aryan" as *the* bearer of civilization are ridiculous, so it is risky to maintain that the African Negroes will never build a civilization simply because they have not built one yet.

There is no such thing as a scientific basis on which to establish a hierarchical classification of civilizations connected with the physical characteristics of the peoples involved. Hereditary transmission of physical features, on the one hand, and transmission of cultural traits by education, imitation, and influence, on the other, are two entirely separate phenomena.

Race, then, as we have seen, should not be confused with culture. Similarly, "culture" or "civilization" should not be equated with society; that is an error of which we find many examples in Toynbee's monumental work. The postclassical civilization of Mexico was common to societies, cities, or tribes of different origins and speaking a great variety of languages. The civilization of the Roman Empire embraced Italian, Greek, Syrian, Celtic and other societies which continued to be heterogeneous in relation to one another, even after the Edict of Caracalla instituted equality before the law throughout the Mediterranean basin. Our own civilization develops through societies in the form of nations which continue to exist as such, both politically and culturally. France, for instance, is one cultural province of our civilization and England is another; each province has features which are peculiar to it alone and give it a certain physiognomy, so to speak.

It comes to pass that at some point, necessarily late, in the history of a civilization, one state, having grown out of one of the societies which belong to that civilization, tries to bring all of the other societies under its control and form a political entity whose borders will coincide as closely as possible with those of the civilization concerned. This is what happened in the third century B.C. when the principality of Ts'in overcame resistance from the other kingdoms and formed what we today call China. The government of ancient Rome became supreme all along the shores of the Mediterranean and even, in Gaul and in Spain, as far as the ocean, by superimposing its laws and its power upon the cities, tribes, and kingdoms of the Greek and Celtic worlds and Asia Minor. The Inca Empire in Peru covered the peoples of the coastal and Andean regions with a political, economic, and religious network that spread outward from Cuzco. The Mexican city of Tenochtitlán may have been on the point of forming an empire around itself; its political confines would have been essentially those of the Toltec-Aztec civilization. Thus far, within our own civilization, all attempts toward hegemony on the part of any single state have failed, but this does not mean that the situation will never change. Islam, however, is one example to prove that, apparently, the "Caesar" phase —i.e., the political unification of the geographical area occupied by a civilization—is not something every civilization has to go through.

It may also come to pass that for a very long period of time a civilization ceases to be embodied in a specific society and yet continues to exist as a complex of cultural traits and themes. Judaism is a case in point. The Jewish civilization had apparently reached its apogee in the reigns of David and Solomon, when culture, society, and government all coincided in Palestine in the period between 1000 and 900 B.C. But then the Jewish society split into two states and invasions by Sargon and Nebuchadnezzar caused dispersal of the Jews. These events were the first in a series of terrible blows culminating in the destruction of the temple in Jerusalem during the reign of Titus and the suppression of the rebellion of Bar Kochba in 135. For eighteen centuries thereafter there was no more Jewish state, not even a people gathered into one territory subject to the authority of another state. Instead, throughout the Christian and Moslem worlds, there was a multitude of scattered communities and, dozens of times, they were expelled, exiled, persecuted, or exterminated. Yet the Hebrew civilization survived, although there was no material vehicle for survival in the form of a "race." Not only is there no Jewish "race" but, in fact, the history of the Diaspora shows that in the course of time the Semitic stock from Palestine has been joined by various other ethnic strains, especially as the result of conversions to Judaism. Two factors contributed to survival. First of all, Hebrew continued to be the ritual language in communities where Aramaic, Arabic, Yiddish, or Ladino were the languages of day-to-day life. Second and most important, although this civilization had no territorial base and no political structures, it became crystallized around a system of religious and moral ideas, rules of conduct, attitudes to the world and to life. The civilization was expressed in the holy books and the commentaries on them—the Bible (Torah) and explanations of the Biblical text (Midrash), then oral teaching and traditions (Mishnah). Codification of the latter, with the glosses, anecdotes and apologues, rules and laws of all sorts which arise from it, formed the Babylonian and Palestinian Talmud. The remarkable thing is that the immense labor which was to provide a landless, stateless civilization with an intellectual and moral structure was carried on and completed after the territorial basis and political framework had collapsed, between the second and the sixth centuries.

The Hebraic civilization went its own way despite dispersal, but, like the Islamic and European civilizations with which it has been associated but has never merged, it felt the Greek influence in two forms: neo-Platonic through Philo from Alexandria and Ibn Gabirol from Spain; and Aristotelian, through Maimonides. Conversely, the Hebraic civilization influenced both Arabs and Westerners. Despite periodic clashes, that civilization and its contemporaries acted on one another in the same way as civilizations whose territories touch one another. Such books as Ibn Gabirol's *Fons Vitae* or Maimonides' *Guide of the Perplexed*, and later the mystical theology of the Zohar, had extensive repercussions both in the Arab world and among Christian thinkers. Like all civilizations, that of the Hebrews tried to adapt itself to changing circumstances; since it was unable to do so in the way that others did—that is, by means of institutions governing a social body gathered onto one land—it reacted through the exchange of questions and answers among the communities scattered throughout Europe and the Ottoman Empire, or through the meditation and studies of such schools as that of Safed in Palestine and the *yeshivoth* in Poland, Lithuania, and the Ukraine. In this way, the Hebrew civilization avoided the danger of becoming fossilized and gave rise to the Cabala and other mystical movements, to Hassidism, modern reformism, and Zionism. Throughout all of these spiritual adventures interwoven with terrible material tribulations, its fundamental structures—exclusive monotheism, the capital importance of ethics, the very special combination of universalism with the doctrine of the Covenant with God—remained intact. That is why, when it became possible to restore a Hebrew state, a territorial and political framework, that state was able to welcome a great many groups which, although physically heterogeneous and speaking a number of separate languages, embodied a single civilization that had preserved its identity despite nearly two thousand years of exile.

The case we have just considered is an extreme one and, like all such cases, it bears a very special illustrative value. It brings out the autonomy of "civilization" as a fact in relation to the biological, economic, and political phenomena which are too often confused with it. It also shows that civilizations, such as we know them and as they appear during a very brief period of human history, are specific phenomena and that it is very risky to try to reduce them to a set of general laws.

Spengler believed it was possible to spell out such laws, applicable to all known civilizations. Each civilization is an organism which, from the time of its birth to the time of its death, has had to pass (or, in the case of our own, will have to pass) through very distinct stages. It follows that each civilization has its own particular life span, which is not measured in the same way as time in the abstract; consequently, a given period of a given civilization is "contemporary" with the corresponding period of another, even if they are centuries or millennia apart. For instance, the setting up of the Chinese Empire (third century B.C.) is "contemporary" with the era of Augustus, and Alexander is a "contemporary" of Napoleon. From this, it could be deduced that our own civilization has reached the phase which corresponds, in Chinese history, to that of the "Contending States" or, in Greek and Roman history, to the phase lasting from Sulla to Caesar and, therefore, that in our third millennium (A.D. 2000 to 2200), the cultural world will be united under a single "Imperium."[15] But when we try to apply this outline, we run into what I consider some insurmountable obstacles. As for the analogies on which Spengler relies in certain instances, it is impossible to continue them in any great detail. If he maintains that Alexander is "contemporary" with Napoleon, he is then obliged to equate Pericles with Louis XIV, which is indefensible. There is no denying that the period of the "Contending States" (Chankwo, 480 to 230 B.C.) bears a marked resemblance to the period of wars we ourselves have been living through since the last century; but can it be that our civilization, with its apparent tendency to split its old European main body from its two (American and Euro-Asian) wings, is really moving toward imperial unification? Although we have no right to overlook this theory altogether, I do find it very difficult to believe that it is well founded.

The internal logic of his own system leads Spengler to deny one fact which is undeniable, namely, the transmission of cultural traits and

15. Spengler, *The Decline of the West*, London, 1932. Table at the end of the first volume.

patterns in space and in time from one civilization to another and, thereby, the affiliation of a recent civilization to an older civilization. He is obliged to deny this, obvious though it is, because he wants to take into account only the biological duration of each civilization, considered as an organism, and not historical time. "Men of two different kinds are parted, each in his own spiritual loneliness, by an impassable gulf. Even though Indians and Chinese in those days both felt as Buddhists, they were spiritually as far apart as ever. The same words, the same rites, the same symbol—but two different souls, each going its own way."[16] Similarly, he goes on to say, it would be illusory to believe that anything whatever of the philosophy or art of classical antiquity subsists in our civilization, or that the "magian" Christianity of the first centuries after Christ lives on in the "Faustian" Christianity of Western man. In other words, there is neither diffusion nor tradition; instead, every civilization is its own closed world wrapped around its own incommunicable "soul."

It must be said that in the course of their transmission through time and space cultural traits and patterns do undergo processes of adaptation and refashioning and acquire new content, in the same way that a language which is adopted by a people which had not formerly spoken it is altered by the "substratum" on which it is superimposed. The Koine, Κοινή, or Greek which became generalized, was not Attic Greek; the Latin spoken by the Romanized Celts in Gaul was not the language of Cicero and Virgil. Christianity, when transposed to Indian America, took on forms and meanings in which the native religions were clearly discernible. But diffusion remains a fact for all that, and from it follows another: civilizations cannot be placed side by side but instead end to end. Their individual life spans are inscribed within time in general. In other words, there are civilizations which proceed from earlier civilizations. If we wanted to make a comparison, we would have to compare civilizations like that of the Greeks or the Toltecs to plants; the plants themselves are dead but the offshoots that have grown out of them have had time to take root and grow in turn.

As a result, a statement to the effect that a given phase of an ancient

16. *Op. cit.*, II, p. 57.

civilization is "contemporary" with a given phase of our own is false. There is a real succession of cultural phenomena in time. Plato's work, for instance, is separated from modern philosophy not only by a specific number of sidereal revolutions, which are nonhuman phenomena, but also, on the strictly human level, by the fact that we can trace the development of classical ideas and their successors up to our own ideas through the meditation of the thinkers and the schools of the ancient world, of Christianity, Judaism, and Islam. In the same way, there can be no doubt that the Toltec architecture of Tula was earlier than that of the Aztecs, not only because it appeared five centuries earlier (as measured in objective time, that is, five hundred revolutions of the earth about the sun) but also because the builders of the monuments at Tenochtitlán—with their pyramids and colonnades, their *coatepantli*, their railings made of plumed serpents, their flag-bearers— incorporated into them a host of features which characterized the Tula architecture.

Toynbee[17] acknowledged the existence of civilizations "affiliated" with others and stemming more or less directly from them. For instance, he states that the Hellenic civilization was "loosely" affiliated with that of Minoan Crete and that our Western civilization is affiliated with the Hellenic. Like Toynbee, we can distinguish between two categories of civilizations. The first includes those which did not have any "parent" civilizations (or which we imagine did not have any, because of our limited archaeological findings); this is the case of Sumer, Egypt, and ancient China. The second category includes such civilizations as our own, that is, "offshoots" of earlier civilizations. Toynbee further recognizes that "fusions" can occur. Unfortunately, the example he gives for Mexico is inaccurate, since it was not a Yucatec civilization and a "Mexic" civilization which fused to form a "Central American" civilization but rather the Toltec civilization and that of the Maya of Yucatán which were associated and formed the postclassic Maya civilization.

Now, whereas many civilizations, in the course of their historical

17. *A Study of History*, Abridgment of Vols. I–VI by D. D. Somervell, Oxford University Press, 1946, Table V.

development, have certainly gone through a "time of troubles," there is nothing to show that that is a general rule nor that such a time of troubles has always been followed by the setting up of a "universal state." We have no reason for agreeing with Toynbee when he says that the time of troubles of the Maya civilization occurred between some undetermined date and the beginning of the fourth century A.D., not any more than when he says that during the so-called "ancient empire" period of Maya civilization a "universal state" was set up and imposed peace throughout the territory occupied by that civilization. Quite the contrary. That period was characterized by the fragmentation of the Maya country into a number of small states which sometimes co-operated and sometimes made war on one another.

In point of fact, although carefully dated inscriptions enable us to retrace the history of the Maya civilization with exceptional certainty, that civilization does not seem to fit easily into Toynbee's scheme of things.

My own view is that, at our present level of knowledge, it is not possible to make any such outlines or, as a result, to lay down any such laws. Human societies and their cultures evolve under the influence of the many forces acting upon them; the effects of those forces overlap and react upon one another. If we try to simplify the matter by reducing everything to a single cause—a material one for Marx and Engels, spiritual for Spengler—we make it impossible for ourselves to understand the reality, which is infinitely more complex than any dogmatic outline can be.

No one can deny that economic phenomena play a vital role in the birth, the development, and the disappearance of cultures. Marx and Engels, in fact, were responsible for certain progress in this respect, by replacing a mechanistic type of economic determinism with infinitely more flexible explanatory concepts. The economic substratum does not *directly* determine the other phenomena of a civilization—the social structures to which it gives rise, the reciprocal influences between the different groups into which a society is divided, the way economic and social conditions are reflected in the human consciousness, all of those interrelated factors that help us to understand history. But, even apart from the old-fashioned Hegelianism of Marxism and the cumbersome store of dogma that Marxism drags behind it like a ball and chain, the explanatory principle is still inadequate since it is powerless to account for the specific diversity, the originality of the facts of civilization.

Furthermore, there are few notions as difficult to prove as the notion of "an end to history," either by the installation of a classless society once and for all, as in the Marxist view (the hypostatic proletariat would play the part of Messiah in a lay Parousia), or by the Teilhardian myth of an "omega point" and a "total amorization." If, as we have already said, it is not possible to reduce the evolution of civilizations to a set of general laws, then it is also impossible to predict the future of our own civilization or, a fortiori, of all mankind.

Cultural history is woven by the dissemination of cultural phenomena in space, by their transmission down through time, by the infinitely complex interplay of influences and borrowings, and also by the rejection of an influence or the refusal to borrow. It is difficult to say to what external or internal necessity most of these facts correspond. Of course, it is easy enough to understand why peoples who had no metal tools eagerly adopted them as soon as they had a chance to, or why domestic animals and cultivable plants crossed one political and cultural frontier after another. It is more difficult to explain why Buddhism died out in the country which had given birth to it, whereas it flourished when transplanted; or why the Maya and the other civilized peoples of Mexico adopted their type of calendar, so original in its remoteness from visible phenomena, instead of the lunar-solar calendar which is used almost everywhere else throughout the world; or why an Eskimo, who lives in a glacial climate, wraps himself up in warm clothing from head to foot, whereas an Indian living in the equally hostile climate of Tierra del Fuego goes practically naked. Survival of certain complexes of ideas and types of behavior does not seem to be linked either to their intrinsic value or to their usefulness or again to any specific social requirement. Why, for instance, has so-called "tarantism"[18]—that peculiar set of beliefs, symbols, dances, and

18. *See:* Ernesto de Martino, *La Terra del Rimorso,* Milan, 1961.

rites so curiously combining myths about the tarantula with worship of Saint Paul—survived until now in southern Italy?

Fashion is not the frivolous topic it may appear to be. The way in which men and women dress, adorn themselves, and wear their hair is an important cultural phenomenon. Didn't the Romans distinguish between *Gallia bragata* and *Gallia togata*? In classical antiquity, trousers were the typical garment of the barbarians. Herodotus tells how in 499 B.C., Aristagoras, tyrant of Miletus, explained to the Spartan king, Cleomenes, that the Greeks would easily defeat the Persians because, among other things, the Persians wore cloth trousers and not metal leg guards. In his ethnography courses, Marcel Mauss always stressed the contrast between two types of clothing—the draped garment and the sewn and fitted garment that eventually became current throughout most of the world.[19] There are shaven eras and bearded eras, as we can see simply by looking at the busts and portraits in any museum, from antiquity to our own day, or by leafing through a family photograph album. These imperceptible variations in taste which cause people to be clean-shaven at one period and to wear mustaches in another or to prefer a broad beard to a small "imperial," and which account for the different meanings that a given style of hair or beard has for a society at a given time,[20] all of these have some analogy with fluctuations of artistic sensitivity and even with ideal values. There are fashions —in the twofold sense of a fashion in dress or adornment and of a fashion, or way, of thinking and feeling—which are passed on, imitated, borrowed, and which emerge, change, or disappear. The "climate" of a society or an era is made up of thousands of choices among all the possibilities in all realms, from ethical ideas down to the shape of a hat.

19. The Aztecs were eclectic in this respect. They generally wore a very Greek-looking draped mantle but, when fighting, they donned a sort of sewn and padded one-piece suit.
20. In the fourth century, the partisans of Greek philosophy, who opposed Christianity, wore beards, just like the emperor Julian; he wrote a pamphlet entitled "Misopogon," or "beard hater"—a clear indication of how important that symbol was for him. In our own civilization, men have sometimes worn long hair (or wigs) and sometimes short hair. Today, the beatniks' long hair is a revolutionary symbol, in the same way that the trousers of the "sans-culottes" was during the French Revolution. In the nineteenth century, the top hat was a "progressive" symbol in the United States whereas, in the political imagery of recent years, it has come to symbolize the reactionaries.

The overwhelming role which arbitrary, coincidental, irrational, accidental things play in history can never be too strongly emphasized. Talk about "the meaning of history" is merely illusion and empty words, or else a cunning myth exploited by cunning people for their own private ends.

For a Moslem in Spain early in the eighth century, the meaning or purpose of History was the extension of Islam to all of Europe; but the Berber-Arabs were defeated at Poitiers in 732 and Islam fell back. For an Aztec in 1518, the purpose of History was the irresistible expansion of the Mexican Empire; but then there was the invasion by Cortés and his troops. In Palestine under the procurator Pontius Pilate, the meaning of History scarcely seemed to be that Jesus' religion would become the religion of the Empire three centuries later; and yet, that is what happened. History is not a person, a deity, a soul or a set of souls, an idea which is embodied or a unique force which grows irresistibly. History is no more or less than what happens. It does not mete out either prizes or punishment, it does not tend toward any specific end. No idea could be more basically absurd than the Hegelian notion, *Weltgeschichte ist Weltgerichte*.

With this in mind, it becomes impossible to make any prediction about the future of our own civilization. It is a river; we are floating on it and it carries us along, but we cannot tell whether it is flowing toward some peaceful ocean or will hurl itself over a gigantic waterfall. Spengler concluded that the West was declining; but I hope I have shown that his philosophy, or rather his mythology, of history is based on unproved and debatable statements. At the other extreme, Teilhard de Chardin allows himself to hail our civilization as the ultimate, planetary form of civilization as such, and this is just as unacceptable.

When we take a look at our Western world—and here we are obliged, despite national and political contradictions, to include both America and Russia—we cannot help noticing two essential aspects. On the one hand, our techniques are developing constantly, our mastery of the material universe is becoming surer and surer; on the other, most of the aesthetic and moral values around which that civilization formed and grew are quaking or collapsing. The wholesale massacres we have witnessed show that the most refined technology can be found in conjunction with the most profound scorn for the individual human being. Oh, we talk a great deal these days about dignity, justice, and peace, but the fact of the matter is that hardness and cynicism are everywhere, both in international relations and in human relations within each nation. In addition, moral structures, whether religious or lay, are worn away in the striving for money or power as means to reach a higher level of consumption. In the process, the individual becomes bewildered, and confusion reigns.

It is almost a commonplace to point out the contrast between the way technology has progressed while other areas have stagnated or even regressed. Already, Bergson had sounded the alarm, calling for "more soul" in order to save our civilization; but that need is easier to express than to satisfy. This is certainly a grave symptom, but it does not necessarily mean that a civilization has already reached its final phase. Although the technology of the ancient world was relatively feeble, its inventive capacities and the practical applications of those inventions in such fields as architecture, weapons, and shipping reached a summit at the same time (shortly before and shortly after the beginning of the Christian era) as its moral values shrank; yet that world was still far from its decline.

Another point worth considering is the sterility which seems to have blighted certain aesthetic forms for about a century. At the present time, our civilization does not have any style. Only in a few instances—and they are to be found mostly, if not exclusively, in America—has architecture managed to avoid either cold utilitarianism or academic plagiary. We live amidst styleless furniture and styleless objects except when we draw on our heritage from the past and make more or less faithful copies of what we find there. But to offset this, we can point to the vitality of painting, sculpture, letters and the new art of motion pictures, and say that they demonstrate a certain capacity for renewal.

There is no denying that our civilization has been constantly losing ground since the start of the century, partly as a result of the internal conflicts which have drained and exhausted it on two occasions. Although our techniques have become widespread and continue to develop, Western civilization has gone into reverse gear. The backward movement has been accentuated since the Second World War, and it is not merely a matter of geography. It is happening below the surface. It is the retreat of a civilization which has called its own values into question and now has self-doubts. Some people maintain that the crisis is only temporary and may even be a good thing. Others, recalling that the ultimate collapse of classical antiquity was heralded by the same symptom, say that it indicates a graver illness and an irremediable decline.

In the third century A.D., despite the avalanche of civil wars and devastation, the fate of the Greco-Roman world did not yet seem to be sealed; that came in the two centuries that followed, when the Romans, who had become disillusioned and skeptical, relied on the Barbarians more and more often and the Barbarians gradually ceased to be their auxiliaries and became their masters. The Barbarians' fashions, garments, and names appeared everywhere. The Franks and the Gauls no longer Romanized themselves; instead, the Romans modeled themselves on the Barbarians. An exhausted civilization lost its hold, its attractiveness; in the Barbarian countries, some even fled the Roman civilization. Priscus of Panium relates that in 448 he met a Greek in the entourage of Attila the Hun. That Greek lived among the Huns, dressed like a Hun, had married a Barbarian woman, and had even fought against the imperial armies. He was happy in his adoptive tribe because, he explained, that way he escaped from the crushing burden of Roman administration, the greed of Roman tax collectors, and the corruption of Roman magistrates. When the members of a society turn away from their own civilization, then a process of profound disintegration is under way.

Of course, one reason which can make us imagine that our civilization is sturdy is that, to use Toynbee's words, we do not see what "external proletariat" could hurl themselves on us in the way that the Barbarians—Germanic, Slavic, and Hun—hurled themselves on the Roman Empire. Nor do we see any civilization separate from our own and contemporary with it which could deal it the same kind of blows as the Arabs dealt the Greek Empire or destroy it as the Spaniards destroyed Tenochtitlán. In short, it does not seem that an attack launched from the exterior could bring our evolution to an end. But this can be countered with two arguments. First, security of this kind is short-term security because we do not know what may emerge, in the space of only a century or two, from other areas of the globe, such as China. Too sure of themselves, our not-very-distant descendants may well experience the abrupt awakening of the inhabitants of Antioch.[21] Second, a civilization can perish from within, fall in on itself, or rip itself apart in conflicts which a high level of technology makes all the more deadly and destructive.

In order to have a clearer idea of the phase we have now reached, we have to put labels on the phases that have gone before. Kroeber estimates that the "detachment" of Western Europe from Greco-Roman civilization became effective between A.D. 500, and 700, that its preliminary phase went on until about A.D. 900 that the first (medieval) phase lasted from the tenth to the fourteenth century and the second (modern) from the sixteenth to the twentieth, and that these latter two phases were both separated and linked by a transition period of which the Renaissance was the most conspicuous part. Attempting to draw conclusions from that analysis, he wonders whether the phase which began in approximately 1900 should be considered as the beginning of a total disintegration or, instead, as a transition toward a third phase:

> . . . the course of a large multinational civilization may be more complex than a smooth rise-culmination-decline . . . it may come in successive surges or pulses . . . the intervals between the pulses may be, at least over most of the area of the civilization, periods of pattern dissolution, preparatory to pattern reconstruction. Consequently, even if the mid-twentieth century is suffering from a breakdown of its cultural patterns . . . the question still remains

21. Ammianus Marcellinus tells how, in the belief that they were perfectly safe, the inhabitants of Antioch had all gathered at the theater. Suddenly one of the actors interrupted the play to cry, "Do I dream, or are these really Persians that I see?" Whereupon the spectators turned around and beheld the archers of King Shapur I already standing at the top of the tiered seats with their bows bent (A.D. 241).

open whether such a breakdown is part of the final death of our civilization . . . or . . . is merely symptomatic of an interpulse reconstruction.[22]

We can approach the problem in another way, by trying to imagine what different forms our future may take in the first two or three centuries of the third millennium. There would seem to be five possibilities:

1. Following an interval between two pulses, Western civilization starts up again; this third phase lasts for approximately the same amount of time—four hundred years—as the first two. This means that there will be, in the terms used by prehistorians or archaeologists, an "Occidental III" just as there was a "Teotihuacán I" or a "Minoan II," and so on. That is one term of the alternative that Kroeber postulates. The other is the "death" of our civilization, but it can be pictured from various angles.

2. Both variants of our civilization—that is, the American (with its two subvariants, the Anglo-Saxon and the Indo-Latin) and the Russian—grow autonomously and undergo such mutations, by comparison with the mother civilization, that they become scions, or new civilizations affiliated with our own. In essence, this is what happened in the Euro-Asiatic world when the ancient civilization disappeared and at the same time left two offshoots, Western Europe and Byzantium.[23]

Another possibility is that only one of those variants will be fully realized.

3. Western civilization can collapse from within or suffer total disintegration. A world war waged with thermonuclear weapons borne by intercontinental missiles or space satellites would probably wipe out all the centers of culture on all of the territory covered by our civilization from San Francisco eastward to Vladivostok and render

22. *A Roster of Civilizations and Culture*, p. 94.
23. Since its religion, its writing, and a number of its fundamental structures come from Byzantium, Russia could be considered an offshoot of the Greco-Asiatic civilization, the "daughter" of Byzantium and "granddaughter" of Rome. Moscow, in this view, is "the third Rome." But the process of Westernization which has been going on without interruption since Peter the Great and the Western nature of the ideology that dominates the scene today make us link the civilization of modern Russia with that of the West in general, calling it a very individualized variant of the latter.

huge expanses of that territory uninhabitable for a long time. If only we could count, with some degree of certainty, on men's common sense and instinct for self-preservation, we would be able to eliminate this apocalyptic vision. But the history of our species shows that moral or even selfish considerations have never prevented the "phenomenon of war"[24] from growing. From the Peloponnesian Wars, those twenty-seven years of fierce fighting which toppled ancient Greece over the brink and into the abyss below, to the world wars from which we have barely emerged, the human spectacle is a monotonously horrible and almost uninterrupted succession of invasions, raids, battles, massacres, reprisals, extermination, forced emigration, lives and property destroyed, monuments razed, libraries burned, harvests and food supplies wiped out, famine and devastation. Not only nations but tribes, churches, sects, and political factions as well have constantly resorted to the use of arms. There is no doubt that if it had taken no more than the exhortations of wise men to make the rest of humanity shrink before the sad consequences of war—which are there anyhow for all to see with the naked eye—then swords would long ago have been beaten into plowshares. But the fact is that no lesson has been forceful enough, until now, to bring us to our senses. From the African prehumans who invented ways of killing even then, right down to modern man and his devices for mass destruction, not one link is missing from the chain. So we cannot say with certainty that our civilization will not eventually commit suicide as atomic weapons become increasingly common. A gigantic holocaust of war can very well be lighted by a minor incident brought about by a nation of only secondary rank, just as the disastrous war which ravaged the entire Hellenic world between 431 and 401 B.C. grew out of a local quarrel between two cities, Corinth and Corcyra (Corfu), over a third, obscurer city.[25] If that were to happen again, the most important areas might be neutralized and it would be in the outlying areas, which would have been spared, that our ruined civilization might find a

24. Gaston Bouthoul, *Le phénomène guerre*, Paris, Payot, 1957.
25. Thucydides, *The Peloponnesian Wars*, Book I, Chap. 1. The spark which was to set the whole Greek world on fire flew from Epidamnus, a small Greek colony on the Illyrian coast, in "barbarian" territory.

9

chance for survival. Japan or Australia, for instance, or some of the Latin American countries might be its only remaining representatives.

4. A new civilization might emerge at some particular point on the globe, then come into conflict with our own and destroy it. Today that does not seem very likely. But in the years before the Hegira, who would ever have imagined that Islam was going to form a flood tide that would submerge the Middle East, North Africa, and Spain?

5. Lastly, it has already happened that certain civilizations wither, or ossify; that was the case with ancient Egypt, India, and the Arab world. The outer forms remain but the sap dries up. Appearances may continue to be impressive for a long, long time; the sterile and senseless agitation of individuals and groups goes on behind the decor of a changeless society. If a younger, more powerful civilization surges onto the scene, the stagnant society more or less readily accepts its hegemony and mechanically continues to make the same gestures as before, empty now of the creative force which first gave rise to them. Where we are concerned, there is nothing improbable about this idea; ways of living are becoming uniform, minds are dominated by mass communication media, consumption is taken as a goal in itself, almost to the exclusion of any other. All of these factors spell sclerosis.

All in all, and contrary to what Kroeber implies, I myself am inclined to believe that our civilization is not suspended between two "pulses" but, instead, that it has entered into the first few decades of its disintegration. But I must admit that that is a subjective conclusion, although the signs do seem to me to point in that direction.

Furthermore, if, as I have emphasized, cultural evolution is largely a matter of arbitrary and coincidental elements, then there is no such thing as historic fatality. We are not confronted with a Juggernaut that crushes all who resist it. Clearly, the deliberate will of human beings is but one factor among a good many others; only with the greatest of difficulty, and only if circumstances are favorable, can we get the better of the scourges that have beset our species for several thousand years. Yet little islets have emerged here and there amidst an ocean of poverty, wars, and cruelty. They were imperfect—only utopia is perfect—but on these peaks of religion, art, social and political organization human life was elevated for a time to a high degree of brilliance and sweetness. Athens, between the Median wars and the war against Sparta, was one such peak; the Roman Empire from Trajan to Marcus Aurelius, another; the Maya cities of the great classical era and Moslem Spain, exemplified in Córdoba and Granada, were others. There is no golden age behind us and none awaits us in the future, but sometimes, and as briefly as a flash between two interminable nights, humanity manages to find a precarious equilibrium, a radiant exception in the course of its somber history.

It is probably not coincidence that ethnography has appeared at just this point in our civilization, precisely because today that civilization is in the beginning of its late phase. At an earlier point, each man cleaves so closely to his own culture that he cannot detach himself from it sufficiently to turn a sympathetic, as well as a curious, gaze upon the others. At a later point, vision is likely to be blurred by the imminence of decline, the wave of what Spengler calls "second religiousness." The age of ethnology comes when a civilization is neither too sure of itself, nor too convinced of its own inherent superiority, nor haunted by the horrors of disintegration. Ethnology is the science of relativity, and it is relative itself, since it can thrive only in a given age and in certain conditions. Man is both the object and the subject, both what ethnology observes and the person observing. The result is a "generalized relativity." Not only do civilizations and cultures move in relationship to one another like the heavenly bodies in space, each on its own orbit, including the one which carries the observer along, but even the science he brings into action is possible only within certain civilizations and not within others, only at a particular point on their trajectory and not at others. The ethnologist exists as such only insofar as he stands off from his own civilization, and that is not possible unless its attractive force, or gravitational pull, is temporarily weakened. Should the world collapse and should that attraction be totally missing from the despair that would ensue, then weightless man would go knocking around among the stars. When the Vandals struck North Africa like a tidal wave, Augustine, bishop of Hippo, turned toward the City of God.

Thus, the ethnologist is necessarily the man of a particular time and a particular country. Not only do his conscious and his subconscious mind bear the stamp of his birth, his education, and the tradition which envelops him, but, moreover, he would not be an ethnologist at all if he were not living at a certain period of a given civilization. More than anyone else, he resists the temptation of dogmatism because he realizes, better than anyone else, how limited our knowledge is, partly because its object—vanished cities, forgotten tongues, peoples who fade away—eludes our grasp, but mostly because the ethnologist himself is part of the human condition he is trying so earnestly to understand.

In its pathetic quest for knowledge, mankind is like a nomadic tribe that gathers around the fire in the chilly evening. The flame of the coals hold the camp in their glow, but the shadows begin just beyond. A menacing wall of darkness encircles the light radiating from the hearth. If wood is fed into the fire, the flames climb higher and the wall of night shrinks back, but no matter how bright the light from the hearth in the middle, and even though the circle of radiance is larger, the eye tries vainly to pierce the dark immensity that is still present all around. In the same way, no matter what conquests our reason may make, the zone of mystery in the world and in ourselves remains infinitely more vast than the area which is known to us. Confronted with that wall of night, some stop and wonder, others have recourse to other lights. Who are we to impose our truth and mock the truth of other people?

Our planet is just a speck of dust in the universe. It lived for billions of years without us, and when the curtain has fallen on the human comedy and a species which believes itself privileged has become extinct, the order of the world will not be disturbed in the least. When the play is over, when there are no more actors and no more spectators, what will remain of the passions and the struggles, the blood and the tears, the beauty and the wisdom? And, for that matter, what importance should we place upon the life and death of a civilization, what meaning should we attach to those brief throbbings of the pulse in an infinite duration?

Every man who meditates on our fate cannot help but ask himself these questions. Inevitably, he wonders why he should undertake to learn, why he should make an effort to act. Aren't knowledge and action both "vanity of vanities"?

While camping with his army along the Danube, which marked the end of the civilized world at that time (the second half of the second century A.D.), Marcus Aurelius noted down his thoughts at the same time as he directed the fighting against the Germanic tribes. "In the life of man, what of duration? A point. Of substance? An unstable flow. Of feeling? Blunted. The assembly of the body? Putrescible. The soul? A whirlwind. Fate? An enigma. . . . All that is of the body is but a river, all that is of the soul is a dream, a vapor." Or this: "Asia, Europe are corners of the universe; all the sea is but one drop of water in the world, Mount Athos but a lump of earth, all the present, a point in time . . . Alexander the Macedonian and his mule driver, once dead, were both reduced to the same condition." Yet, at the same time, the very same Marcus Aurelius governed an immense state, led a war to defend his empire against invasion, administered, decreed. And on the same tablets he exhorted himself, "Apply yourself, as a Roman and a man, at all times and with all your care, to do what is in your hands." Contradictory? No doubt. But what other choice was there, except a monk's or a lama's existence or the cave of Zarathustra. The emperor-philosopher chose to accept his role, his part in the play at the risk of straining logic, of making mistakes and acting unjustly, for who can govern without making mistakes and acting unjustly? In other words, he chose not to withdraw from the world, although he *knew very well where he stood*.

Now, what is valid where action is concerned is also valid with respect to knowledge. Knowledge knows in advance that it is fallible and limited, and that its efforts are doomed, anyhow, to the nothingness that hovers over all human effort. "He that increaseth knowledge increaseth sorrow" (Ecclesiastes, 1:18). But should we prefer ignorance? Something in us answers no.

Although knowledge makes only a feeble glow, is it or will it one day be capable of lighting man's way sufficiently to guide him toward those oases of beauty and peace which, at rare moments in history, civilizations can cause to bloom in the desert? Ethnology is to mankind what anatomy and physiology are to the human body. If that science becomes reliable enough, it is possible that techniques analogous to the science of medicine will be based on it. There will be doctors of human society. They will observe existing phenomena and compare them with earlier ones, make their diagnosis, and prescribe remedies for avoiding mistakes, relieving suffering and disasters, prolonging the life of a civilization and postponing its old age. Man today is still as helpless to deal with the forces that agitate society as prehistoric man was to face illness and the senile decay of his own body. Will this always be the case? Won't there come a day when man will stop investing all his efforts in the material world and the resources he can extract from it (the "gathering phase", as it were, in the search for happiness) and turn toward himself, toward the cultures and the civilizations which—like the Huaxtec statue of Chilitujú—have a smiling face of flesh and a grimacing mask of death?

Of course, even if this hope were to become reality, it would never be more than an ephemeral enterprise in an ephemeral universe. But it is our universe, the one which is given us, given mankind, during the time allotted to us. Nothing is vain if it can lighten by even so much as one grain of sand the burden of suffering and terror that we have been bowed under for thousands of years. Even if all effort ultimately proved to be useless, it would be justified by the attempt itself, by man's boldness in rising up against nature to introduce a parcel of beauty and goodness into the world. Those, after all, are values which have nothing to do with the *things* of this world and have meaning only for us.

Knowledge is not a consolation but a liberation. We can gaze on human history as it really is, already so long and yet so brief, a mixture of many things—impulses which are quickly shattered, a little progress, dull stagnation and dragging relapses; a stormy chaos with no apparent meaning where, amidst the prevailing sound and fury, the light and gentle murmur of a highly alert or graceful art is faintly audible; a night stretching from one age to the next and relieved by the glimmer of little lamps held high by peoples proceeding toward a fate they cannot know. When we gaze on this, each of us discovers the others and finds himself all over again. Stripping away illusion, we attain serenity without succumbing to indifference. We loosen the chains of the human condition as much as we can by the very fact that we assume it lucidly, voluntarily.

Index